COOKIES, MUFFINS & CAKES

THE **COMPLETE** COOKBOOK

COOKIES, MUFFINS & CAKES

TASTY RECIPES FOR EVERY DAY

Contents

You will find the following cookery ratings on the recipes in this book:

A single pot symbol indicates a recipe that is simple and generally straightforward to make—perfect for beginners.

Two symbols indicate the need for just a little more care and a little more time.

Three symbols indicate special recipes that need more investment in time, care and patience—but the results are worth it.

Perfect Muffins & Scones

PERFECT MUFFINS

Muffins must be one of the most rewarding things to cook. They're simple, tasty and can be ready in next to no time! If you follow a few simple rules, you'll find your muffins will turn out perfect every time. The first step is to assemble all your ingredients and utensils before you start and remember to always make sure the oven is preheated. Preparing the muffin tin for baking is very important. Even though most tins have non-stick surfaces, it is still well worth greasing the holes, especially when making sweet muffins, as the sugar can make them very sticky. Always sift the flour into a mixing bowl as it will aerate the flour and ensure your muffins are light. The next step is to gently fold in the liquid ingredients with a metal spoon until just combined.

Be careful not to over-beat or the muffins will become tough and rubbery. The mixture should still be quite lumpy at this stage. Divide the mixture evenly among the holes using two metal spoons—fill each hole to about three-quarters full. Always try to use the hole size indicated in the recipe as the cooking time changes if you use a different size. The larger the hole, the longer the baking time.

Bake the muffins for 20–25 minutes, or until they are risen, golden and come away slightly from the sides of the holes. Test them by pressing lightly with your fingertips, they are cooked if they feel firm and spring back after you touch them.

Another test is to insert a skewer into the centre of the muffin—if it comes out clean they are ready. Most muffins should be left in the tin for a couple of minutes once out of the oven, but don't leave them too long or trapped steam will make the bases soggy. Using a flat-bladed knife, loosen the muffins and transfer to a wire rack to cool completely before serving or storing.

If you like the idea of having freshly baked muffins for breakfast but don't want to start the day making a mess in the kitchen, simply make a muffin mixture, spoon it into the muffin tin and refrigerate it overnight, ready for baking the following day. Uncooked mixture for the plainer muffins such as chocolate or blueberry, or those without fillings, can be frozen in paper-lined muffin tins for up to a month. When you want to cook the muffins, remove them from the freezer and bake in a preheated 200°C (400°F/Gas 6) oven for 25–30 minutes, or until golden and slightly shrunk away from the sides.

STORAGE

Muffins will freeze very well. Once they have cooled after baking, place in a freezer bag and freeze for up to three months. When required, thaw and wrap in foil before reheating in a 180°C (350°F/ Gas 4) oven for about 8 minutes, or until heated through.

PERFECT SCONES

Making great scones is not difficult and they get even easier with practice. All scones are made according to the same principles: add wet ingredients to the dry and mix the dough as briefly and lightly as possible. Because the

---

WHAT WENT WRONG?

Perfect The texture of the muffin is even with a nicely risen centre and good golden coloring. If a skewer is inserted in the centre it will come out clean. The muffin has started to come away from the side of the holes. Muffins need to be cooked in a preheated 200°C (400°F/Gas 6) oven so the batter will set and peak correctly as it has above.

Too peaked The crust is too colored and the muffin too peaked. This is caused by over-beating or baking in an oven that is too hot. The result is rubbery muffins with an uneven shape. Be sure all the dry ingredients are evenly distributed by sifting and mixing them before adding them to the wet ingredients.

Poorly risen The muffin texture is too heavy and dense. This can be caused by insufficient raising agent or a missing ingredient. To avoid leaving out any vital ingredient, check that you have all the ingredients assembled and correctly weighed out before you start.

moisture content of flour varies, you may not need all the liquid stated in your recipe. The amount of liquid the flour absorbs can also change according to the room temperature and even the altitude. Although our recipe uses self-raising flour, some people prefer to use plain flour and add more raising agents such as baking powder. Salt is added to enhance the flavor of all scones, even sweet ones.

It's simple to achieve a good batch of high, light and golden scones. Remember that unlike bread, which requires vigorous kneading, scone dough simply needs quick, light handling.

Before you begin mixing, preheat the oven to 220°C (425°F/Gas 7) and lightly grease the baking tray or line it with baking paper. Sift the dry ingredients into a mixing bowl. Sifting aerates the dry ingredients and helps achieve lighter scones, so many bakers sift the flour twice. Rub in the butter briefly and lightly with your fingertips until the mixture is crumbly and resembles fine breadcrumbs. Make a well in the centre and add the liquid ingredients. Mix with a flat-bladed knife, using a cutting action, until the dough comes together in clumps, rotating the bowl as you work. Use the remaining milk if the mixture seems dry.

Handle the mixture with great care and a very light hand. If you are heavy-handed and mix too much, or knead, your scones will be very tough. The dough should feel slightly wet and sticky. With floured hands, gently gather the dough together, lift onto a lightly floured surface and pat into a smooth ball. Do not knead. Cut the dough as indicated in the recipe and place on the prepared tray. Gather the dough scraps together and, without too much handling, press out again and cut out more scones.

It is important to cook scones at a high temperature, otherwise the raising agents will not work. If you aren't sure they are cooked, break one open. If it is still doughy in the centre, cook for a few more minutes. For soft scones, wrap them in a dry tea towel while hot. For scones with a crisp top, transfer to a wire rack to cool slightly before wrapping.

STORAGE

As scones generally contain little fat, they dry out quickly so are best eaten soon after baking. However, they will freeze very successfully for up to three months.

WHAT WENT WRONG?

Perfect The scone is evenly risen, has a soft crust and soft inside texture and is light golden. The dough should not be overworked, but lightly mixed with a flat-bladed knife until combined.

Poorly risen If the scone texture feels heavy and dense, the dough may have been either too dry or too wet. Overworking or mixing the dough too much will also result in heavy scones.

Undercooked The scone is pale, sticky in the centre and has a dense texture. The cooking time was too short or the oven temperature too low. The oven must be 220°C (425°F/Gas 7).

Overcooked The scone has a dark crust and dry texture. Either the cooking time was too long or the oven temperature was too hot, so always check the temperature and cooking time.

Overflowing mixture It is very important to make sure you use the size of muffin tin suggested in the recipe you are using. Do not fill the muffin holes more than two-thirds full. This leaves room for the batter to rise as it will often rise by half its volume.

Undercooked The finished muffin is moist in the centre with insufficient peaking. The muffin is not properly colored and didn't shrink away from the tin. The oven was probably not sufficiently preheated or not hot enough, or the cooking time may have been too short.

Perfect Cookies

Nothing compares with the scintillating aroma of freshly baked biscuits. Whether you prefer nutty, fruity, plain or creamy biscuits, you will feel extremely satisfied about not just ripping open a packet.

CREAMING METHOD

With the following recipe, which uses the creaming method, you can make a basic butter biscuit and variations. To make about 30 biscuits, line two baking trays with baking paper or lightly grease them with melted butter instead. Allow 125 g (4 oz) butter to soften to room temperature, then cut it into cubes. This will make it easier to work with. Preheat the oven to 210°C (415°F/Gas 6–7). Cream the softened butter with the $\frac{1}{2}$ cup (125 g/4 oz) caster sugar in a small bowl with electric beaters, or by hand, until light and fluffy. This should take about 3–5 minutes with electric beaters, or 10 minutes by hand. Scrape down the side of the bowl occasionally with a spatula. The mixture should look pale and be quite smooth, and the sugar should be almost dissolved. Add $\frac{1}{4}$ cup (60 ml/2 fl oz) milk and $\frac{1}{4}$ teaspoon vanilla essence and beat until combined. Add $1\frac{1}{2}$ cups (185 g/ 6 oz) self-raising flour and $\frac{1}{2}$ cup (60 g/2 oz) custard powder and use a flat-bladed knife to bring to a soft dough together. Rotate the mixing bowl as you work and use a cutting motion to incorporate all the dry ingredients. Don't overwork the dough or you will end up with tough biscuits. Roll level teaspoons of the dough into balls and place on trays, leaving 5 cm (2 inches) between each biscuit. Flatten the balls lightly with your fingertips, then press with a fork. The biscuits should be about 5 cm (2 inches) in diameter. Bake the biscuits for 15–18 minutes or until lightly golden.

MELT AND MIX

This quick method involves mixing the dry ingredients, then quickly mixing in the melted butter (and any other ingredients in the recipe) with a wooden spoon until the dry ingredients are well moistened.

RUBBING IN

This involves cutting cold butter into small pieces and rubbing it into the flour with your fingertips until the mixture is crumbly and resembles fine breadcrumbs. Then almost all the liquid is added and cut into the dry ingredients with a knife, adding the remaining liquid if necessary to bring the mixture together. Do not add the liquid all at once as flour varies a great deal so the full amount of liquid may not be required.

BAKING

The biscuit mixture should be put on a baking tray that is at room temperature. When re-using baking trays, don't put the biscuit mixture on a hot tray because the biscuits will spread too much and lose their shape.

Don't use trays or tins that have high sides, otherwise the heat distribution during cooking will not be even. Most biscuits are best baked in or close to the centre of the oven. Avoid opening the oven door until at least two-thirds of the way through baking. When cooked, cool the biscuits on the baking trays for about 3 minutes before transferring them to a wire rack to allow to cool completely.

STORAGE

Moisture is absorbed easily by biscuits so they lose their crispness if not in an airtight jar. Try not to store different types of biscuits in the same jar and never store with cakes. Biscuits that are to be filled should be stored without their filling and filled just before serving. To freeze, place in freezer bags and seal, label and date. Unfilled and un-iced cooked biscuits can be frozen for up to two months. After thawing, refresh in a 180°C (350°F/Gas 4) oven for a few minutes, then cool and decorate with icing or sifted icing sugar. Biscuit dough also will freeze well if wrapped in plastic.

WHAT WENT WRONG?

DROP BISCUITS

Perfect The biscuit has a golden coloring on both the top and base and an even thickness.

Undercooked, sticking Pale and soft to touch, the cooking time for these biscuits may not have been long enough. Alternatively, the oven temperature may have been too low or the oven insufficiently preheated.

Overcooked These biscuits are too dark, indicating that the oven temperature was too high or the cooking time too long. The mixture may also have had too much sugar. Be sure to only rest the biscuits for a couple of minutes on the tray after cooking or they will continue to cook.

MIXTURE ROLLED OUT AND CUT INTO SHAPES

Perfect The biscuit has a light golden coloring and even thickness.

Thin, overcooked The mixture may have been rolled too thinly, the oven may have been too hot, or perhaps the biscuits were overcooked.

Too thick The mixture was rolled and cut too thickly. These biscuits would need extra baking time to cook properly.

MIXTURE SHAPED BY HAND OR PIPED

Perfect The biscuit has an even, golden coloring on both the top and base. It is also the correct thickness.

Undercooked These pale biscuits may not have been cooked enough. The oven may also have not been preheated or the temperature too low.

Overcooked and spread too much The oven may have been too hot or the biscuits cooked too long.

Perfect Cakes

Cake pans Using the correct size of cake pan plays an important part in the success of the finished cake. There are many shapes and sizes of pans from which to choose. Metal cake pans give consistently good results. Avoid using shiny or very dark pans and glass bakeware.

Changing pan sizes If you wish to substitute one shape of pan for another, measure the volume of the batter and pour the same amount of water into the pan you intend to use. As long as the water comes at least halfway but no higher than two-thirds of the way up the pan, you can use it. Be sure to check the cake before the minimum baking time so you can adjust the baking time, if necessary.

INGREDIENTS

Each ingredient used in cake baking has a specific role.
Flour This forms the structure of the cake. It is not necessary to sift the flour unless specified.
Eggs These are also essential to the structure of the cake. They bind the other ingredients together and add flavor and color. We have used large (60 g/2 oz) eggs in all of our recipes. For baking, eggs should be at room temperature.
Butter Butter supplies flavor, texture and aroma. We have used unsalted butter in our recipes because it gives cakes a much richer, sweeter flavor. Make sure it is at room temperature so it creams correctly. If colder, it will not cream or aerate well. If it is too soft and oily, it will not aerate at all.
Margarine This can be substituted for butter in most cakes but will give some difference in flavor. Avoid diet and whipped margarines as these products contain too much water for use in successful baking.
Oil In carrot and zucchini cakes, oil gives very moist results. Use a good quality vegetable oil but avoid olive oil and peanut oil because their

flavors are too pronounced.
Sugar Adds sweetness, color and fine grain to cakes. Granulated sugar is commonly used in baking. Caster sugar is too fine for general cake making. Brown sugar produces moist, flavorsome results in fruit cakes. Dark brown sugar gives a more intense flavor than light brown sugar.
Milk Regular milk is the most commonly used liquid in cake baking. Low-fat milk works equally well.

TECHNIQUES

Cakes are often classified by the method used to make them. In general, they'll fall into one of four categories: creaming, whisking (beating of whole eggs and/or egg whites), cutting in, and quick mixing. It is important to understand the differences between these methods and to follow the correct procedures for each one.

Creaming Method

This is the most frequently used method in cake baking. It is used for butter cakes, chocolate cakes, light fruit cakes and many others. The proportion of butter to sugar varies from recipe to recipe. The best results are obtained by beating butter (which is at room temperature) and sugar in a small mixing bowl with electric beaters. If the recipe has a high proportion of

Creaming method Beat the butter and sugar, scraping the sides of the bowl occasionally.

butter to sugar, the mixture will become light and fluffy. If the recipe uses a much greater quantity of sugar than butter, the mixture won't be very light or fluffy, so just beat until the ingredients are well mixed.

Scrape the sides of the bowl with a spatula several times during the creaming process to make sure the sugar and butter are well incorporated. This initial creaming process should take several minutes. Whole eggs or egg yolks are then added. Be sure to beat these lightly before adding them to the butter mixture. Add the beaten eggs gradually, beating thoroughly after each addition.

Vanilla, grated citrus zest and other flavorings are added at this stage. The mixture is then transferred to a large mixing bowl. Add the dry ingredients and liquid alternately (about one-quarter to one-third of each at a time), stirring gently with a large spoon after each addition. Stir until just combined and the mixture is almost smooth. Take care with this final stage, mixing the ingredients together lightly yet evenly as any over enthusiastic beating can undo previous good work and produce a heavy, coarse-textured cake.

Whisking Method

This is generally used for sponge cakes and light and airy cake rolls. Eggs are the chief ingredient,

Whisking method Whisk eggs together until thick and pale yellow.

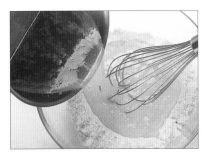

Quick mix method Make a well in the dry ingredients and pour melted butter and sugar into the centre. Whisk until well combined.

Folding technique Run the spoon along the underside of the mixture and up in one sweeping motion. Cut through the centre on the next fold.

Beating egg whites Use a clean glass or metal bowl for beating egg whites. Beat until firm peaks form, then add sugar.

used whole or separated. Use the freshest eggs and always have them at room temperature. Whole-egg sponge cakes are made by beating whole eggs in a small mixing bowl with an electric mixer for 5 minutes or until thick and pale yellow.

Sugar is added gradually, about a tablespoon at a time. Beat constantly about 10 minutes or until the sugar is dissolved and the mixture is pale yellow and glossy. The sifted dry ingredients are then quickly and lightly folded in.

Eggs can also be beaten with sugar in a heatproof bowl over simmering water (Génoise-style) until mixture is pale yellow and thick; a hand-held electric mixer should be used. The mixture is then removed from the heat and beaten with an electric mixer until it has almost doubled in volume. The sifted dry ingredients are then gently folded in.

Most sponge cake recipes call for the eggs to be separated and beaten separately. Take care when separating eggs, because just one small particle of egg yolk (or any type of fat) can ruin beating quality. Separate one at a time into a small glass bowl, then transfer to the bowl for beating.

Quick Mix Method

This fast and simple method is gaining popularity. Melt the butter with flavorings such as brown sugar and chocolate and then pour over the sifted dry ingredients. Make a well in the centre of the dry ingredients beforehand. Stir mixture with a wooden spoon until combined.

The eggs are then stirred in, taking care not to overmix.

The Folding Technique

Using a large metal spoon, fold in the dry ingredients, running the spoon along the underside of the mixture and up in one sweeping action that takes the dry ingredients under and over the egg mixture. Cut down through the centre of the bowl on the next fold, rotating the mixing bowl as you fold. Repeat these actions until the mixture is well combined. Work quickly and lightly to ensure even distribution of ingredients and to avoid over-mixing.

Beating the Egg Whites

Beating egg whites to the correct consistency is a vital stage in cake making. Use a glass or metal mixing bowl that is clean and dry. Use an electric mixer to beat the egg whites until firm peaks form; the whites should hold a straight peak when you lift the beaters out. The sugar is then added gradually while beating constantly and the mixture is beaten until the sugar is completely dissolved. Rub some of the beaten egg white mixture between your fingers to make sure that there aren't any undissolved sugar crystals in it. The mixture should be very glossy and thick and hold in stiff peaks.

The lightly beaten egg yolks are then added and the mixture is transferred to a large mixing bowl. Use a metal spoon to fold in the sifted dry ingredients quickly and lightly.

STEPS TO SUCCESSFUL CAKES

- Make sure you read the whole recipe before you start baking.
- Assemble all the ingredients and equipment before proceeding.
- Preheat the oven to the correct temperature and prepare all the baking tins you are going to use.
- Do not allow room temperature ingredients such as butter and eggs to get too warm.
- Measure ingredients accurately; do not judge quantities by eye but use standard measuring cups and spoons.
- Stir together or sift dry ingredients as directed.
- Beat together butter and sugar mixtures as directed.
- Add lightly beaten eggs gradually, making sure they are well incorporated.
- Do not over-beat the egg whites.
- Take care with folding-in procedures.
- Spoon the batter into prepared cake tin and spread evenly.
- Check the oven temperature and avoid opening the oven door until your cake is at least two-thirds of the way through baking.
- Remember that all the baking times given for cakes are approximate as baking times can vary according to your oven and where the cake is placed in the oven.
- Place the cake in the tin on a wire rack and let it stand for the specified time before turning it out onto a wire rack to cool completely.

Cookies

LEBKUCHEN

Preparation time: 25 minutes
Total cooking time: 30 minutes
Makes 35

2¹/₃ cups (290 g/10 oz) plain flour
¹/₂ cup (60 g/2 oz) cornflour
2 teaspoons cocoa powder
1 teaspoon mixed spice
1 teaspoon ground cinnamon
¹/₂ teaspoon ground nutmeg
100 g (3¹/₂ oz) unsalted butter, cubed
³/₄ cup (260 g/8 oz) golden syrup
2 tablespoons milk
150 g (5 oz) white chocolate melts
¹/₄ teaspoon mixed spice, extra

1 Preheat the oven to 180°C (350°F/ Gas 4). Line two baking trays with baking paper.
2 Sift the plain flour and cornflour, cocoa and spices into a large bowl and make a well in the centre.
3 Place the butter, golden syrup and milk in a small saucepan, and stir over low heat until butter has melted and mixture is smooth. Remove from the heat and add to the dry ingredients. Mix with a flat-bladed knife until ingredients come together in small beads. Gather together with your hands and turn out onto a sheet of baking paper.
4 Roll the dough out to about 7 mm (³/₈ inch) thick. Cut into heart shapes using a 6 cm (2¹/₂ inch) biscuit cutter. Place on the prepared trays and bake for 25 minutes, or until lightly browned. Cool slightly, then transfer to a wire rack until biscuits are completely cool.
5 Place the chocolate in a heatproof bowl. Bring a saucepan of water to the boil, then remove from heat. Sit the bowl over the pan, making sure the base does not touch the water. Stir until the chocolate has melted.
6 Dip one half of each biscuit into the chocolate and place on a sheet of baking paper until set. Sprinkle with mixed spice.

Carefully transfer the dough shapes to the prepared baking tray using a flat-bladed knife.

If the chocolate starts to set, place it over the hot water until it melts again.

Beat the butter and icing sugar then add the egg yolks and vanilla essence.

Carefully pipe the mixture directly onto the prepared tray.

VIENNESE FINGERS

Preparation time: 20 minutes
Total cooking time: 12 minutes
Makes 20

100 g (3¹/₂ oz) unsalted butter, softened
¹/₃ cup (40 g/1¹/₄ oz) icing sugar
2 egg yolks
1¹/₂ teaspoons vanilla essence
1 cup (125 g/4 oz) plain flour
100 g (3¹/₂ oz) dark cooking chocolate, chopped
30 g (1 oz) unsalted butter, extra, for icing

1 Preheat the oven to 180°C (350°F/ Gas 4). Line two baking trays with baking paper.
2 Using electric beaters, cream the butter and icing sugar in a small mixing bowl until light and fluffy. Gradually add the egg yolks and vanilla essence and beat thoroughly. Transfer the mixture to a large mixing bowl, then sift in the flour. Using a flat-bladed knife, mix until just combined and the mixture is smooth.
3 Spoon the mixture into a piping bag fitted with a fluted 1 cm (¹/₂ inch) piping nozzle and pipe the mixture into wavy 6 cm (2¹/₂ inch) lengths on the prepared trays.
4 Bake the cookies for 12 minutes, or until golden brown. Allow to cool slightly on the trays, then transfer to a wire rack to cool completely.
5 Place the chocolate and extra butter in a small heatproof bowl. Half-fill a saucepan with water and bring to the boil, then remove from the heat. Sit the bowl over the pan, making sure the base of the bowl does not sit in the water. Stir occasionally until the chocolate and butter have melted together and the mixture is smooth.

Dip half of each biscuit into the melted chocolate mixture and leave to set on greaseproof paper or foil.

STORAGE: Store in an airtight container for up to 2 days.
NOTE: To make piping easier, fold down the bag by 5 cm (2 inches) before adding the mixture, then unfold. The top will be clean and easy to twist, stopping any mixture from squirting out the top.

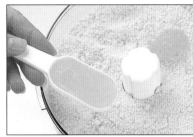

Add the lemon rind and juice to the mixture in the food processor.

Use a 6 cm (2½ inch) cutter to cut the star shapes out of the dough.

SHORTBREAD STARS WITH LEMON GLAZE

Preparation time: 20 minutes
Total cooking time: 15 minutes
Makes 35

2 cups (250 g/8 oz) plain flour
2 tablespoons rice flour
200 g (6½ oz) unsalted butter
⅓ cup (40 g/1¼ oz) icing sugar
1 teaspoon finely grated lemon rind
2 tablespoons lemon juice
silver cachous, to decorate

LEMON GLAZE
1 cup (125 g/4 oz) pure icing sugar
2 tablespoons lemon juice, strained
yellow or orange food coloring

1 Preheat the oven to 180°C (350°F/ Gas 4). Line two baking trays with baking paper. Place the flours, butter and sugar in a food processor and process for 30 seconds or until the mixture is fine and crumbly. Add the lemon rind and juice and process for 20 seconds or until the mixture forms a soft dough.
2 Turn out onto a lightly floured surface and knead for 20 seconds or until smooth. Roll the dough out to 7 mm (¼ inch) thickness. Using a 6 cm (2½ inch) star cutter, cut out shapes. Bake for 15 minutes. Transfer to wire rack to cool.
3 To make the lemon glaze, place the icing sugar and lemon juice in a heatproof bowl over a pan of hot water. Stir until smooth. Dip the biscuits face down in glaze and drain any excess. Dip a skewer into food coloring and draw lines into icing before it sets. Decorate with a cachou.

STORAGE: Store for up to 5 days in an airtight container.

Beat the softened butter and sugar together until they are pale and fluffy.

Use a flat-bladed knife to mix ingredients together with a cutting, rather than a stirring, motion.

JAM DROPS

Preparation time: 20 minutes
Total cooking time: 15 minutes
Makes 32

80 g (2³/₄ oz) unsalted butter, softened
¹/₃ cup (90 g/3 oz) caster sugar
2 tablespoons milk
¹/₂ teaspoon vanilla essence
1 cup (125 g/4 oz) self-raising flour
¹/₃ cup (40 g/1¹/₄ oz) custard powder
¹/₃ cup (105 g/3¹/₂ oz) raspberry jam

1 Preheat the oven to 180°C (350°F/ Gas 4). Line two baking trays with baking paper.
2 Cream the butter and sugar in a small mixing bowl with electric beaters until light and fluffy. Add the milk and vanilla essence and beat until well combined. Add the sifted flour and custard powder and mix to form a soft dough. Roll heaped teaspoons of the mixture into balls and place on the prepared trays.
3 Make an indentation in each ball using the end of a wooden spoon. Fill each hole with a little jam.
4 Bake for 15 minutes, cool slightly on the trays, then transfer to a wire rack to cool completely.

Add the walnuts and choc bits to the sifted flours, then make a well in the centre.

Roll the mixture into balls and place on the prepared tray, allowing a little room for spreading.

CHOCOLATE FUDGE BROWNIES

Preparation time: 15 minutes + 1 hour refrigeration
Total cooking time: 12 minutes
Makes 30

³/₄ cup (90 g/3 oz) plain flour
¹/₂ cup (60 g/2 oz) self-raising flour
1 cup (125 g/4 oz) chopped walnuts
¹/₂ cup (90 g/3 oz) choc bits
125 g (4 oz) unsalted butter, chopped
200 g (6¹/₂ oz) dark chocolate, chopped
2 tablespoons golden syrup
2 eggs, lightly beaten

1 Line a baking tray with baking paper. Sift the plain and self-raising flours into a large mixing bowl. Add the walnuts and choc bits and make a well in the centre.
2 Combine the butter and chocolate in a small pan. Stir over low heat for 5 minutes, or until the chocolate has melted and the mixture is smooth. Remove the pan from heat, add the syrup and beaten eggs, mixing well.
3 Pour the chocolate mixture into a large mixing bowl with the dry ingredients. Using a metal spoon, stir until just combined. Cover with plastic wrap and refrigerate for 1 hour.
4 Preheat the oven to 180°C (350°F/ Gas 4). Roll 1 level tablespoon of mixture at a time into a ball. Arrange the balls on the prepared tray and bake for 12 minutes. (The biscuits will still be soft at this stage, but they will become firm on standing.) Remove the biscuits from the oven and transfer to a wire rack to cool completely.

STORAGE: The brownies may be stored in an airtight container for up to 2 days.
NOTE: These rich, chocolate brownies have a delicious fudge-like texture. Sprinkle brownies with chocolate sprinkles before baking, if desired. This brownie mixture can also be baked in a tin as a slice and cut into fingers when cooked. Spread with your favorite rich chocolate icing before cutting, if desired.

PASSIONFRUIT SHORTBREAD

Preparation time: 45 minutes
Total cooking time: 20 minutes
Makes about 40

250 g (8 oz) butter
1/3 cup (90 g/3 oz) caster sugar
2 1/4 cups (280 g/9 oz) plain flour
1/4 cup (45 g/1 1/2 oz) rice flour
40 g (1 1/4 oz) white choc melts, melted

PASSIONFRUIT ICING
1 1/4 cups (155 g/5 oz) icing sugar, sifted
2 tablespoons passionfruit pulp
20 g (3/4 oz) softened butter
1 tablespoon water

1 Preheat the oven to 160°C (315°F/ Gas 2–3). Line two baking trays with baking paper. Using electric beaters, beat the butter and sugar in a small mixing bowl until light and creamy. Fold in the sifted flours and mix until a soft dough forms. Turn out onto a lightly floured surface. Knead gently for 1 minute or until smooth.
2 Roll out the dough between two sheets of baking paper to 5 mm (1/4 inch) thickness. Using a sharp knife, cut into 4 x 4 cm (1 1/2 x 1 1/2 inch) diamonds. Place on the prepared trays, allowing room for spreading. Re-roll the pastry and cut out diamonds in the same way. Bake for 15 minutes, or until the biscuits are lightly brown. Stand for 5 minutes before transferring onto a wire rack to cool.
3 To make the passionfruit icing, combine the icing sugar, passionfruit pulp, butter and water in a bowl to form a smooth paste. Stand the bowl in pan of simmering water, stirring until the icing is smooth and glossy. Remove the pan from heat but leave the bowl of icing to stand in the warm water while icing the biscuits. Using a flat-bladed knife, spread each diamond with 1/2 teaspoon of icing.
4 Leave the biscuits to stand for 15 minutes to set, then drizzle or pipe a decorative pattern on top with the melted white chocolate.

STORAGE: These biscuits can be stored in an airtight container for up to 2 days.
NOTE: Overheating the icing will make it dull and grainy. Try to work as quickly as possible and dip the knife into hot water occasionally to give the icing a smooth finish.

Use a large metal spoon to fold the flour into the butter mixture.

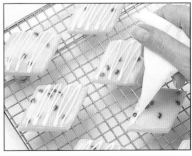

Drizzle the white chocolate over the biscuits in a decorative pattern and leave to set.

Add the dry ingredients to the mixture and gently stir together with a metal spoon.

Drop tablespoons of the mixture onto the prepared baking tray.

AFGHANS

Preparation time: 20 minutes
Total cooking time: 20 minutes
Makes 25

150 g (5 oz) unsalted butter, softened
$1/3$ cup (60 g/2 oz) lightly packed soft brown sugar
1 egg, lightly beaten
1 teaspoon vanilla essence
1 cup (125 g/4 oz) plain flour
2 tablespoons cocoa powder
$1/3$ cup (30 g/1 oz) desiccated coconut
$1^{1}/2$ cups (45 g/$1^{1}/2$ oz) lightly crushed cornflakes
$1/2$ cup (90 g/3 oz) dark choc bits

1 Preheat the oven to 180°C (350°F/ Gas 4). Line two baking trays with baking paper.
2 Using electic beaters, cream the butter and sugar in a large mixing bowl until light and fluffy. Add the egg and vanilla essence and beat well.
3 Add the sifted flour and cocoa powder to the bowl with the coconut and cornflakes. Stir with a metal spoon until the ingredients are just combined. Put level tablespoons of mixture on the prepared trays, allowing room for spreading. Bake for 20 minutes, or until lightly browned, then leave on the tray to cool completely.
4 Place the choc bits in a small heatproof bowl. Bring a saucepan of water to the boil, then remove the pan from the heat. Sit the bowl over the pan, making sure the base of the bowl does not sit in the water. Stir until the chocolate has melted and the mixture is smooth. Spread the top of each biscuit thickly with the melted chocolate and allow to set.

Mix in the dry ingredients with a flat-bladed knife, using a cutting action.

Use your favorite cutters to cut out the gingerbread — a person shape is traditional.

GINGERBREAD PEOPLE

**Preparation time: 40 minutes + 15
 minutes refrigeration
Total cooking time: 10 minutes
Makes 16**

125 g (4 oz) unsalted butter, softened
1/3 cup (60 g/2 oz) lightly packed soft brown
 sugar
1/4 cup (90 g/3 oz) golden syrup
1 egg, lightly beaten
2 cups (250 g/8 oz) plain flour
1/4 cup (30 g/1 oz) self-raising flour
1 tablespoon ground ginger
1 teaspoon bicarbonate of soda
1 tablespoon currants

ICING
1 egg white
1/2 teaspoon lemon juice
1 1/4 cups (155 g/5 oz) icing sugar, sifted
assorted food colorings

1 Preheat the oven to 180°C (350°F/ Gas 4).
Line two baking trays with baking paper.
2 Using electric beaters, cream the butter, sugar
and golden syrup in a large mixing bowl until
light and fluffy. Add the egg gradually, beating
well after each addition. Sift the dry ingredients
over the butter mixture and mix with a knife until
just combined. Combine the dough with your
hands. Turn onto a well-floured surface and
knead for 1–2 minutes, or until smooth. Roll out
on a chopping board, between two sheets of
baking paper, to 5 mm (1/4 inch) thick. Chill on
the board for 15 minutes to firm.

3 Cut the dough into shapes with a 13 cm
(5 inch) gingerbread person cutter. Press the
remaining dough together and re-roll. Cut out
shapes and place the biscuits on the trays.
Place the currants as eyes and noses. Bake for
10 minutes, or until lightly browned. Cool on
the trays.
4 To make the icing, beat the egg white with
electric beaters in a small, clean, dry bowl until
foamy. Gradually add the lemon juice and icing
sugar and beat until thick. Divide the icing
among several bowls and add the food
colorings. Spoon into small paper icing bags.
Seal ends, snip the tips off the bags and pipe
on faces and clothing.

STORAGE: These biscuits can be stored in an
airtight container for up to 3 days.

Add the cooled syrup to the beaten butter, beating constantly.

Pipe icing onto each biscuit and top with a small rosette of coffee cream.

HAZELNUT COFFEE BISCUITS

Preparation time: 1 hour + 20 minutes refrigeration
Total cooking time: 25–35 minutes
Makes 50–60

125 g (4 oz) butter
$^1\!/_2$ cup (125 g/4 oz) caster sugar
1 teaspoon grated lemon rind
1 egg yolk
1 teaspoon lemon juice
1 cup (125 g/4 oz) hazelnuts, ground
$1^1\!/_4$ cups (155 g/5 oz) plain flour

ICING
1 cup (125 g/4 oz) icing sugar
30 g (1 oz) unsalted butter, melted
3–4 teaspoons lemon juice

COFFEE CREAM
$^1\!/_2$ cup (125 g/4 oz) caster sugar
$^1\!/_4$ cup (60 ml/2 fl oz) water
1 tablespoon instant coffee powder
80 g ($2^3\!/_4$ oz) unsalted butter

1 Preheat the oven to 180°C (350°F/ Gas 4). Line two baking trays with baking paper. Using electic beaters, beat the butter and sugar in a mixing bowl until light and creamy. Add the rind, egg yolk, juice and nuts. Beat until well combined. Using a metal spoon, stir in the sifted flour. Shape the dough into a smooth ball and cover in plastic wrap. Refrigerate for 20 minutes.
2 Divide the mixture in half. Roll one portion between two sheets of baking paper until 5 mm ($^1\!/_4$ inch) thick. Using a 3 cm ($1^1\!/_4$ inch) fluted cutter, cut out rounds and place on the prepared trays. Repeat with remaining dough. Bake for 10 minutes, or until the biscuits are golden. Remove from oven and transfer to wire racks to cool.

3 To make the icing, combine the sifted icing sugar and butter in a mixing bowl. Add enough lemon juice to form a smooth mixture. Place into a paper piping bag, snip off tip. Pipe the icing onto each biscuit.
4 To make the coffee cream, combine the sugar, water and coffee in a pan. Stir over low heat, without boiling, until the sugar dissolves. Bring to the boil, reduce heat and simmer, uncovered, without stirring for 4–5 minutes. Beat butter in a mixing bowl until light and creamy. Pour cooled syrup in a thin stream, beating constantly until thick and glossy.
5 Place into a paper piping bag, snip off tip to an inverted 'V'. Pipe small rosettes on top of iced biscuits.

STORAGE: Make up to a week in advance but ice just before serving.

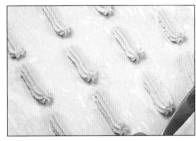

Pipe lengths of the mixture onto the prepared trays and place in the oven for baking.

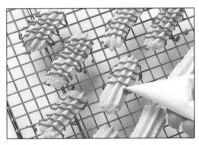

Drizzle the melted chocolate across the biscuits in a zigzag pattern and leave to set.

CHOCOLATE BUTTER FINGERS

Preparation time: 30 minutes
Total cooking time: 15 minutes
Makes 40

125 g (4 oz) butter
$^1/_3$ cup (40 g/1$^1/_4$ oz) icing sugar
$^1/_2$ teaspoon vanilla essence
$^1/_2$ teaspoon grated lemon rind
1 teaspoon cream
$^1/_2$ cup (60 g/2 oz) cornflour
$^1/_2$ cup (60 g/2 oz) plain flour
60 g (2 oz) chocolate melts, melted

1 Preheat the oven to 180°C (350°F/ Gas 4). Lightly grease two baking trays and line with baking paper. Using electric beaters, beat the butter and sugar until light and creamy. Add the vanilla essence, rind and cream, beat until combined. Add the sifted flours and beat until the mixture is smooth enough for piping.

2 Spoon the mixture into a piping bag fitted with a 1.5 cm ($^5/_8$ inch) star nozzle. Pipe 4 cm (1$^1/_2$ inch) lengths onto the prepared trays. Bake the biscuits for 15 minutes, or until lightly golden. Cool the biscuits on the trays before transferring to a wire rack.

3 Place the melted chocolate into a small paper icing bag and snip off the tip. Drizzle diagonally over the fingers. Allow to set. Serve.

STORAGE: The biscuits can be made up to 3 days in advance. Store in an airtight container in a cool, dark place.
NOTE: Decorate with dark or white chocolate, or dust with combined icing sugar and cocoa. When melting the chocolate, take care not to let water come into contact with the melting mixture or it will begin to seize and start to harden immediately.

Spread the dough with chocolate hazelnut spread and then carefully roll up.

Place the dough roll onto a clean work surface and cut into slices.

CHOC-HAZELNUT SCROLLS

Preparation time: 25 minutes
Total cooking time: 15 minutes + 30
minutes refrigeration
Makes 35

2 cups (250 g/8 oz) plain flour
$1/2$ cup (60 g/2 oz) ground hazelnuts
100 g ($3^1/2$ oz) unsalted butter
$1/2$ cup (125 g/4 oz) caster sugar
1 egg, lightly beaten
2 tablespoons iced water
$1/4$ cup (80 g/$2^3/4$ oz) chocolate hazelnut
   spread

1 Line two baking trays with baking paper. Place dry ingredients in a food processor and add the butter and sugar. Process until the mixture resembles fine breadcrumbs. Add the combined egg and water and process until the mixture forms a dough. Turn out onto a lightly floured surface and knead for 30 seconds or until the dough is smooth.

2 Place the dough onto a large sheet of baking paper and roll out into a rectangle of 25 x 35 cm (10 x 14 inch). Trim the edges. Spread the dough evenly with the chocolate hazelnut spread. Using the baking paper to lift the dough, roll up from the long side in Swiss-roll style. Wrap tightly in paper and refrigerate for 30 minutes.

3 Preheat the oven to 180°C (350°F/ Gas 4). Cut the roll into 1 cm ($1/4$ inch) slices, wiping the knife's blade between each cut. Place the slices on the prepared baking trays and bake for 15 minutes. Transfer to a wire rack to cool completely.

STORAGE: Store for up to 3 days in an airtight container.
VARIATION: Use ground macadamia nuts in place of the hazelnuts.
HINT: Chocolate hazelnut spread can be found in the jam and spread section of most supermarkets.

Fold the golden syrup mixture into the dry ingredients with a metal spoon.

Make sure the biscuits are well spaced on the baking trays as they will spread during baking.

COCOA SESAME BISCUITS

Preparation time: 15 minutes
Total cooking time: 12 minutes
Makes about 33

¾ cup (90 g/3 oz) plain flour
¼ cup (25 g/¾ oz) cocoa powder
¾ cup (75 g/2½ oz) rolled oats
1 cup (150 g/5 oz) sesame seeds
¾ cup (190 g/6½ oz) caster sugar
100 g (3½ oz) unsalted butter
2 tablespoons golden syrup
1 tablespoon boiling water
1 teaspoon bicarbonate of soda
185 g (6 oz) milk chocolate melts, melted

1 Preheat the oven to 160°C (315°F/ Gas 2–3). Line two baking trays with baking paper. Sift the flour and cocoa powder into a large mixing bowl. Add the rolled oats, sesame seeds and sugar and combine.

2 Combine the butter and golden syrup in a pan. Stir over a low heat until the butter is melted and the mixture is smooth. Pour boiling water into a small mixing bowl, add the soda and stir until dissolved. Add to the golden syrup mixture. Using a metal spoon, fold the mixture into the dry ingredients until well combined.

3 Drop 3 level tablespoons of mixture onto the prepared trays, allowing room for spreading. Flatten each one slightly with your fingertips. Bake for 12 minutes, or until lightly golden. Cool the biscuits on the trays for 5 minutes before transferring to a wire rack to cool completely. Spread approximately 1 teaspoon of chocolate into a 3 cm (1¼ inch) round in the centre of each biscuit.

Add the cocoa and melted chocolate to half the mixture and mix with a flat-bladed knife.

Assemble the biscuits by placing smaller shapes inside bigger pieces of a different color.

TWO-TONE BISCUITS

**Preparation time: 20 minutes + 20
 minutes refrigeration**
Total cooking time: 10–12 minutes
Makes about 40

125 g (4 oz) butter
³/₄ cup (90 g/3 oz) icing sugar
1 egg
1¹/₂ cups (185 g/6 oz) plain flour
1 tablespoon cornflour
2 tablespoons cocoa powder
50 g (1³/₄ oz) dark cooking chocolate, melted

1 Preheat the oven to 180°C (350°F/ Gas 4). Line two baking trays with baking paper. Using electric beaters, beat the butter and icing sugar in a large mixing bowl until light and creamy. Add the egg and beat until smooth. Add the sifted plain flour and cornflour and mix with a flat-bladed knife until well combined.
2 Divide the mixture evenly between two bowls. Only add the cocoa powder and melted chocolate to one portion, then mix both until well combined. Wrap the dough portions separately in plastic wrap and refrigerate for 20 minutes, or until firm.
3 Roll the dough portions separately between sheets of baking paper until 5 mm (¹/₄ inch) thick. Use two sizes of biscuit cutter of the same shape. Cut large shapes from each sheet of dough. Then take the smaller cutter and cut a shape from inside the larger dough shape; swap inner shapes and assemble to make two-tone biscuits. Place on the prepared trays and bake for 10–12 minutes, or until just golden. Cool on the tray.

STORAGE: These biscuits may be stored in an airtight container for up to 4 days.

Generously sprinkle the sugar mixture over the sheet of puff pastry.

Fold the sides of the pastry inwards and then again so that they almost meet in the centre.

SUGAR AND SPICE PALMIERS

Preparation time: 20 minutes +
15 minutes refrigeration
Total cooking time: 20 minutes
Makes 32

1 sheet frozen butter puff pastry
2 tablespoons raw sugar
1 teaspoon mixed spice
1 teaspoon ground cinnamon
40 g (1¼ oz) butter, melted
icing sugar, to dust

1 Preheat the oven to 210°C (415°F/ Gas 6–7). Lightly grease two baking trays and line with baking paper. Thaw the pastry sheet as directed on the packet. Combine the sugar and spices in small mixing bowl. Cut the pastry sheet in half and brush with the melted butter. Sprinkle with the sugar mixture until the pastry sheet is well covered, reserving 2 teaspoons.

2 Fold the long edges of the pastry inwards, then fold again so that the edges almost meet in the centre. Fold once more, place the pastry on a baking tray and refrigerate for 15 minutes. Using a small, sharp knife, cut the pastry pieces into 32 slices.

3 Arrange the palmiers cut-side up onto the prepared trays, brush with butter and sprinkle lightly with the reserved sugar mixture. Bake for 20 minutes, or until golden. Transfer palmiers to a wire rack to cool completely. Dust lightly with icing sugar before serving.

STORAGE: Store for up to a day in an airtight container. Palmiers may be re-crisped in a 180°C (350°F/Gas 4) oven for 5 minutes before serving.

Roll the mixture into balls, place on the baking trays and flatten with a fork.

Beat together the butter and icing sugar, then add the passionfruit pulp.

PASSIONFRUIT MELTING MOMENTS

Preparation time: 40 minutes
Total cooking time: 20 minutes
Makes 14 filled biscuits

250 g (8 oz) unsalted butter
$1/3$ cup (40 g/1$1/4$ oz) icing sugar
1 teaspoon vanilla essence
1$1/2$ cups (185 g/6 oz) self-raising flour
$1/2$ cup (60 g/2 oz) custard powder

PASSIONFRUIT FILLING
60 g (2 oz) butter
$1/2$ cup (60 g/2 oz) icing sugar
1$1/2$ tablespoons passionfruit pulp

1 Preheat the oven to 180°C (350°F/ Gas 4). Line two baking trays with baking paper. Place the butter and sugar in a large mixing bowl and beat until light and creamy. Add the vanilla essence and beat until combined. Sift in the flour and custard powder and mix to a soft dough. Roll level tablespoons of mixture into 28 balls and place on the prepared trays. Flatten slightly with a fork.

2 Bake for 20 minutes, or until lightly golden. Cool on a wire rack.

3 To make the filling, beat the butter and sugar until light and creamy. Fold in the passionfruit pulp until well combined. Use the filling to sandwich the biscuits together and leave to firm before serving.

STORAGE: The biscuits will keep for up to 4 days in an airtight container.

VARIATION: You can vary the flavor of the filling. For example, to make a coffee filling dissolve 2 teaspoons instant coffee in 2 teaspoons water and add to the butter and sugar mixture. Beat until well combined.

Add the nuts and ginger and mix until the mixture becomes a soft dough.

Place the dough on the prepared baking tray and shape into a log shape.

GINGER PECAN BISCOTTI

Preparation time: 30 minutes + cooling
Total cooking time: 1 hour 20 minutes
Makes about 20

1 cup (100 g/3½ oz) pecans
2 eggs
⅔ cup (155 g/5 oz) firmly packed soft
    brown sugar
1 cup (125 g/4 oz) self-raising flour
¾ cup (90 g/3 oz) plain flour
100 g (3½ oz) glacé ginger, finely chopped

1 Preheat the oven to 160°C (315°F/ Gas 2–3). Spread the pecans onto a baking tray and bake for 10–12 minutes, or until toasted. Tip the pecans onto a board to cool, then roughly chop. Line the baking tray with baking paper.

2 Using electric beaters, beat the eggs and sugar in a large mixing bowl until pale and creamy. Sift the self-raising flour and plain flour into the bowl, and add the pecans and glacé ginger. Mix to a soft dough, then place onto a prepared tray and carefully shape into a 9 x 23 cm (3½ x 9 inch) loaf.

3 Bake for 45 minutes, or until lightly golden. Cool completely on a wire rack for 15 minutes each side, then cut into 1 cm (½ inch) slices with a serrated bread knife. The biscotti will be crumbly on the edges so work slowly and, if possible, try to hold the sides as you cut. Arrange slices in a single layer on baking trays. Bake for 10 minutes each side. Don't worry if they don't seem fully dry as they will become crisp on cooling.

STORAGE: Cool before storing in an airtight container for 2–3 weeks.

RASPBERRY COCONUT BISCUITS

Preparation time: 40 minutes
Total cooking time: 10 minutes each tray
Makes 28

BISCUIT PASTRY
60 g (2 oz) butter
1/2 cup (125 g/4 oz) caster sugar
1 egg
2/3 cup (100 g/3 1/2 oz) plain flour
2/3 cup (100 g/3 1/2 oz) self-raising flour

ICING
100 g (3 1/2 oz) packet pink marshmallows
    (see VARIATION)
40 g (1 1/4 oz) butter
1/4 cup (40 g/1 1/4 oz) icing sugar, sifted
1/2 cup (45 g/ 1 1/2 oz) desiccated coconut
1/3 cup (100 g/3 1/2 oz) raspberry jam (see
    VARIATION)

1 Preheat the oven to 180°C (350°F /Gas 4).
Line two baking trays with baking paper. To
make the pastry, beat the butter and sugar with
electric beaters in a small mixing bowl until
light and creamy. Transfer to a large mixing
bowl. Add the egg and beat until combined.
Using a metal spoon, fold in the sifted flours.
Turn the dough onto a lightly floured surface.
Knead gently for 1 minute or until smooth. Roll
out the dough between sheets of baking paper
until 5 mm (1/4 inch) thick. Using a knife or
fluted pastry wheel, cut the dough into 4.5 x 6 cm
(1 3/4 x 2 1/2 inch) rectangles. Place the dough
rectangles on the prepared trays, making sure
they are well spaced to allow enough room for
spreading during baking. Re-roll the remaining
pastry and repeat cutting. Bake for 10 minutes,
or until lightly golden. Transfer to a wire rack
when cool.

2 To make the icing, combine the
marshmallows and butter in a small saucepan.
Stir over low heat until the marshmallows and
butter are melted and smooth. Stir in the icing
sugar and mix until smooth. Place the coconut
on a sheet of baking paper. Working very
quickly, spread about 1/4 teaspoon of icing along
each side of the biscuit, leaving a strip for the
jam in the centre. Dip the iced biscuit into the
desiccated coconut and shake off any excess.

3 Place the jam in small pan and heat gently
until thinned and warm. Using a teaspoon,
carefully spread a little jam down the centre of
each biscuit.

STORAGE: Biscuits can be stored for 3 days in a
single layer in an airtight container.
VARIATION: For a totally different look, use
white marshmallows and apricot jam.
HINT: Stand the icing in a bowl of hot water
while you are icing the biscuits. This will
prevent it from setting too quickly.

Spread icing down the sides of the biscuits and
then quickly coat with coconut.

Using a teaspoon, fill the centre strip of the
biscuits with warmed raspberry jam.

Beat the butter, sugar and egg until light and creamy then add the orange rind and juice.

Using a metal spoon, fold in the flour and poppy seeds until well combined.

ORANGE POPPY SEED COOKIES

Preparation time: 30 minutes
Total cooking time: 15 minutes
Makes 60

75 g (2½ oz) unsalted butter
¾ cup (185 g/6 oz) caster sugar
1 egg
1½ teaspoons finely grated orange rind
2 teaspoons orange juice
1¼ cups (155 g/5 oz) plain flour
¼ cup (35 g/1¼ oz) cornflour
¼ teaspoon bicarbonate of soda
1 tablespoon buttermilk
2 tablespoons poppy seeds
185 g (6 oz) white chocolate melts

1 Preheat the oven to 180°C (350°F/ Gas 4). Line two baking trays with baking paper. Using electric beaters, beat butter, sugar and egg in a small mixing bowl until light and creamy. Add the orange rind and juice and beat until combined. Transfer the mixture to a medium bowl.

2 Add the sifted flour, cornflour, bicarbonate of soda, buttermilk and poppy seeds. Using a metal spoon, mix to a soft dough.

3 Drop mixture, 2 teaspoons at a time, onto the prepared trays. Press a white chocolate melt into the centre of each cookie. Bake for 15 minutes, or until just golden. Cool the cookies on trays for 5 minutes before transferring to a wire rack to cool completely.

STORAGE: Cookies may be stored up to 3 days in an airtight container.
HINT: These cookies are also delicious if topped with an orange glaze icing, if desired.

Beat the butter and sugar with electric beaters until the mixture is light and creamy.

Shape the mixture into crescent-shaped biscuits and place on prepared baking tray.

MOCHA HAZELNUT CRESCENTS

Preparation time: 40 minutes
Total cooking time: 10 minutes
Makes 30

150 g (5 oz) unsalted butter
1/4 cup (60 g/2 oz) caster sugar
1 cup (125 g/4 oz) plain flour
1/2 cup (60 g/2 oz) self-raising flour
2 teaspoons instant coffee powder
250 g (8 oz) dark chocolate, chopped (see HINT)
1/4 cup (25 g/3/4 oz) ground hazelnuts (see VARIATION)

1 Preheat the oven to 180°C (350°F/ Gas 4). Line two baking trays with baking paper. Using electric beaters, beat the butter and sugar in a large mixing bowl until light and creamy. Sift the flours over the mixing bowl, and using a metal spoon, fold in with the coffee powder. Mix until a soft dough forms.

2 Shape 2 teaspoons of mixture into crescents and place on the prepared tray. Bake for 10 minutes. Transfer the biscuits to a wire rack and allow to cool completely before decorating.

3 Place the chocolate in a small heatproof bowl. Stand over a pan of simmering water and stir until chocolate is melted and mixture is smooth. Cool slightly.

4 Working with one at a time, place a crescent into the melted chocolate. Using a spoon, carefully coat the whole crescent in chocolate and lift out on a fork, allowing any excess chocolate to drain away. Place on a wire rack, and sprinkle half the top of the crescent with hazelnuts before the chocolate sets. Repeat with the remaining crescents.

STORAGE TIME: Store biscuits in an airtight container for up to 3 days.
VARIATION: Use ground almonds, walnuts or other ground nuts of choice in place of the hazelnuts, if preferred.
HINT: If the weather is warm, use 250 g (8 oz) compound chocolate or dark chocolate melts in place of the dark chocolate. Compound chocolate will set at room temperature.

Using a flat-bladed knife and a spoon, shape macaroons out of the mixture.

After the macaroons have cooled, dip each one into the bowl of melted chocolate.

COCONUT MACAROONS

Preparation time: 15 minutes
Total cooking time: 15–20 minutes
Makes 60

3 egg whites
1¼ cups (310 g/10 oz) caster sugar
½ teaspoon coconut essence
1 teaspoon grated lemon rind
2 tablespoons cornflour, sifted
2 cups (180 g/6 oz) desiccated coconut
125 g (4 oz) dark chocolate melts, melted

1 Preheat the oven to 180°C (350°F/ Gas 4). Line two baking trays with baking paper. Place egg whites in a small dry mixing bowl. Using electric beaters, beat the egg whites until firm peaks form. Add the sugar gradually, beating constantly until mixture is thick and glossy and all the sugar is dissolved. Add the coconut essence and rind and beat until just combined.

2 Transfer the mixture to a large mixing bowl and add cornflour and coconut. Using a metal spoon, stir until just combined.

3 Drop 2 level teaspoons of mixture onto prepared trays about 3 cm (1¼ inch) apart. Bake on the top shelf for 15–20 minutes, or until golden.

4 Leave the macaroons to completely cool on the trays. Dip half of each biscuit into the melted chocolate and allow to set before serving.

STORAGE: Store in an airtight container for up to 2 days.
HINT: Sprinkle biscuits with shredded coconut before baking. Drizzle with melted chocolate, instead of dipping, for decoration.

Roll the dough into balls, place on the prepared trays and press firmly with a fork.

Sandwich the cooled biscuits together with the jam and butter mixture.

MONTE CREAMS

Preparation time: 30 minutes
Total cooking time: 20 minutes
Makes 25

125 g (4 oz) unsalted butter
1/2 cup (125 g/4 oz) caster sugar
3 tablespoons milk
1 1/2 cups (185 g/6 oz) self-raising flour
1/4 cup (30 g/1 oz) custard powder
1/3 cup (30 g/1 oz) desiccated coconut

FILLING
75 g (2 1/2 oz) unsalted butter, softened
3/4 cup (90 g/3 oz) icing sugar
2 teaspoons milk
1/3 cup (105 g/3 1/2 oz) strawberry jam

1 Preheat the oven to 180°C (350°F/ Gas 4). Line two baking trays with baking paper.
2 Using electric beaters, cream the butter and sugar in a small mixing bowl until light and fluffy. Add the milk and beat until combined. Sift the flour and custard powder together and add to the bowl with the coconut. Mix to form a soft dough.
3 Roll 2 teaspoons of the mixture into balls. Place on the prepared trays, making sure they are spaced to allow for spreading during baking, and press with a fork. Dip the fork in custard powder occasionally to prevent it from sticking. Bake for 15–20 minutes, or until just golden. Transfer the biscuits to a wire rack to cool completely before filling.
4 For the filling, beat the butter and icing sugar in a small bowl with electric beaters until light and creamy. Beat in the milk. Spread one biscuit with half a teaspoon of the filling and one with half a teaspoon of jam, then press them together.

STORAGE: These will keep for up to 4 days in an airtight container.

Remove cooked biscuits from oven and transfer to a wire rack to completely cool.

Using a bag with a fluted nozzle, pipe coffee buttercream on the biscuits.

COFFEE KISSES

Preparation time: 30 minutes
Total cooking time: 10 minutes
Makes about 30

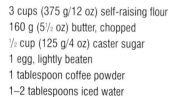

3 cups (375 g/12 oz) self-raising flour
160 g (5½ oz) butter, chopped
½ cup (125 g/4 oz) caster sugar
1 egg, lightly beaten
1 tablespoon coffee powder
1–2 tablespoons iced water

COFFEE BUTTERCREAM
80 g (2¾ oz) butter
1 cup (125 g/4 oz) icing sugar, sifted
2 teaspoons water
2 teaspoons coffee powder
100 g (3½ oz) white chocolate, melted

1 Preheat the oven to 180°C (350°F/ Gas 4). Brush two baking trays and line with baking paper. Sift the flour into a large bowl. Add the butter and rub into the flour, using your fingertips, until it resembles fine breadcrumbs. Add combined sugar, egg and coffee powder, dissolved in water, all at once. Mix with a flat-bladed knife until ingredients come together to form a soft dough. Lightly knead until smooth.
2 Roll out the dough between two sheets of baking paper to 5 mm (¼ inch) thickness. Cut into 5 cm (2 inch) rounds, using a fluted biscuit cutter. Place on the prepared trays and bake for 10 minutes, or until lightly golden. Transfer biscuits to a wire rack to cool.
3 To make coffee buttercream, using electric beaters, beat butter and icing sugar until light and creamy. Add combined water and coffee powder and beat until combined. Place the mixture in a piping bag fitted with a fluted nozzle and pipe buttercream onto half of the biscuits. Top with another biscuit and sandwich together. Drizzle or pipe with melted chocolate. Top with a chocolate-coated coffee bean, if desired.

Turn dough out onto a floured surface and press together until smooth.

Using a sharp knife, carefully cut each chilled dough log into slices.

LEMON AND LIME BISCUITS

Preparation time: 30 minutes + 1 hour refrigeration
Total cooking time: 12–15 minutes
Makes 30

150 g (5 oz) butter, softened
³/₄ cup (190 g/6¹/₂ oz) caster sugar
1 egg, lightly beaten
1 tablespoon lime juice
2 teaspoons grated lime rind
2 teaspoons grated lemon rind
1 cup (125 g/4 oz) plain flour
¹/₂ cup (60 g/2 oz) self-raising flour
60 g (2 oz) marzipan, grated
silver cachous, to decorate

LIME ICING
1 cup (125 g/4 oz) icing sugar, sifted
1 teaspoon finely grated lime rind
1 tablespoon lime juice
2 teaspoons water

1 Line two baking trays with baking paper. Using electric beaters, beat the butter and sugar in a large mixing bowl until light and creamy. Add the egg, juice and rinds. Beat until the mixture is well combined.

2 Add the flours and marzipan and, using a knife, mix until a soft dough forms. Divide the mixture in two. Turn one portion out onto a lightly floured surface and press together until smooth.

3 Roll the biscuit dough into a log shape about 4 cm (1¹/₂ inch) diameter. Roll in plastic wrap and refrigerate for 1 hour. Repeat with the remaining dough. Preheat the oven to 180°C (350°F/Gas 4). Cut the dough roll into 1 cm (¹/₂ inch) slices. Place on the prepared baking trays and bake for 10–15 minutes, or until lightly golden. Cool on the trays.

4 To make the lime icing, combine the icing sugar, rind, juice and water in a small bowl. Beat the mixture until smooth then either dip the biscuits in icing or pipe with an icing bag. Decorate with silver cachous.

STORAGE: Store the biscuits in an airtight container for up to 4 days.

Place the dough balls on the tray. Press each one with a fork, leaving a crisscross pattern.

After the white chocolate has set, dip the cookies into melted dark chocolate.

TRIPLE CHOCOLATE PEANUT BUTTER COOKIES

Preparation time: 20 minutes
Total cooking time: 30 minutes
Makes about 34

125 g (4 oz) unsalted butter
³/₄ cup (140 g/4¹/₂ oz) lightly packed soft
    brown sugar
1 egg, lightly beaten
³/₄ cup (185 g/6 oz) peanut butter (see
    HINTS)
1 cup (150 g/5 oz) plain flour, sifted
¹/₂ teaspoon bicarbonate of soda
¹/₄ cup (25 g/³/₄ oz) cocoa powder
175 g (6 oz) white chocolate melts
175 g (6 oz) dark chocolate melts

1 Preheat the oven to 180°C (350°F/ Gas 4). Line two 32 x 28 cm (13 x 11 inch) baking trays with baking paper. Using electric beaters, beat the butter and sugar in a mixing bowl until light and creamy. Add the egg gradually, beating thoroughly after each addition. Add the peanut butter and beat until combined.

2 Using a metal spoon, add the flour, soda and cocoa powder and mix to a soft dough. Roll level tablespoons of mixture into balls. Place the dough balls on the prepared trays and flatten with a fork in a crisscross pattern. Bake for 20 minutes. Leave the biscuits to cool on the trays for 5 minutes before transferring to wire racks. Allow the biscuits to cool completely before decorating.

3 Place the white chocolate melts in a small heatproof bowl. Stand over a pan of simmering water, making sure the bottom of bowl does not touch the water, and stir until the chocolate is melted and smooth. Dip one-third of each cookie in the white chocolate. Place on a wire rack to set. Melt the dark chocolate melts in the same way, and dip the opposite one-third of each cookie in the melted chocolate, leaving a plain band in the centre.

STORAGE: These cookies may be stored for up to 3 days in an airtight container.
HINTS: Before the chocolate sets, sprinkle the cookies with crushed nuts, if desired. Crunchy or smooth peanut butter may be used, as preferred.

Roll the dough into lengths before folding in half and plaiting together.

Dip the biscuits into the cooled chocolate and then set aside to set.

JAFFA RINGS

Preparation time: 30 minutes
Total cooking time: 20 minutes
Makes about 45

180 g (6 oz) unsalted butter
$^1/_2$ cup (125 g/4 oz) caster sugar
1 egg, lightly beaten
1$^1/_2$ teaspoons finely grated orange rind
50 g (1$^3/_4$ oz) milk chocolate, grated
1 cup (125 g/4 oz) self-raising flour, sifted
2 cups (250g/8 oz) plain flour, sifted
100 g (3$^1/_2$ oz) milk chocolate melts (see HINT)

1 Preheat the oven to 180°C (350°F/ Gas 4). Line two 32 x 28 cm (13 x 11 inch) baking trays with baking paper. Using electric beaters, beat the butter, sugar and egg in a large mixing bowl until light and creamy. Add the rind and grated chocolate and beat until combined.
2 Using a flat-bladed knife, fold in the flours and mix together to form a soft dough. Turn onto a lightly floured surface and knead for 30 seconds or until the dough is smooth.
3 Roll 3 teaspoonsful of mixture into small oblongs. Continue rolling into lengths of 20 cm (8 inch). Carefully fold in half and twist. Form the twisted rope into a ring. Place on the prepared trays. Bake for 12 minutes and transfer to a wire rack to cool.
4 Place the milk chocolate melts in a small heatproof bowl. Sit over a pan of simmering water, making sure the bottom of the bowl does not sit in the water, and stir until the chocolate is melted and smooth. Cool slightly. Dip bases of the biscuits into the melted chocolate. Stand on a wire rack to set.

STORAGE: Biscuits may be kept up to 4 days in an airtight container.
HINT: To decorate these biscuits quickly, the melted chocolate can be simply drizzled off the end of the prongs of a fork.

Press the mixture together with your fingers until a soft dough forms.

Roll the dough out into lengths, fold in half then twist and press the ends together.

SPICY WHOLEMEAL TWISTS

Preparation time: 20 minutes + 30 minutes refrigeration
Total cooking time: 15 minutes
Makes about 40

1 cup (125 g/4 oz) self-raising flour
$^1/_2$ cup (100 g/3$^1/_2$ oz) wholemeal self-raising flour
$^1/_4$ cup (30 g/1 oz) ground walnuts (see HINT)
125 g (4 oz) unsalted butter, chopped
$^1/_3$ cup (80 g/2$^3/_4$ oz) firmly packed soft brown sugar
3 teaspoons mixed spice
1 egg, lightly beaten
1 tablespoon sugar

1 Preheat the oven to 180°C (350°F/ Gas 4). Grease two 32 x 28 cm (13 x 11 inch) baking trays. Place the flours, walnuts, butter, brown sugar and spice in a food processor. Process for 10 seconds or until the mixture resembles fine breadcrumbs. Add the egg and process for another 10 seconds or until just combined.
2 Transfer the mixture to a mixing bowl. Mix until a soft dough forms. Cover with plastic wrap and refrigerate for 30 minutes, or until firm.
3 Roll 2 teaspoons of mixture into 14 cm (5$^1/_2$ inch) lengths. Fold lengths in half. Twist and press the ends together. Place onto the prepared trays. Sprinkle with the sugar. Bake for 15 minutes, or until golden. Transfer the biscuits to a wire rack to cool.

STORAGE: Biscuits may be stored up to 4 days in an airtight container or up to 2 months in the freezer.
VARIATION: Dust biscuits with icing sugar when cold.
HINT: Ground walnuts are found in supermarkets and delicatessens, or they may be freshly ground in a food processor or blender.

Remove the cookies from the oven and set aside on a wire rack to cool.

Work quickly with the icing as overbeating will make it dull, flat and grainy.

CITRUS COOKIES

Preparation time: 10 minutes
Total cooking time: 15 minutes
Makes about 30

125 g (4 oz) unsalted butter
¾ cup (90 g/3 oz) icing sugar, sifted
1½ cups (185 g/6 oz) plain flour
2 teaspoons finely grated lime rind
2 teaspoons finely grated lemon rind
⅓ cup (80 ml/2¾ fl oz) sour cream
1 tablespoon lemon juice

ORANGE ICING
1 cup (125 g/4 oz) pure icing sugar
2 teaspoons finely grated orange rind
2 tablespoons orange juice

1 Preheat the oven to 180°C (350°F/ Gas 4). Lightly grease two 32 x 28 cm (13 x 11 inch) baking trays. Place the butter, icing sugar, flour and rind in a food processor. Process for 10 seconds or until the mixture resembles fine breadcrumbs. Add the sour cream and lemon juice and process for 10 seconds or until the mixture is well combined.

2 Drop level tablespoons of mixture onto the prepared trays, allowing room for spreading. Bake for 15 minutes, or until lightly golden. Cool completely on a wire rack.

3 To make the orange icing, combine the icing sugar, rind and juice in a small bowl. Stand the bowl over a pan of simmering water, stirring until the icing is smooth and glossy. Spread the icing over cookies with a flat-bladed knife.

STORAGE: Store up to 3 days in an airtight container or up to 2 months in the freezer, without icing.

Fold oats, coconut, apple and flour into the mixture using a metal spoon.

Make sure the balls of mixture are well spaced as they will spread during baking.

APPLE AND CINNAMON OATCAKES

Preparation time: 15 minutes
Total cooking time: 20 minutes
Makes about 20

1 cup (90 g/3 oz) chopped dried apple (see VARIATION)
1/2 cup (125 ml/4 fl oz) boiling water
125 g (4 oz) unsalted butter
1/2 cup (95 g/3 oz) lightly packed soft brown sugar
1 egg, lightly beaten
3/4 cup (75 g/2 1/2 oz) rolled oats
1 cup (125 g/4 oz) self-raising flour, sifted
1 tablespoon cinnamon sugar (see HINT)
1/4 cup (25 g/3/4 oz) desiccated coconut

1 Preheat the oven to 180°C (350°F/ Gas 4). Lightly grease two 32 x 28 cm (13 x 11 inch) baking trays. Combine the apple and water in a small bowl and stand for 5 minutes, or until all the water is absorbed. Using electric beaters, beat the butter and sugar in a small mixing bowl until light and creamy. Add the egg and beat well.
2 Transfer the mixture to a large mixing bowl and add the oats, coconut, apple and flour. Using a metal spoon, stir until just combined.
3 Drop heaped tablespoons full of mixture onto the prepared trays, making sure to allow room for spreading during baking. Sprinkle with the cinnamon sugar. Bake for 20 minutes, or until the biscuits are lightly golden. Transfer to wire racks to cool.

STORAGE: Store for 2 days in an airtight container or freeze for 2 months.
VARIATION: Use chopped dried apricots instead of apples.
HINT: You can buy cinnamon sugar in the supermarket, or simply make your own by combining equal quantities of caster sugar and ground cinnamon.

Place the rounds at well spaced intervals on the baking tray to allow for spreading during baking.

Pipe the peppermint cream onto each biscuit and top with a choc bit.

CHOC-MINT SWIRLS

Preparation time: 30 minutes
Total cooking time: 15 minutes
Makes 22

65 g (2¼ oz) unsalted butter
¼ cup (60 g/2 oz) caster sugar
½ cup (60 g/2 oz) plain flour
⅓ cup (40 g/1¼ oz) self-raising flour
2 tablespoons cocoa powder
1–2 tablespoons milk
22 choc bits

FILLING
100 g (3½ oz) unsalted butter, extra
1⅓ cups (165 g/5½ oz) icing sugar
few drops peppermint essence

1 Preheat the oven to 180°C (350°F/ Gas 4). Line two 32 x 28 cm (13 x 11 inch) baking trays with baking paper. Using electric beaters, beat the butter and sugar in a small mixing bowl until light and creamy. Add the sifted flours, cocoa and milk. Stir with a flat-bladed knife until the mixture forms a soft dough. Turn out onto a piece of baking paper and knead for 1 minute or until smooth.

2 Roll the dough out to 5 mm (¼ inch) thickness. Cut into rounds, using a 4 cm (1½ inch) plain biscuit cutter. Place on the prepared tray and bake for 15 minutes. Transfer to a wire rack to cool completely before decorating.

3 To make the filling, beat the butter with electric beaters until soft. Add the icing sugar and beat until smooth, creamy and light. Add the peppermint essence and beat until combined. Using a piping bag fitted with a large fluted nozzle, carefully pipe a flower of peppermint cream onto each biscuit. Place a choc bit in the centre of each flower.

STORAGE: Store for up to 2 days in an airtight container
VARIATION: Dust the biscuits with one teaspoon each of icing sugar and cocoa powder, sifted together.

Roll mixture into balls and place on a prepared baking tray before slightly flattening.

Place softened butter and essence in a small bowl and beat with a wooden spoon.

VANILLA CUSTARD KISSES

Preparation time: 15 minutes
Total cooking time: 12 minutes
Makes 40

125 g (4 oz) unsalted butter
1/2 cup (125 g/4 oz) caster sugar
2 egg yolks
2 teaspoons vanilla essence
1/3 cup (60 g/2 oz) custard powder
3/4 cup (120 g/4 oz) plain flour
3/4 cup (120 g/4 oz) self-raising flour

VANILLA CREAM
40 g (1 1/4 oz) unsalted butter, softened
2/3 cup (110 g/3 1/2 oz) icing sugar
1 teaspoon vanilla essence
1 tablespoon milk

1 Preheat the oven to 180°C (350°F/ Gas 4). Grease two 32 x 28 cm (13 x 11 inch) baking trays and line with baking paper. Using electric beaters, beat the butter and sugar in a small mixing bowl until mixture is light and creamy. Add the egg yolks one at a time, beating thoroughly after each addition. Add the essence and beat until combined.

2 Transfer the mixture to a large mixing bowl. Using a metal spoon, fold in the sifted custard powder and flours. Stir until ingredients are just combined and the mixture is almost smooth. Press the mixture together with fingertips to form a soft dough.

3 Roll 1 level teaspoon of mixture at a time into balls. Arrange about 5 cm (2 inch) apart on the prepared trays. Flatten lightly with the base of a glass into 2.5 cm (1 inch) rounds. Bake for 12 minutes, or until golden.

4 To make the vanilla cream, beat the butter and essence in a small bowl with a wooden spoon until smooth. Add the sifted icing sugar and milk gradually, stirring until the mixture is smooth. Leave the biscuits on the trays for 5 minutes then transfer to a wire rack to cool. Spread half the biscuits with filling and sandwich together with the remaining biscuits.

STORAGE: Store the biscuits in an airtight container for up to 2 days.

Add beaten eggs gradually to the mixture, making sure they are well combined.

Roll balls of mixture in the crushed cornflakes on a piece of baking paper.

CORNFLAKE COOKIES

Preparation time: 15 minutes
Total cooking time: 20 minutes
Makes 36

125 g (4 oz) unsalted butter, softened
³/₄ cup (185 g/6 oz) sugar
2 eggs, lightly beaten
1 teaspoon vanilla essence
2 tablespoons currants
1¹/₂ cups (135 g/4¹/₂ oz) desiccated coconut
¹/₂ teaspoon bicarbonate of soda
¹/₂ teaspoon baking powder
2 cups (250 g/8 oz) plain flour
3 cups (90 g/3 oz) cornflakes, lightly
    crushed (see NOTE)

1 Preheat the oven to 180°C (350°F/ Gas 4). Line two baking trays with baking paper.
2 Cream the butter and sugar in a small bowl with electric beaters until light and fluffy. Gradually add the eggs, beating thoroughly after each addition. Add the essence and beat until combined.
3 Transfer the mixture to a large bowl and stir in the currants and coconut. Fold in the sifted bicarbonate of soda, baking powder and flour with a metal spoon and stir until the mixture is almost smooth. Put the cornflakes in a shallow dish, drop level tablespoons of mixture onto the cornflakes and roll into balls. Arrange on the trays, allowing room for spreading.
4 Bake for 15–20 minutes, or until crisp and golden. Cool slightly on the tray, then transfer to a wire rack to cool. When completely cold, store in an airtight container.

NOTE: A mess-free method for crushing cornflakes is to put them in a plastic bag and lightly crush with your hands or a rolling pin.

Knead the dough until smooth on a lightly floured work surface.

Using the base of a glass, slightly flatten the balls of dough after they are placed on the tray.

CHOCOLATE JAMAICAN ROUNDS

Preparation time: 15 minutes
Total cooking time: 25 minutes
Makes 30

100 g (3½ oz) unsalted butter
⅓ cup (90 g/3 oz) caster sugar
1 teaspoon coconut essence
2 tablespoons coconut cream
60 g (2 oz) milk chocolate, melted
2 teaspoons grated lime rind
½ cup (45 g/1½ oz) desiccated coconut,
   plus 2 tablespoons extra
1¾ cups (220 g/7 oz) plain flour

ICING
60 g (2 oz) grated dark cooking chocolate,
   chopped
30 g (1 oz) unsalted butter
2 teaspoons coconut cream
¼ teaspoon coconut essence

1 Preheat the oven to 180°C (350°F/ Gas 4). Line a 32 x 28 cm (13 x 11 inch) baking tray with baking paper. Using electric beaters, beat the butter and sugar in small mixing bowl until light and creamy. Add the essence, cream, chocolate and rind and beat until well combined.

2 Add the coconut and flour and press together to form a soft dough. Turn onto a lightly floured surface and knead for 1 minute or until the dough is smooth.

3 Roll 3 teaspoons of the mixture at a time into balls. Place on the prepared tray. Flatten the balls slightly, using the base of a glass. Bake for 20 minutes, or until lightly browned. Leave the biscuits to cool on the tray.

4 To make the icing, place the butter and chocolate in a small heatproof bowl. Stand over a pan of simmering water, making sure the base does not touch the water, and stir until mixture is smooth. Remove from heat. Add the coconut essence and cream and stir to combine. When the biscuits cool, dip the tops in the icing. Sprinkle with the extra coconut and leave to set.

Make sure the mixture is well combined by stirring with a flat-bladed knife.

Spoon the mixture, 1 tablespoon at a time, onto the prepared baking tray.

CHOCOLATE CHERRY OATIES

Preparation time: 12 minutes
Total cooking time: 15 minutes
Makes 30

¼ cup (30 g/1 oz) plain flour
¼ cup (30 g/1 oz) self-raising flour
1½ cups (150 g/5 oz) rolled oats
½ cup (125 g/4 oz) caster sugar
½ cup (125 g/4 oz) glacé cherries,
    quartered
½ cup (60 g/2 oz) chopped pecan nuts
¼ cup (45 g/1½ oz) choc bits
⅓ cup (60 g/2 oz) chopped white chocolate
125 g (4 oz) unsalted butter, melted
2 eggs, lightly beaten
80 g (2¾ oz) white chocolate melts, melted

1 Preheat the oven to 180°C (350°F/ Gas 4). Line a 32 x 28 cm (13 x 11 inch) baking tray with baking paper. Sift the flours into a large mixing bowl. Add the oats, sugar, cherries, nuts and chocolate and stir. Make a well in the centre of the ingredients, then add the butter and eggs.
2 Using a flat-bladed knife, stir until all ingredients are well combined.
3 Drop 1 level tablespoon of mixture at a time onto the prepared tray, allowing room for spreading during baking. Bake for 12–15 minutes, or until lightly browned. Transfer to a wire rack to cool completely. Pipe a spiral of white chocolate on top of each biscuit.

Lightly knead the dough with your fingertips and then roll into balls.

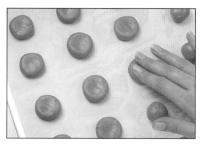

Place the balls of dough on the prepared trays and press with your fingertips to flatten.

GINGERNUTS

Preparation time: 15 minutes
Total cooking time: 15 minutes
Makes 50

2 cups (250 g/8 oz) plain flour
$^{1}/_{2}$ teaspoon bicarbonate of soda
1 tablespoon ground ginger
$^{1}/_{2}$ teaspoon mixed spice
125 g (4 oz) unsalted butter, chopped
1 cup (185 g/6 oz) lightly packed soft brown sugar
$^{1}/_{4}$ cup (60 ml/2 fl oz) boiling water
1 tablespoon golden syrup

1 Preheat the oven to 180°C (350°F/ Gas 4). Line two baking trays with baking paper.
2 Sift the flour, bicarbonate of soda, ginger and mixed spice into a large mixing bowl. Add the butter and sugar and rub into the flour with your fingertips until the mixture resembles fine breadcrumbs.
3 Pour the boiling water into a small heatproof jug, add the golden syrup and stir until dissolved. Add to the flour mixture and mix to a soft dough with a flat-bladed knife.
4 Roll into balls using 2 heaped teaspoons of mixture at a time. Place on the prepared trays, allowing room for spreading, and flatten out slightly with your fingertips. Bake for 15 minutes, or until well-colored and firm. Leave to cool on the trays for 10 minutes before transferring to a wire rack to cool completely. Repeat with the remaining mixture.

STORAGE: Store biscuits in an airtight container for up to 5 days.
VARIATION: If you want to dress the biscuits up, make icing by combining 2–3 teaspoons lemon juice, $^{1}/_{2}$ cup (60 g/2 oz) sifted icing sugar and 10 g ($^{1}/_{4}$ oz) melted butter in a bowl. Mix until smooth, then spread over the biscuits and allow to set.

Place the caramel on top of the biscuits after spreading with melted chocolate.

Push a choc bit into the caramel centre until it is firmly placed.

CHOCOLATE CARAMEL ROUNDS

Preparation time: 30 minutes
Total cooking time: 25 minutes
Makes 30

1½ cups (185 g/6 oz) plain flour
1 tablespoon cocoa powder
180 g (6 oz) unsalted butter, chopped
½ cup (95 g/3 oz) lightly packed soft brown sugar
1 egg yolk
2 tablespoons grated milk chocolate
1 cup (200 g/6½ oz) choc bits, plus 30 choc bits, extra

CARAMEL FILLING
200 g (6½ oz) jersey caramels, chopped
1 tablespoon unsalted butter
1 tablespoon cream

1 Preheat the oven to 180°C (350°F/ Gas 4). Line two 32 x 28 cm (13 x 11 inch) baking trays with baking paper. Sift the flour and cocoa powder into a large mixing bowl. Add the butter and sugar and, using your fingertips, rub butter into the flour for 2 minutes, or until the mixture is fine and crumbly. Add the egg yolk and grated chocolate and press together to form a soft dough. Turn the dough onto a lightly floured surface and knead for 1 minute.

2 Roll the pastry to 5 mm (¼ inch) thickness. Using a fluted biscuit cutter, cut into 5 cm (2 inch) rounds and place on the prepared tray. Bake for 15 minutes. Transfer the biscuits to a wire rack to cool.

3 To make the caramel filling, combine the caramels, butter and cream in a small pan. Stir over low heat for 3 minutes, or until the caramels have melted. Remove from the heat and beat until smooth. Cool.

4 To melt the choc bits for the top of the biscuits, place in a small heatproof bowl. Stand the bowl over a pan of simmering water, making sure the base does not touch the water, and stir

until the chocolate is melted and smooth. Spread a little melted chocolate over each biscuit and place half a teaspoon of filling in the centre. Push one of the extra choc bits on top.

Sift the flour and cocoa powder into the bowl and stir with a metal spoon.

Pipe swirls of mixture onto the prepared baking tray and place the mixed peel on top.

CHOCOLATE LEMON SWIRLS

Preparation time: 12 minutes
Total cooking time: 12 minutes
Makes 60

125 g (4 oz) unsalted butter
²/₃ cup (85 g/3 oz) icing sugar
1 egg, lightly beaten
2 teaspoons grated lemon rind (see VARIATION)
1¹/₄ cups (155 g/5 oz) plain flour
¹/₄ cup (25 g/³/₄ oz) cocoa powder
2 tablespoons finely chopped mixed peel

1 Preheat the oven to 180°C (350°F/ Gas 4). Line a 32 x 28 cm (13 x 11 inch) baking tray with baking paper. Using electric beaters, beat the butter and sugar until light and creamy. Add the egg and rind, beat until well combined.

2 Add the flour and cocoa. Using a metal spoon, stir until the ingredients are just combined.

3 Spoon the mixture into a piping bag fitted with a fluted 1 cm (¹/₂ inch) piping nozzle and pipe swirls about 3 cm (1¹/₄ inch) in diameter onto the prepared tray. Top each swirl with a few pieces of the mixed peel. Bake for 12 minutes. Leave the biscuits to cool on the trays.

STORAGE: The biscuits may be stored in an airtight container for up to 2 days.
VARIATION: Use orange rind in place of the lemon rind, if preferred.

Pour the combined butter, sugar, honey and peanut butter into the flour mixture.

Coat one side of the cookie with icing and then dip into the chopped nuts.

PEANUT BUTTER COOKIES

Preparation time: 15 minutes
Total cooking time: 10 minutes
Makes about 30

1 cup (150 g/5 oz) plain flour
1/2 cup (75 g/2 1/2 oz) self-raising flour
1 cup (90 g/3 oz) rolled oats
125 g (4 oz) unsalted butter
1/2 cup (110 g/3 1/2 oz) caster sugar
1/3 cup (120 g/4 oz) honey
2 tablespoons peanut butter
1 cup (150 g/5 oz) roasted unsalted
   peanuts, finely chopped

TOPPING
3/4 cup (120 g/4 oz) icing sugar
25 g (3/4 oz) butter, softened
1 tablespoon warm water

1 Preheat the oven to 180°C (350°F/ Gas 4). Grease two baking trays. Sift the flours into a large mixing bowl and stir in the oats.
2 Combine the butter, sugar, honey and peanut butter in a pan and stir over medium heat until melted. Add to the flour mixture. Using a metal spoon, stir to just combine the ingredients. Roll heaped teaspoons of mixture into balls. Arrange on the prepared trays and press lightly to flatten. Bake for 10 minutes, or until golden. Cool the cookies on the trays.
3 To make the topping, combine the icing sugar, butter and water in a small bowl. Stir until smooth. Dip the tops of the cookies into the topping, then into the nuts.

STORAGE: Store for up to 4 days in an airtight container.

It is essential to work as fast as possible once the cookies are removed from the oven.

Fold each cookie in half, than in half again over the edge of a bowl.

FORTUNE COOKIES

Preparation time: 45 minutes + 15 minutes standing
Total cooking time: 50 minutes
Makes 30

3 egg whites
1/2 cup (60 g/2 oz) icing sugar, sifted
45 g (1 1/2 oz) unsalted butter, melted
1/2 cup (60 g/2 oz) plain flour

1 Preheat the oven to 180°C (350°F/ Gas 4). Lightly grease a baking tray. Draw three 8 cm (3 inch) circles on a sheet of baking paper, turn over and use to line the tray.

2 Place the egg whites in a clean, dry bowl and whisk until just frothy. Add the icing sugar and butter and stir until smooth. Add the flour, mix until smooth, and leave for 15 minutes. Using a flat-bladed knife, spread 2 level teaspoons of mixture over each circle. Bake for 5 minutes, or until slightly brown around the edges.

3 Working quickly, remove from the trays by sliding a flat-bladed knife under each round. Place a written fortune message in each cookie. Fold in half, then in half again, over the edge of a bowl or a flat-bladed knife. Keep a tea towel handy to use when folding the cookies. The tray is hot and you need to work fast, so take care not to burn your hands. Cool on a wire rack. Cook the remaining mixture the same way. Make two or three cookies at a time, otherwise they will harden too quickly and break when folding.

STORAGE: The cookies will keep for 2 days in an airtight container.
NOTE: These were originated by Chinese Americans. Each biscuit contains a message, usually a proverb or horoscope, or more recently a joke. The biscuits are served at the end of a Chinese meal to wish good fortune.

Using your fingertips, rub the butter into the flour until the mixture is fine and crumbly.

Shape the rolled lengths of dough into pretzel shapes on a floured work surface.

CHOCOLATE APRICOT PRETZELS

Preparation time: 25 minutes
Total cooking time: 20 minutes
Makes 40

¹/₂ cup (80 g/2³/₄ oz) finely chopped dried apricots
¹/₃ cup (80 ml/2³/₄ fl oz) orange juice
20 g (³/₄ oz) unsalted butter
³/₄ cup (120 g/4 oz) self-raising flour
¹/₂ cup (75 g/2¹/₂ oz) plain flour
60 g (2 oz) unsalted butter, chopped
¹/₄ cup (55 g/2 oz) caster sugar
2 egg yolks
¹/₂ cup (70 g/2¹/₄ oz) grated milk chocolate
150 g (5 oz) white chocolate melts
10 g (¹/₄ oz) white vegetable shortening

1 Preheat the oven to 180°C (350°F/ Gas 4). Line a 32 x 28 cm (13 x 11 inch) baking tray with baking paper. Combine apricots, juice and butter in a small saucepan. Stir over low heat for 5 minutes; remove from heat, cool.

2 Sift the flours into a large mixing bowl. Add the butter and sugar. Using fingertips, rub butter into flour for 2 minutes, or until the mixture resembles fine breadcrumbs. Add the yolks, chocolate and cooled apricot mixture. Press mixture together to form a soft dough.

3 Turn onto lightly floured surface and knead for 2 minutes until smooth. Roll 2 level teaspoons of mixture at a time into balls. Roll the dough into 15 cm (6 inch) x 5 mm (¹/₄ inch) lengths. Shape and loop into pretzels. Bake for 15 minutes, or until lightly browned. Transfer to a wire rack to cool. Combine the chocolate melts and shortening in a small saucepan and stir over low heat until melted. Dip half of each pretzel diagonally into the melted chocolate mixture.

FRUITY SHORTBREAD PILLOWS

Preparation time: 1 hour
Total cooking time: 15–20 minutes
Makes 18

2 cups (250 g/8 oz) plain flour
1/2 cup (60 g/2 oz) icing sugar
185 g (6 oz) chilled unsalted butter, chopped
1 egg
1/4 cup (45 g/1 1/2 oz) fruit mince (see VARIATION)
1 egg, extra, lightly beaten
icing sugar, to serve

1 Preheat the oven to 180°C (350°F/ Gas 4). Line two baking trays with baking paper. Place the flour, sugar and butter in a food processor. Process for 20 seconds or until the mixture resembles fine breadcrumbs. Add the egg and process for a further 15 seconds or until the mixture comes together. Turn onto a lightly floured surface and knead for 2–3 minutes, or until the dough is smooth. Leave the dough, covered with plastic wrap, in the refrigerator for 10–15 minutes.
2 Divide the pastry in two. Roll half the pastry on a sheet of baking paper to 5 mm (1/4 inch) thickness. Lightly mark round circles with a 4 cm (1 1/2 inch) cutter. Spoon 1/2 teaspoon of the fruit mince into the centre of each circle. Brush the pastry with egg.

3 On a sheet of baking paper, roll the remaining pastry to 2.5 mm (1/8 inch) thickness. (Pastry should be rolled into a slightly larger circle, approximately 1.5 cm (5/8 inch) extra in diameter.) Carefully lift the pastry, using the rolling pin as a lever, over the top of first pastry sheet. Press down between the filling to seal the edges. Cut the biscuits, using a floured 4 cm (1 1/2 inch) round cutter. (The biscuits should look like little pillows.) Place on the prepared baking trays. Bake for 15–20 minutes, or until pale golden. Cool biscuits on trays. Dust liberally with icing sugar before serving.

STORAGE: The biscuits may be stored in an airtight container for up to 3 days.
VARIATION: Add 1 tablespoon of chopped walnuts to the fruit mince, for a fruit and nut variation. If fruit mince is not available, use 1/4 cup (45 g/1 1/2 oz) of finely chopped mixed dried fruit, with 2–3 teaspoons of rum or brandy. Mix well and leave to stand for 30 minutes, or until the fruit has absorbed the liquid. Fruit juice can be used in place of rum or brandy.
HINT: Make the biscuits a different shape by using a square or oval cutter, instead of round.

Mark the pastry with a biscuit cutter, then place fruit mince in the centre of the circles.

Once you have sealed the edges, cut out the biscuits with a round cutter.

Roll dough into balls and place on the prepared baking tray, allowing room for spreading.

After the biscuits have cooled, sandwich together with the ginger filling.

GINGER SHORTBREAD DREAMS

Preparation time: 25 minutes
Total cooking time: 15 minutes
Makes 22

¹/₂ cup (60 g/2 oz) plain flour
¹/₂ cup (60 g/2 oz) self-raising flour
2 tablespoons cornflour
100 g (3¹/₂ oz) unsalted butter, chopped
2 tablespoons soft brown sugar

FILLING
60 g (2 oz) unsalted butter
¹/₃ cup (40 g/1¹/₄ oz) icing sugar
1 tablespoon finely chopped glacé ginger

1 Preheat the oven to 180°C (350°F/ Gas 4). Line two 32 x 28 cm (13 x 11 inch) baking trays with baking paper. Place the flours, butter and sugar in a food processor. Process until the mixture forms a dough. Turn out onto a lightly floured surface and knead for 20 seconds or until smooth.

2 Roll level teaspoons of mixture into balls. Place on the prepared trays and press with a fork in a crisscross pattern. Bake for 15 minutes, until just golden. Transfer the biscuits to a wire rack to cool completely before filling.

3 To make the filling, beat the butter and sugar until light and fluffy. Add the ginger and beat until combined. Spread half the biscuits with the filling and sandwich with the plain ones.

STORAGE: This shortbread can be stored for up to 3 days in an airtight container.
VARIATION: Add 1 teaspoon of ground ginger to biscuit mixture.

Place the dry ingredients in a large mixing bowl then add the butter and eggs.

Gently press a banana chip on top of each ball of mixture and then place in the oven.

CHOC-BANANA CHIP BISCUITS

Preparation time: 20 minutes
Total cooking time: 20 minutes
Makes about 40

150 g (5 oz) banana chips (see NOTE)
¼ cup (30 g/1 oz) plain flour
¼ cup (30 g/1 oz) self-raising flour
2 tablespoons cocoa powder
½ cup (125 g/ 4 oz) caster sugar
40 g (1¼ oz) unsalted butter, melted
2 eggs, lightly beaten
60 g (2 oz) dark chocolate melts

1 Preheat the oven to 180°C (350°F/ Gas 4). Line two 32 x 28 cm (13 x 11 inch) baking trays with baking paper. Reserve 40 small banana chips for decoration and place the rest in a food processor. Process until the chips resemble coarse breadcrumbs.

2 Sift the flours with the cocoa powder and caster sugar into bowl. Add the banana chips. Make a well in the centre. Stir in the melted butter and eggs. Using a metal spoon, mix until well combined. Do not over-beat.

3 Drop 2 teaspoons of mixture at well spaced intervals onto the prepared trays. Top each with a banana chip and bake for 15 minutes. Leave to cool on the trays for 10 minutes before transferring to a wire rack to cool completely. Place the chocolate melts in a small heatproof bowl and stand over a pan of simmering water. Stir until melted. Put the melted chocolate in a paper piping bag, snip the corner off, and pipe the desired design over each biscuit.

STORAGE: the biscuits may be stored for up to 2 days in an airtight container.
NOTE: Banana chips are available at super-markets and health food stores.

Using a metal spoon, fold flour and nuts through the beaten egg whites.

Slice the biscotti loaf and bake for 15 minutes, or until lightly golden and crisp.

MIXED NUT BISCOTTI

Preparation time: 30 minutes
Total cooking time: 45 minutes
Makes about 50

25 g (³/₄ oz) almonds (see VARIATION)
25 g (³/₄ oz) hazelnuts
75 g (2¹/₂ oz) unsalted pistachios
3 egg whites
¹/₂ cup (125 g/4 oz) caster sugar
³/₄ cup (90 g/3 oz) plain flour

1 Preheat the oven to 180°C (350°F/ Gas 4). Lightly grease a 26 x 8 x 4.5 cm (10¹/₂ x 3 x 1³/₄ inch) bar tin and line base and sides with baking paper. Spread the almonds, hazelnuts and pistachios onto a flat baking tray and place in the oven for 2–3 minutes, until nuts are just toasted. Leave to cool. Place the egg whites in a small, clean, dry bowl. Using electric beaters, beat egg whites until stiff peaks form. Add the sugar gradually, beating constantly until the mixture is thick and glossy and all the sugar has dissolved.
2 Transfer the mixture to a large mixing bowl. Add the sifted flour and nuts. Using a metal spoon, gently fold the ingredients together until well combined. Spread into the prepared tin and smooth the surface with a spoon. Bake for 25 minutes. Leave to cool completely in tin.
3 Preheat the oven to 160°C (315°F/ Gas 2–3). Using a sharp, serrated knife, cut the baked loaf into 5 mm (¹/₄ inch) slices. Spread the slices onto the prepared trays and bake for about 15 minutes, turning once halfway through cooking, until the slices are lightly golden and crisp. Serve with coffee, or a sweet dessert wine.

STORAGE: The biscotti will keep for up to a week in an airtight container.
VARIATION: Use any combination of nuts, or a single variety, to the weight of 125 g (4 oz).

Roll the mixture into balls and place on the prepared tray.

Dip the cooled macaroons into melted chocolate and leave to set.

CHOC-DIPPED MACAROONS

Preparation time: 25 minutes
Total cooking time: 15 minutes
Makes about 24

1 egg white
⅓ cup (90 g/3 oz) caster sugar
2 teaspoons cornflour
1 cup (90 g/3 oz) desiccated coconut
65 g (2¼ oz) dark compound chocolate

1 Preheat the oven to 160°C (315°F/ Gas 2–3). Line a baking tray with baking paper. Place the egg white in a small, dry bowl. Using electric beaters, beat until firm peaks form. Add the sugar gradually, beating constantly until the mixture is thick and glossy and all the sugar has dissolved. Add the cornflour and beat until the ingredients are just combined.

2 Add the coconut to the egg white mixture. Using a metal spoon, stir until just combined. Roll heaped teaspoons of mixture into balls and place on the prepared tray. Bake for 15–20 minutes, or until the macaroons are lightly golden. Remove from the oven and leave to cool on the tray.

3 Place the chocolate in a small bowl over a pan of barely simmering water. When the chocolate is beginning to soften, stir until smooth. Dip the macaroons into the chocolate and allow the excess to drain. Place on a foil-lined tray and leave to set.

STORAGE: Store the macaroons in an airtight container for 1 day.
HINT: These are delicious served with a soft, creamy dessert.

Spread the mixture out into a circle with a flat-bladed knife and bake for 10 minutes.

Leave the tuiles to cool on the rolling pin and they will retain their curled shape.

ORANGE AND ALMOND TUILES

Preparation time: 10 minutes
Total cooking time: 30 minutes
Makes about 15

90 g (3 oz) butter
$1/3$ cup (90 g/3 oz) caster sugar
$1/4$ cup (30 g/1 oz) plain flour
$1/4$ cup (25 g/$3/4$ oz) flaked almonds, crushed
   slightly
1 tablespoon finely chopped mixed peel

1 Preheat the oven to 180°C (350°F/ Gas 4). Lightly grease a large baking tray and dust lightly with flour. Using electric beaters, beat the butter and sugar in a small mixing bowl until light and fluffy. Add the flour and stir until combined. Add the flaked almonds and mixed peel. Stir until well combined.
2 Cook in batches. Place heaped teaspoonfuls of the mixture about 10 cm (4 inch) apart on the prepared tray. Spread each spoonful of the mixture out into a 5 cm (2 inch) circle. Bake for 10 minutes or until brown.
3 Remove the tray from the oven and stand for 1 minute. Carefully lift each circle off the tray with a flat-bladed knife and drape immediately over a rolling pin to curl. Leave to cool on the rolling pin. Repeat with the remaining circles.

STORAGE: Tuiles can be stored in an airtight container for several days before use.
HINT: Cook only about 4–6 tuiles at a time, as they cool and harden very quickly. Grease and flour the tray again before baking each batch.

Shape the dough into crescent shapes and place on the prepared tray.

Dust the crescent-shaped biscuits with icing sugar while they are still warm.

FROSTED CRESCENTS

Preparation time: 50 minutes
Total cooking time: 12 minutes
Makes 50

60 g (2 oz) roasted macadamia nuts or
   almonds
1 cup (125 g/4 oz) plain flour
$^1/_4$ cup (60 g/2 oz) sugar
$^1/_2$ teaspoon grated orange rind (see
   VARIATION)
125 g (4 oz) butter, chopped
1 egg yolk
icing sugar, to dust

1 Preheat the oven to 180°C (350°F/ Gas 4). Lightly grease two baking trays. Place the macadamia nuts or almonds in a food processor and process until finely crushed. Sift the flour into a medium bowl and add the sugar, orange rind and butter. Using your fingertips, rub the butter into the flour mixture for 5 minutes, or until the mixture is fine and crumbly. Add the egg yolk and ground nuts. Mix until well combined and the mixture forms a soft dough.
2 Shape level teaspoonfuls of the dough into small crescents and place on the prepared trays. Bake for 12 minutes or until pale golden in color.
3 While the crescents are still warm, sift a generous amount of icing sugar over them. Stand the crescents for 2 minutes. Transfer to wire racks to cool completely.

STORAGE: Make the crescents up to 1 week in advance. Store in an airtight container in a cool, dry place.
VARIATION: Use lemon rind in place of the orange rind, if desired. Add $^1/_2$–$^1/_4$ teaspoonful of orange-flower water or rosewater to the dough for extra flavor.

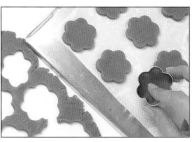

Using a fluted biscuit cutter, cut into shapes and place on the prepared tray.

Pipe a swirl of chestnut cream filling onto each biscuit then dip in melted chocolate.

CHOCOLATE CHESTNUT CREAMS

Preparation time: 25 minutes
Total cooking time: 12 minutes
Makes 35

1 cup (125 g/4 oz) plain flour
1 teaspoon cocoa powder
$^1/_4$ teaspoon ground cinnamon
50 g (1$^3/_4$ oz) unsalted butter
$^1/_3$ cup (90 g/3 oz) caster sugar
1 egg
200 g (6$^1/_2$ oz) choc dots
1 tablespoon vegetable oil
$^1/_3$ cup (50 g/1$^3/_4$ oz) white chocolate melts, melted

CHESTNUT CREAM FILLING
125 g (4 oz) cream cheese
$^1/_4$ cup (80 g/2$^3/_4$ oz) sweetened chestnut spread (see NOTE)

1 Preheat the oven to 180°C (350°F/ Gas 4). Line two 32 x 28 cm (13 x 11 inch) baking trays with baking paper. Place the flour, cocoa powder and cinnamon in a food processor. Add the butter and sugar and process until the mixture resembles fine breadcrumbs. Add the egg and process for a further 15 seconds or until a soft dough forms.
2 Turn the dough onto a lightly floured surface. Knead for 1 minute until smooth. Roll the dough out to 5 mm ($^1/_4$ inch) thickness. Cut into 4 cm (1$^1/_2$ inch) rounds, using a fluted biscuit cutter. Place on the prepared trays. Bake for 12 minutes, or until lightly golden. Cool on the trays. Place the choc dots into a small heatproof bowl. Stand over a pan of simmering water, making sure the base does not touch the water, and stir until the chocolate is melted. Remove from the heat. Add the oil and beat until the mixture is smooth. Cool slightly.

3 To make the chestnut cream filling, beat the cream cheese with electric beaters in a small bowl until light and creamy. Add the spread and beat for 1 minute or until well combined. Spoon the filling into a piping bag fitted with a fluted piping nozzle and pipe a swirl over each biscuit. Dip each biscuit into the melted chocolate, coating the filling and top of the biscuit only. Place on a wire rack to set. Pipe fine lines over each biscuit with the white chocolate melts.

STORAGE: Store biscuits in an airtight container for up to 2 days.
NOTE: Sweetened chestnut spread is available in cans from some supermarkets, delicatessens and specialty food stores.

Rub the butter with your fingertips into the flour mixture until a soft dough forms.

Decorate the edges of the shortbread by pinching the dough.

SCOTTISH SHORTBREAD

Preparation time: 25 minutes + 20 minutes refrigeration
Total cooking time: 35 minutes
Makes two large rounds

250 g (8 oz) unsalted butter, softened
$1/2$ cup (125 g/4 oz) caster sugar
2 cups (250 g/8 oz) plain flour
$2/3$ cup (125 g/4 oz) rice flour
1 teaspoon sugar, to decorate

1 Preheat the oven to 160°C (315°F/ Gas 2–3). Line two baking trays with baking paper. Mark a 20 cm (8 inch) circle on the paper on each tray and turn the paper over.

2 Sift the flours into a large bowl and add the butter and sugar. Using your fingertips, rub the butter into the flour mixture or until a soft dough forms. Add a pinch of salt and gather together and divide the dough into two portions. Wrap in plastic wrap and refrigerate for 20 minutes.

3 Place one dough portion on each tray and press into a round, using the drawn circle as a guide. Pinch and flute the edges decoratively and prick the surface with a fork. Use a knife to mark each circle into 12 segments. Sprinkle with the sugar and bake for 30–35 minutes, until firm and pale golden. Leave to cool on the trays and break into scored wedges to serve.

STORAGE: When completely cold, store in an airtight container.
NOTE: Usually no liquid is used, but if the mixture is very crumbly add not more than 1 tablespoon of milk or cream.

Spread the bottom of one biscuit with the vanilla cream and press together.

Roll the assembled biscuit in chocolate sprinkles, making sure the join is well covered.

CHOC-VANILLA CREAMS

Preparation time: 45 minutes
Total cooking time: 10 minutes
Makes 15

125 g (4 oz) unsalted butter
$^1/_3$ cup (40 g/1$^1/_4$ oz) icing sugar
$^2/_3$ cup (85 g/3 oz) plain flour
$^1/_2$ cup (60 g/2 oz) self-raising flour
2 tablespoons cocoa powder
$^2/_3$ cup chocolate sprinkles
2 teaspoons icing sugar, to dust

VANILLA CREAM
75 g (2$^1/_2$ oz) unsalted butter
$^2/_3$ cup (85 g/3 oz) icing sugar
1 teaspoon vanilla essence

1 Preheat the oven to 180°C (350°F/ Gas 4). Line a 32 x 28 cm (13 x 11 inch) baking tray with baking paper. Using electric beaters, beat the butter and sugar in a small mixing bowl until light and creamy. Using a metal spoon, fold in the sifted flours and cocoa and mix to a soft dough. Roll 2 teaspoons of dough into balls. Using the base of a glass, press into 4 cm (1$^1/_2$ inch) rounds. Place on the prepared tray. Bake for 10 minutes. Transfer biscuits to a wire rack to cool completely before decorating.
2 To make the vanilla cream, using electric beaters, beat the butter and sugar until light and creamy. Add the vanilla essence and beat until well combined.
3 To assemble the biscuits, spread one biscuit with the vanilla cream and place another on top to sandwich together. Using a flat-bladed knife, spread vanilla cream around the join.
4 Place the chocolate sprinkles on a plate and roll each biscuit on the side to coat the join. Dust with the icing sugar.

STORAGE: Store for up to 2 days in an airtight container.

Roll the mixture into oval shapes, place on the prepared tray and press pecans on top.

Leave the biscuits to cool on a wire rack and dust with icing sugar.

CINNAMON PECAN BISCUITS

Preparation time: 20 minutes
Total cooking time: 15 minutes
Makes 40

100 g (3¹/₂ oz) dark chocolate
125 g (4 oz) unsalted butter
¹/₂ cup (125 g/4 oz) caster sugar
1 egg, lightly beaten
³/₄ cup (75 g/2¹/₂ oz) finely chopped pecans
¹/₃ cup (40 g/1¹/₄ oz) self-raising flour
²/₃ cup (85 g/3 oz) plain flour
2 teaspoons ground cinnamon (see VARIATION)
¹/₂ cup (50 g/1³/₄ oz) whole pecans, for decoration (see HINT)
1 tablespoon icing sugar, to dust

1 Preheat the oven to 180°C (350°F/ Gas 4). Line two 32 x 28 cm (13 x 11 inch) baking trays with baking paper. Chop the chocolate and place in a small heatproof bowl. Stand over a pan of simmering water. Stir until the chocolate is melted and smooth. Allow to cool but not to reset.

2 Using electric beaters, beat the butter and sugar in a small mixing bowl until light and creamy. Add the egg gradually, beating thoroughly. Add the cooled melted chocolate and beat until combined.

3 Transfer the mixture to a large bowl and add the chopped pecans. Using a metal spoon, fold in the sifted flours and cinnamon. Stir until the ingredients are combined and do not over-beat. Lightly roll 2 teaspoons of the mixture into oval shapes, place on the prepared tray and press a pecan onto each. Bake for 10 minutes.

4 Transfer to a wire rack to cool completely. Lightly dust each biscuit with the icing sugar.

STORAGE: Store for up to 2 days in an airtight container.
VARIATION: Use ground mixed spice or allspice in place of the cinnamon.
HINT: If preferred, bake the biscuits without the pecan on top. When baked and cooled, dip the top of each biscuit in melted chocolate and press a pecan on top.

Spread the filling over the dough with a flat-bladed knife and top with the chopped prunes.

To make the scroll, roll the dough from one long side into the centre and then roll the other side in.

PRUNE AND CREAM CHEESE SCROLLS

Preparation time: 30 minutes + 30 minutes refrigeration
Total cooking time: 15 minutes
Makes 20

1½ cups (185 g/6 oz) plain flour
1 tablespoon custard powder
90 g (3 oz) unsalted butter
¼ cup (60 g/2 oz) caster sugar
1 egg yolk
2–3 tablespoons milk

PRUNE FILLING
250 g (8 oz) cream cheese
⅓ cup (90 g/3 oz) caster sugar, extra
2 teaspoons grated lemon rind
1 cup pitted prunes, chopped

1 Lightly grease two 32 x 28 cm (13 x 11 inch) baking trays. Place the flour, custard powder, butter and sugar in a food processor. Process until the mixture resembles fine breadcrumbs. Add the egg yolk and milk and process for 15 seconds, or until the mixture comes together. Turn onto a lightly floured surface and knead for 1 minute, or until smooth. Roll out the dough on baking paper to form a 30 x 28 cm (12 x 11 inch) rectangle.

2 To make the prune filling, beat the cream cheese, extra sugar and lemon rind with electric beater in a small bowl until light and fluffy. Using a flat-bladed knife, spread the filling evenly over the dough. Top evenly with the prunes.

3 Roll the dough from one long side into the centre. Roll from the opposite side to meet in the centre. Refrigerate for 30 minutes or until firm. Heat oven to 180°C (350°F/Gas 4). Using a sharp knife, cut into 1.5 cm (⅝ inch) slices. Place on the prepared trays, allowing room for spreading during baking. Bake for 15 minutes or until lightly golden. Transfer to wire racks to cool.

STORAGE: Store for 3 days in an airtight container.

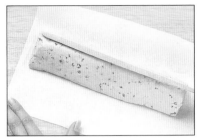

Shape the log into a triangular shape with a flat-bladed knife.

After chilling, use a sharp knife to cut the log into slices. Bake for 10 minutes.

GOLDEN TRIANGLES

Preparation time: 20 minutes + 30 minutes refrigeration
Total cooking time: 10 minutes
Makes 40

125 g (4 oz) unsalted butter
2 tablespoons caster sugar
2 tablespoons golden syrup (see VARIATION)

1/2 cup (75 g/2 1/2 oz) currants
1/2 cup (50 g/1 3/4 oz) rolled oats
3/4 cup (90 g/3 oz) plain flour
1/4 cup (45 g/1 1/2 oz) rice flour

1 Lightly grease two 32 x 28 cm (13 x 11 inch) baking trays. Using electric beaters, beat the butter, sugar and golden syrup in a small bowl until light and creamy. Transfer the mixture to a large bowl and add the currants and oats. Using a metal spoon, stir until combined. Add the sifted flours and stir until combined.

2 Roll the mixture into a log shape, 20 cm (8 inch) long. Press the log into a triangular shape. Refrigerate for 30 minutes or until firm.

3 Preheat the oven to 180°C (350°F/ Gas 4). Remove log from fridge and cut into 5 mm (1/4 inch) slices. Place the slices on the prepared trays. Bake for 10 minutes or until golden. Transfer to a wire rack to cool completely.

STORAGE: Biscuits may be stored up to 4 days in an airtight container or up to 2 months in the freezer.
VARIATION: If preferred, use golden syrup instead of honey.

Oil or wet your hands to stop the mixture from sticking and then roll into balls.

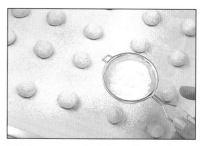

Sift icing sugar over the balls, making sure they are well covered, and bake for 15–20 minutes.

AMARETTI

Preparation time: 15 minutes + 1 hour standing
Total cooking time: 20 minutes
Makes 40

1 tablespoon plain flour
1 tablespoon cornflour
1 teaspoon ground cinnamon
²⁄₃ cup (160 g/5¹⁄₂ oz) caster sugar
1 cup (95 g/3 oz) ground almonds
1 teaspoon grated lemon rind
2 egg whites
¹⁄₄ cup (30 g/1 oz) icing sugar

1 Line two baking trays with baking paper. Sift the flour, cornflour, cinnamon and half the caster sugar into a large bowl, then add the ground almonds and lemon rind.

2 Beat the egg whites in a clean, dry bowl with electric beaters until firm peaks form. Gradually add the remaining caster sugar, beating constantly until the mixture is thick and glossy and all the sugar has dissolved. Using a metal spoon, fold the egg white mixture into the dry ingredients and stir until the ingredients are just combined.

3 Roll 2 level teaspoons of mixture at a time with oiled or wetted hands into balls and arrange on the trays, allowing room for spreading. Set the trays aside, uncovered, for 1 hour.

4 Preheat the oven to 180°C (350°F/ Gas 4). Sift the icing sugar liberally over the uncooked biscuits, then bake for 15–20 minutes, or until crisp and lightly browned. Transfer to a wire rack and leave to cool completely.

STORAGE: These biscuits can be stored in an airtight container for up to 2 days.

Draw guide lines on the baking paper with pencil then turn over before piping mixture onto the tray.

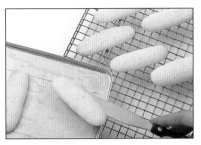

Remove the biscuits from the tray with a flat-bladed knife and leave to cool on a wire rack.

CATS' TONGUES

Preparation time: 12 minutes
Total cooking time: 10 minutes
Makes 40

80 g (2³/₄ oz) unsalted butter, chopped
²/₃ cup (80 g/2³/₄ oz) icing sugar, sifted
2 egg whites
2 tablespoons caster sugar
³/₄ cup (90 g/3 oz) plain flour
ice-cream, to serve

1 Preheat the oven to 180°C (350°F/ Gas 4). Lightly grease a 32 x 28 cm (13 x 11 inch) baking tray and line base with baking paper. Grease the baking paper. Using electric beaters, beat the butter and icing sugar in a small bowl until light and fluffy. Transfer the mixture to a large bowl.

2 Place the egg whites in a mixing bowl. Using electric beaters, beat the egg whites until firm peaks form. Add the sugar gradually, beating until the mixture is thick and glossy and all the sugar is dissolved. Using a metal spoon, fold the egg mixture into the butter mixture. Add the sifted flour and fold in quickly and lightly, making sure not to overmix.

3 Spoon the mixture into a piping bag fitted with a 1 cm (¹/₂ inch) plain piping nozzle. Pipe the mixture into 8 cm (3 inch) lengths onto the prepared tray, allowing room for spreading.

4 Bake for 10 minutes, or until lightly golden. Leave the biscuits to stand on the tray for 1 minute before transferring to a wire rack to cool completely. Dust with the icing sugar before serving. Serve with ice-cream.

STORAGE: Store biscuits in an airtight container for up to 2 days.
VARIATION: Add ¹/₂ teaspoon finely grated orange or lemon rind to the mixture, if desired.

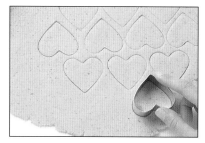

Roll the dough out on a lightly floured surface and cut out shapes.

Place on the prepared baking tray and brush with maple syrup.

PECAN-MAPLE SHORTBREADS

Preparation time: 20 minutes
Total cooking time: 20 minutes
Makes about 35

1 cup (125 g/4 oz) plain flour
$^1/_2$ cup (60 g/2 oz) ground pecans
2 tablespoons icing sugar
90 g (3 oz) butter, chopped
2 tablespoons maple syrup
50 g (1$^3/_4$ oz) white choc melts, melted

1 Preheat the oven to 180°C (350°F/ Gas 4). Line a baking tray with baking paper. Place the flour, pecans, sugar and butter in a food processor and process for 1 minute or until the mixture comes together.

2 Turn onto a lightly floured surface, press together to form a smooth dough. Roll out on a sheet of baking paper to a thickness of 5 mm ($^1/_4$ inch). Using a 4 cm (1$^1/_2$ inch) heart-shaped cutter, cut out shapes.

3 Transfer to the prepared tray, bake for 10 minutes and remove from the oven. Brush each shortbread generously with the maple syrup and bake for another 10 minutes. Transfer to a wire rack to cool completely. Spoon the white chocolate into a small piping bag and pipe an outline around the edge of the biscuits.

STORAGE: Store for up to 4 days in an airtight container.

Using a fluted biscuit cutter, cut out shapes and place on the prepared baking tray.

After the biscuits have cooled on a wire rack, spread with the vanilla icing.

ALMOND CINNAMON BISCUITS

Preparation time: 12 minutes
Total cooking time: 20 minutes
Makes 45

200 g (6½ oz) blanched almonds
⅓ cup (90 g/3 oz) caster sugar
⅓ cup (40 g/1¼ oz) icing sugar
3 teaspoons ground cinnamon (see VARIATION)
¾ cup (90 g/3 oz) plain flour
2 egg whites

VANILLA ICING (SEE VARIATION)
1⅔ cups (210 g/7 oz) pure icing sugar
1 egg white, lightly beaten
½ teaspoon vanilla essence

1 Preheat the oven to 150°C (300°F/ Gas 2). Line a 32 x 28 cm (13 x 11 inch) baking tray with baking paper. Place the almonds, sugars, cinnamon and flour in a food processor. Process for 30 seconds, or until the mixture resembles fine breadcrumbs. Add the egg whites and process for 30 seconds, or until a soft dough forms.

2 Turn the dough onto lightly floured surface. Knead for 1 minute and shape the dough into a ball. Roll the dough between two sheets of plastic wrap to 5 mm (¼ inch) thickness. Cut into shapes, using a 4 cm (1½ inch) plain or fluted biscuit cutter and place on the prepared tray. Bake for 20 minutes, or until the biscuits are lightly golden. Transfer the biscuits to a wire rack to cool completely.

3 To make the vanilla icing, sift the icing sugar into a small bowl. Make a well in centre and add combined egg white and vanilla essence. Beat the mixture constantly with a wooden spoon until all the icing sugar is incorporated and a firm paste is formed. Using a flat-bladed knife, spread the biscuits with icing.

STORAGE: These biscuits may be stored in an airtight container for up to 2 days.
VARIATIONS: Use 1 teaspoon ground nutmeg instead of cinnamon in the biscuits. Spread the biscuits with lemon icing instead of vanilla, if preferred. Simply add 2 teaspoons of finely grated lemon rind in place of vanilla essence.

Icings & Toppings

These delicious toppings will add a special touch to even a basic biscuit. Along with the simple recipe provided, even young cooks can produce a masterpiece — with a bit of help from mum and dad!

BASIC BISCUIT

Preheat the oven to 160°C (315°F/Gas 2–3). Line a baking tray with baking paper. Using electric beaters, beat together 125 g (4 oz) cubed butter and ½ cup (125 g/4 oz) caster sugar until light and fluffy. Add 1 egg and ¼ teaspoon vanilla essence and beat well. Sift 1 cup (125 g/4 oz) plain flour and 1 cup (125 g/4 oz) self-raising flour and fold in to form a soft dough. Turn out onto a sheet of baking paper, cover with another sheet and roll out to 5 mm (¼ inch) thick. Using biscuit cutters, cut out shapes and place on the tray. Bake in batches for 10–15 minutes, or until lightly golden. Cool on a wire rack, then spread with your choice of topping (see below and right). Makes about 50 biscuits.

MAPLE SYRUP ICING

Mix 1 cup (125 g/4 oz) sifted icing sugar, 2 tablespoons maple syrup and 1 tablespoon softened, unsalted butter in a small, heatproof bowl. Stir the mixture over a pan of simmering water until the mixture softens and is smooth and easy to spread.

PASSIONFRUIT GLACE ICING

Mix 2 tablespoons fresh passionfruit pulp and 1¼ cups (155 g/5 oz) sifted icing sugar in a small, heatproof bowl. Stir the mixture over a pan of simmering water until it becomes smooth and glossy. You can use tinned pulp if passionfruit is not in season.

COCONUT ICE TOPPING

Mix 1¼ cups (155 g/5 oz) sifted icing sugar, 1 tablespoon softened butter, ½ cup (45 g/1½ oz) desiccated coconut, ½ teaspoon vanilla essence and a few drops pink food coloring in a bowl. Add 6–8 teaspoons boiling water to make a thick, spreadable mixture.

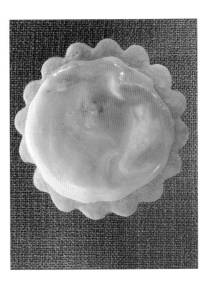

2 oz) sifted icing sugar and ¹/₄ cup (60 ml/2 fl oz) water in a pan. Stir constantly over low heat until the sugar dissolves. Simmer, without stirring, for 5 minutes. Remove the rinds and drain on a wire rack. Mix together 1¹/₄ cups (155 g/5 oz) sifted icing sugar, 1 tablespoon softened butter, 2 teaspoons lemon juice, 3 teaspoons lime juice, 2 teaspoons orange juice and the drained peel in a bowl until they form a spreadable mixture.

VANILLA ICING

Sift 1¹/₄ cups (155 g/5 oz) icing sugar into a small bowl. Add 1 tablespoon cubed and softened unsalted butter, ¹/₂ teaspoon vanilla essence and 1–2 tablespoons boiling water. Stir until the mixture is smooth and spreadable.

CHOC AND NUT TOPPING

Sift 1¹/₄ cups (155 g/5 oz) icing sugar and 1 tablespoon cocoa powder into a bowl. Add 1 tablespoon softened unsalted butter, 1–2 tablespoons boiling water and mix together until smooth. Spread the biscuits with the topping, then sprinkle with chopped, roasted hazelnuts or almonds. The nuts can be replaced by colored sprinkles for a more colorful effect.

MARSHMALLOW TOPPING

Mix 1 cup (125 g/4 oz) sifted icing sugar, 1 tablespoon softened unsalted butter and 1 tablespoon boiling water in a bowl until smooth. Add ¹/₂ cup (25 g/³/₄ oz) mini marshmallows. Stir

over a pan of simmering water for 1 minute, or until the marshmallows have just melted. Spread quickly onto the biscuits.

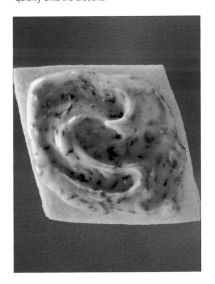

CHOCOLATE FLECK ICING

Sift 1¹/₄ cups (155 g/5 oz) icing sugar into a bowl. Add 1 tablespoon softened unsalted butter, ¹/₂ teaspoon vanilla essence and 5 teaspoons boiling water. Stir until smooth. Gently mix in 2 tablespoons grated dark chocolate, then spread on the biscuits.

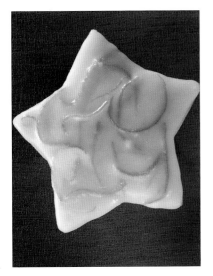

CITRUS FRUIT ICING

Put 2 teaspoons each of finely shredded lime rind, lemon rind and orange rind, ¹/₂ cup (60 g/

Cakes

HAWAIIAN MACADAMIA CAKE

Preparation time: 10 minutes
Total cooking time: 1 hour 15 minutes
Serves 10–12

3 cups (375 g/12 oz) self-raising flour
1 teaspoon ground cinnamon
1½ cups (185 g/6 oz) caster sugar
1 cup (90 g/3 oz) desiccated coconut
5 eggs, lightly beaten
440 g (14 oz) can crushed pineapple in
    syrup
1½ cups (375 ml/12 fl oz) vegetable oil
¾ cup (100 g/3½ oz) macadamia nuts,
    chopped

1 Preheat the oven to 180°C (350°F/ Gas 4). Lightly grease a 23 cm (9 inch) round deep cake tin. Line the base and side with two sheets of baking paper, cutting it to make a collar that sits 2–3 cm (¾–1 inch) above the side of the tin. Sift the flour and cinnamon into a bowl, add the sugar and coconut and stir to combine. Add the eggs, pineapple and oil and mix well. Stir in the macadamia nuts.

2 Spoon the mixture into the prepared tin and level the surface. Bake for 1 hour 15 minutes, or until a skewer comes out clean when inserted into the centre of the cake. Cover the cake with oil if it browns too much. Leave in the tin for 30 minutes before turning out onto a wire rack to cool completely.

Make sure all the ingredients are well combined before folding in the chopped macadamia nuts.

Test to see if the cake is cooked by inserting a skewer in the middle.

Make sure you place the peaches closely together over the sugar mixture.

Use a metal spoon to gently fold the flour and yoghurt into the mixture.

CARAMEL PEACH CAKE

Preparation time: 15 minutes + 30 minutes standing
Total cooking time: 1 hour 25 minutes
Serves 10–12

250 g (8 oz) unsalted butter, softened
1/3 cup (60 g/2 oz) lightly packed soft brown sugar
825 g (1 lb 11 oz) can peach halves in natural juice
1 cup (250 g/8 oz) caster sugar
3 teaspoons finely grated lemon rind
3 eggs, lightly beaten
2 1/2 cups (310 g/10 oz) self-raising flour, sifted
1 cup (250 g/8 oz) plain yoghurt

1 Preheat the oven to 180°C (350°F/ Gas 4). Lightly grease a deep 23 cm (9 inch) round cake tin and line the base with baking paper. Melt 50 g (1 3/4 oz) of the butter and pour on the base of the tin. Evenly sprinkle the brown sugar on top. Drain the peaches, reserving 1 tablespoon of the liquid. Arrange the peach halves, cut-side up, over the sugar mixture.

2 Beat the caster sugar, lemon rind and remaining butter with electric beaters for 5–6 minutes, or until pale and creamy. Add the egg gradually, beating well after each addition. The mixture may look curdled but it will come together once the flour is added. Using a metal spoon, fold in the flour alternately with the yoghurt (in two batches) then the reserved peach liquid. Spoon the mixture over the peaches in the tin and smooth the surface. Bake for 1 hour 25 minutes, or until a skewer comes out clean when inserted into the centre of the cake. Leave to cool in the tin for 30 minutes before carefully turning out onto a large serving plate.

Use a metal spoon to fold the egg whites into the egg yolk mixture with minimal loss of volume.

Simmer the sugar mixture until it is thick and syrupy. Take care—it will be very hot.

LEMON SEMOLINA CAKE

Preparation time: 15 minutes
Total cooking time: 45 minutes
Serves 8–10

6 eggs, separated
1¼ cups (310 g/10 oz) caster sugar
2 teaspoons finely grated lemon rind
⅓ cup (80 ml/2¾ fl oz) lemon juice
¾ cup (90 g/3 oz) semolina
½ cup (95 g/3 oz) ground almonds
2 tablespoons self-raising flour
thick cream, to serve

1 Preheat the oven to 170°C (325°F/ Gas 3). Grease a 24 cm (9½ inch) springform tin and line with baking paper. Using electric beaters, beat the yolks, 1 cup (250 g/8 oz) of the sugar, the rind and 2 tablespoons of the lemon juice in a mixing bowl for 8 minutes, or until thick and pale and the mixture leaves a trail when the beaters are lifted.

2 Beat the egg whites in a clean bowl with clean electric beaters until firm peaks form. Gently fold the whites with a metal spoon into the egg yolk mixture alternately with the combined semolina, ground almonds and flour. Take care not to overmix. Carefully pour the mixture into the prepared tin and smooth the surface. Bake for 35–40 minutes, or until a skewer comes out clean when inserted into the centre of the cake. Leave the cake in the tin for 5 minutes then turn out onto a wire rack to cool completely. Pierce a few holes in the cake with a skewer.

3 Place the remaining lemon juice and sugar in a small saucepan with ½ cup (125 ml/4 fl oz) water. Stir over low heat until the sugar has dissolved. Increase the heat and simmer for 3 minutes, or until thick and syrupy. Pour the hot syrup over the cooled cake. Serve with thick cream.

Start with the electric beaters on low speed then increase to high after a few minutes.

Spoon the mixture into the tin and smooth the surface to ensure your cake has an even top.

DEVIL'S FOOD CAKE

Preparation time: 15 minutes
Total cooking time: 50 minutes
Serves 8

1¹/₃ cups (165 g/5¹/₂ oz) plain flour
²/₃ cup (85 g/3 oz) cocoa powder
1 teaspoon bicarbonate of soda
1 cup (250 g/8 oz) sugar
1 cup (250 ml/8 fl oz) buttermilk
2 eggs, lightly beaten
125 g (4 oz) unsalted butter, softened
¹/₂ cup (125 ml/4 fl oz) cream, whipped
icing sugar, to dust
250 g (8 oz) fresh berries

1 Preheat the oven to 180°C (350°F/ Gas 4). Lightly grease a deep 20 cm (8 inch) round cake tin and line the base with baking paper. Sift the plain flour, cocoa powder and bicarbonate of soda into a large bowl.

2 Add the sugar to the bowl. Combine the buttermilk, eggs and butter, then pour onto the dry ingredients. Using electric beaters, beat on low speed for 3 minutes, or until just combined. Increase the speed to high and beat for another 3 minutes, or until the mixture is free of any lumps and increased in volume.

3 Spoon the mixture into the prepared tin and smooth the surface. Bake for 40–50 minutes, or until a skewer comes out clean when inserted into the centre. Leave the cake in the tin for 15 minutes before turning out onto a wire rack to cool completely. Cut the cake in half horizontally and fill with the whipped cream. Dust with icing sugar and garnish with fresh berries.

STORAGE: Unfilled, the cake will keep for 3 days in an airtight container or up to 3 months in the freezer.

Beat the butter and sugar until the mixture is pale in color but not creamy.

Gently fold in the cherries, taking care not to break them up with the spoon.

SOUR CHERRY CAKE

Preparation time: 10 minutes
Total cooking time: 50 minutes
Serves 8–10

125 g (4 oz) unsalted butter, softened
³/₄ cup (185 g/6 oz) caster sugar
2 eggs, lightly beaten
¹/₂ cup (95 g/3 oz) ground almonds
1 cup (125 g/4 oz) self-raising flour
¹/₂ cup (60 g/2 oz) plain flour
¹/₂ cup (125 ml/4 fl oz) milk
680 g (1 lb 6 oz) jar pitted morello cherries, well drained
icing sugar, to dust

1 Preheat the oven to 180°C (350°F/ Gas 4). Grease and flour a 23 cm (9 inch) fluted baba tin, shaking out any excess flour. Beat the butter and sugar with electric beaters until pale. Add the beaten egg gradually, beating well after each addition.

2 Stir in the ground almonds, then fold in the sifted flours alternately with the milk. Gently fold in the cherries. Spoon the mixture into the prepared tin and smooth the surface. Bake for 50 minutes, or until a skewer comes out clean when inserted into the centre of the cake. Leave to cool in the tin for 10 minutes before turning out onto a wire rack to cool. Dust with icing sugar before serving.

NOTE: This cake is best eaten on the day it is made.

Lightly fold the chopped nuts and fruit into the mixture with a large metal spoon.

Spoon the mixture into the prepared tin and smooth the surface.

HONEY, NUT AND FRUIT LOAF

Preparation time: 20 minutes
Total cooking time: 1 hour
Makes one loaf

1 cup (350 g/11 oz) honey
45 g (1¹/₂ oz) butter
1 egg
2¹/₂ cups (310 g/10 oz) self-raising flour
¹/₂ teaspoon bicarbonate of soda
¹/₂ teaspoon ground cinnamon
³/₄ cup (185 ml/6 fl oz) milk
¹/₂ cup (80 g/2³/₄ oz) chopped pecans
¹/₄ cup (40 g/1¹/₄ oz) chopped almonds
¹/₄ cup (60 g/2 oz) chopped pitted prunes
¹/₄ cup (45 g/1¹/₂ oz) chopped dried apricots
¹/₄ cup (30 g/1 oz) raisins

1 Preheat the oven to 180°C (350°F/ Gas 4). Grease a 15 x 23 cm (6 x 9 inch) loaf tin and line base with baking paper. Using electric beaters, beat the honey and butter until well combined. Add the egg and beat well. Transfer mixture to a large bowl.
2 Fold the sifted flour, bicarbonate of soda and cinnamon into the creamed mixture alternately with the milk. Fold in the nuts and fruit.
3 Spoon the cake mixture into the prepared tin and smooth the surface. Bake for 45 minutes, then cover the cake with foil and bake for another 15 minutes, or until a skewer comes out clean when inserted in the centre of the cake. Let the cake cool in the tin for 10 minutes before turning it out onto a wire rack to cool completely before serving.

STORAGE: This cake will keep in an airtight container for up to 3 days.

Spoon the apple onto half the batter then cover with the remaining batter.

The cake is cooked when a skewer inserted into the middle comes out clean.

APPLE AND SPICE TEACAKE

Preparation time: 35 minutes
Total cooking time: 1 hour
Makes one 20 cm (8 inch) cake

180 g (6 oz) butter
1/2 cup (95 g/3 oz) lightly packed soft brown
 sugar
2 teaspoons finely grated lemon rind
3 eggs, lightly beaten
1 cup (250 g/8 oz) self-raising flour
1/2 cup (75 g/2 1/2 oz) wholemeal flour
1/2 teaspoon cinnamon
1/2 cup (125 ml/4 fl oz) milk
410 g (13 oz) can pie apple (see NOTE)
1/4 teaspoon ground mixed spice
1 tablespoon soft brown sugar, extra
1/4 cup (25 g/3/4 oz) flaked almonds

1 Preheat the oven to 180°C (350°F/ Gas 4). Lightly grease a 20 cm (8 inch) springform pan and line base with baking paper. Using electric beaters, beat the butter and sugar until light and creamy. Beat in rind. Add the egg gradually, beating well.

2 Fold the sifted flours and cinnamon into the creamed mixture alternately with milk. Spoon half of the mixture into the prepared tin, top with three-quarters of the pie apple then top with remaining cake batter. Press the remaining pie apple around the edge of the top. Combine the mixed spice, extra sugar and flaked almonds and sprinkle them over the cake.

3 Bake the cake for 1 hour, or until a skewer comes out clean when inserted in the centre of cake. Remove from the tin and allow to cool completely on a wire rack.

NOTE: Pie apricots can be used instead of apples if desired.

FLOURLESS ORANGE AND ALMOND CAKE

Preparation time: 15 minutes
Total cooking time: 1 hour 30 minutes
Serves 8

2 oranges
1½ cups (280 g/9 oz) ground almonds
1 cup (250 g/8 oz) caster sugar
1 teaspoon baking powder
1 teaspoon vanilla essence
1 teaspoon Cointreau
6 eggs, lightly beaten
icing sugar, to dust

1 Wash the oranges well to remove any sprays or waxes. Place the whole oranges in a large saucepan, add enough water to cover them and place a small plate on top to keep the oranges submerged. Gradually bring the water to the boil, then reduce the heat and leave them to simmer for 40 minutes, or until the oranges are very soft. Preheat the oven to 180°C (350°F/ Gas 4). Place the cake tin on a sheet of baking paper and trace around the outside, then cut out the shape with a pair of scissors. Lightly grease the tin, then place the baking paper, pencil-side down, onto the base of the tin and smooth out any bubbles.
2 Cut each of the oranges into quarters and leave the pieces to cool. Remove any pips, then place the oranges in the bowl of a food processor and blend until they form a very smooth pulp. Add the ground almonds, caster sugar, baking powder, vanilla essence and Cointreau and, using the pulse button, process until all of the ingredients are combined. Add the egg and process again until just combined—take care not to over-process. Pour the orange mixture into the prepared tin and bake for 50 minutes, or until the cake is firm and leaves the side of the tin. Leave to cool completely in the tin. Dust with icing sugar to serve.

NOTES: This makes a great dessert cake served with fruit and cream. Try this cake with an orange syrup. Place 2 cups (500 ml/16 fl oz) of freshly squeezed and strained orange juice in a saucepan with ¾ cup (185 g/6½ oz) caster sugar and ¼ cup (60 ml/2 fl oz) Sauternes. Place the saucepan over a medium heat and stir until the sugar is dissolved. Reduce the heat and simmer for about 20 minutes, or until the liquid is reduced by half and has become slightly syrupy. Skim off any scum that forms on the surface as you go. The syrup will thicken further as it cools. Poke some random holes in the top of the cake to let the syrup absorb, or just drizzle the syrup over the cake before dusting with icing sugar and serving.

The oranges should be quite soft; if a sharp knife cuts into them easily, they are done.

Pour the batter into the prepared tin. It will be quite thick and may look slightly lumpy

Gently fold the flour, lemon rind and juice into the egg mixture with a metal spoon.

Evenly sprinkle caster sugar over the top of the mixture before placing in the oven for baking.

MADEIRA CAKE

Preparation time: 10 minutes
Total cooking time: 1 hour
Serves 6

180 g (6 oz) unsalted butter, softened
³/₄ cup (185 g/6 oz) caster sugar
3 eggs, beaten
1¹/₃ cups (165 g/5¹/₂ oz) self-raising flour, sifted
2 teaspoons finely grated lemon rind
1 teaspoon lemon juice
2 teaspoons caster sugar, extra, to sprinkle
icing sugar, to dust
1 tablespoon lemon zest

1 Preheat the oven to 160°C (315°F/ Gas 2–3). Lightly grease and flour a deep 18 cm (7 inch) round cake tin, shaking out any excess flour. Beat the butter and sugar with electric beaters until pale and creamy. Add the eggs gradually, beating well after each addition. Fold in the flour, lemon rind and juice until combined. When smooth, spoon into the prepared tin and level the surface.

2 Sprinkle the extra sugar over the top. Bake for 1 hour, or until a skewer comes out clean when inserted into the centre of the cake. Allow to cool for 15 minutes in the tin before turning out onto a wire rack to cool completely. If desired, dust with icing sugar and garnish with lemon zest.

Put the mixture into the prepared tin and smooth the surface with a spatula.

Peel the skin off the lime, carefully avoiding the bitter white pith.

PISTACHIO, YOGHURT AND CARDAMOM CAKE

Preparation time: 15 minutes
Total cooking time: 55 minutes
Serves 8

1 cup (150 g/5 oz) unsalted pistachio nuts
$1/2$ teaspoon ground cardamom
150 g (5 oz) unsalted butter, chopped
$1^1/2$ cups (185 g/6 oz) self-raising flour
$1^1/4$ cups (310 g/10 oz) caster sugar
3 eggs
$1/2$ cup (125 g/4 oz) plain yoghurt
1 lime

1 Preheat the oven to 180°C (350°F/ Gas 4). Grease a 20 cm (8 inch) round cake tin and line the base with baking paper. Place the pistachio nuts and cardamom in a food processor and process until just chopped. Add the butter, flour and $3/4$ cup (185 g/6 oz) of the caster sugar and process for 20 seconds, or until the mixture is crumbly. Add the combined eggs and yoghurt and process for another 10 seconds, or until everything is just combined.

2 Spoon into the tin and smooth the surface. Bake for 45–50 minutes, or until a skewer comes out clean when inserted into the centre of the cake. Leave the cake in the tin for 5 minutes before turning out onto a wire rack to cool completely.

3 To make the syrup, peel the skin off the lime with a vegetable peeler and make sure the white pith is removed. Place the remaining caster sugar and 100 ml ($3^1/2$ fl oz) water in a small saucepan and stir it over low heat until the sugar has dissolved. Bring to the boil, then add the lime peel and cook for 5 minutes. Strain and cool slightly. Pierce the cake several times with a skewer then pour the hot syrup over.

Use a metal spoon to fold the egg mixture into the dry ingredients.

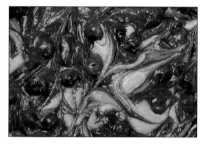

Carefully swirl the different colored mixtures together, making sure not to overmix them.

MARBLED BLUEBERRY CAKE

Preparation time: 30 minutes
Total cooking time: 50–55 minutes
Serves 8

1 tablespoon sugar
1¼ cups (195 g/6½ oz) fresh blueberries,
   plus extra, to serve (see VARIATION)
2 eggs
½ teaspoon vanilla essence
125 g (4 oz) butter
1⅓ cups (165 g/5½ oz) self-raising flour,
   sifted
½ cup (125 g/4 oz) caster sugar
2 tablespoons soft brown sugar
icing sugar, to dust
cream, to serve

1 Preheat the oven to 180°C (350°F/ Gas 4). Lightly grease a 20 cm (8 inch) round springform tin and line the base and side with baking paper. Place the sugar and half the blueberries in a small saucepan. Stir together gently over medium heat for 1–2 minutes or until the juices begin to run. Remove from the heat. Stir in the remaining blueberries, then allow the mixture to cool.

2 Beat the eggs in a small mixing bowl. Add the vanilla essence and butter, mix well. Combine the flour and sugar in a mixing bowl. Make a well in the centre. Using a metal spoon, stir in the egg mixture until smooth.

3 Take out ¾ cup of the cake mixture and stir into the blueberries. Place spoonfuls of both mixtures randomly into the prepared tin. Swirl the mixture with a knife or skewer to produce a marbled effect. Do not overmix the blueberries and cake mixture or they will blend, rather than looking nicely swirled. Sprinkle the brown sugar over the top. Bake for 45–50 minutes, or until a skewer comes out clean when inserted into the centre. Stand the cake in its tin on a wire rack to

cool for 5 minutes before removing and allowing it to cool completely on the rack. Serve the cake dusted liberally with icing sugar, or decorate with extra berries and cream.

STORAGE: The cake is best eaten on the day it is make.
VARIATION: Raspberries can also be used in this cake if blueberries are out of season.

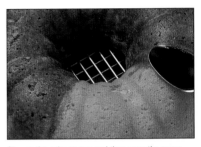

Combine the syrup ingredients over low heat, then simmer until the mixture thickens slightly.

Skewer the cake on top and then pour the syrup over several times so it is well soaked.

COFFEE COGNAC SYRUP CAKE

Preparation time: 45 minutes
Total cooking time: 45–50 minutes
Serves 8

185 g (6 oz) butter
³/₄ cup (185 g/6 oz) caster sugar
3 eggs, separated
1 teaspoon grated lemon rind
1 cup (250 g/8 oz) sour cream
¹/₄ cup (60 g/2 oz) plain yoghurt
1³/₄ cups (215 g/7 oz) self-raising flour
¹/₄ cup (25 g/³/₄ oz) ground almonds
whipped cream, to serve
chocolate curls, to serve

SYRUP
1 cup (250 ml/8 fl oz) strong coffee
¹/₂ cup (125 g/4 oz) caster sugar
2 tablespoons cognac

1 Preheat the oven to 180°C (350°F/ Gas 4). Lightly grease a 23 cm (9 inch) fluted ring tin. Dust the tin with flour, shaking out any excess. Using electric beaters, beat butter and sugar in a mixing bowl until light and creamy. Add the egg yolks one at time, beating after each addition. Add the rind and beat well. Add combined cream and yoghurt alternately with the sifted flour. Stir in the almonds.

2 Using electric beaters, beat the egg whites until stiff peaks form. Fold in the egg whites with a metal spoon into the flour mixture. Spoon into the prepared tin. Bake for 5 minutes. Reduce temperature to 160°C (315°F/ Gas 2–3). Bake another 40 minutes, or until a skewer comes out clean. Stand the cake in the tin for 5 minutes before turning out onto a wire rack to cool.

3 To make the syrup, combine the coffee, sugar and cognac in a saucepan over low heat without boiling until the sugar has dissolved. Bring to the boil, then simmer for 3 minutes to reduce. Remove from heat and cool slightly.

4 Stand the cake on a wire rack over the baking tray and skewer randomly on top. Spoon the syrup over and collect excess syrup from the tray to spoon over again. Cool and decorate with piped, whipped cream and chocolate curls before serving.

Place ricotta and sugar in a mixing bowl, add egg and cream then beat until light and creamy.

Fold remaining ingredients into mixture and place in prepared cake tin.

PRUNE AND RICOTTA CAKE

Preparation time: 10 minutes
Total cooking time: 2 hours
Serves 8

²/₃ cup (150 g/5 oz) pitted prunes, chopped
2 tablespoons marsala
500 g (1 lb) ricotta
1 cup (250 g/8 oz) caster sugar
3 eggs, lightly beaten
¹/₂ cup (125 ml/4 fl oz) cream
¹/₂ cup (60 g/2 oz) cornflour, sifted
¹/₂ cup (60 g/2 oz) grated chocolate

1 Preheat the oven to 160°C (315°F/ Gas 2–3). Lightly grease a 23 cm (9 inch) round cake tin and line the base with baking paper. Combine the chopped prunes and marsala in a small saucepan. Bring to the boil, reduce heat and then simmer for 30 seconds, or until the marsala is absorbed. Allow to cool.

2 Using electric beaters, beat the ricotta and sugar in a mixing bowl for 4 minutes, or until light and creamy. Gradually add the egg, beating well after each addition. Add the cream and beat for 2 minutes. Gently fold in the cornflour, prune mixture and chocolate with a metal spoon.

3 Spoon the mixture into the prepared tin and bake for 2 hours, or until firm and a skewer comes out clean when inserted into the centre of the cake. Leave in the tin for 15–20 minutes before gently turning out onto a wire rack to cool.

NOTE: To make the star pattern, dust with icing sugar. Place cardboard cut-outs of stars (or other shapes) gently on top, then dust liberally with cocoa powder.

Fold the beaten egg white into the cooled strawberry mixture then spread on the cake.

Place the sliced strawberries on top of the layer of mousse and top with remaining cake.

STRAWBERRY MOUSSE SPONGE

Preparation time: 15 minutes + 2–3 hours chilling
Total cooking time: 30 minutes
Serves 8

510 g (1 lb) packet French vanilla cake mix
3 eggs
1/3 cup (80 ml/2¾ fl oz) vegetable oil
500 g (1 lb) fresh strawberries, hulled
1/4 cup (60 g/2 oz) caster sugar
2 teaspoons powdered gelatine
1/2 cup (125 ml/4 fl oz) cream
1 egg white

1 Preheat the oven to 180°C (350°F/ Gas 4). Lightly grease two round 20 cm (8 inch) shallow cake tins and line each base with baking paper. Using electric beaters, beat the cake mix, eggs, oil and 290 ml (9 fl oz) water with electric beaters on low speed for 30 seconds. Increase to medium speed and beat for 2 minutes, or until well combined. Evenly divide into the prepared tins and bake for 25–30 minutes, or until a skewer comes out clean when inserted into the centre of each cake. Leave in the tins for 5 minutes before turning out onto a wire rack to cool completely.

2 Place 250 g (8 oz) of the strawberries in a food processor and blend until smooth. Stir in the sugar. Pour the strawberry mixture into a saucepan and bring to the boil. Sprinkle in the gelatine, whisking until dissolved. Transfer to a bowl and set aside to cool. Slice half of the remaining strawberries and set aside the remaining whole strawberries to decorate the cake. Beat the cream to soft peaks. Using electric beaters, beat the egg white in a clean, dry bowl until soft peaks form. Fold one-third of

the cream into the cooled strawberry mixture, then fold in the egg white until combined.

3 Trim the top off one of the cakes to level the surface, then place on a serving plate. Fill with three-quarters of the mousse and arrange the sliced strawberries on top. Spread underside of the other cake with the remaining mousse so it will stick and place it on top. Spread the top of the cake with the remaining cream and decorate with the whole strawberries. Chill for 2–3 hours before serving.

Spoon the cake mixture into the tin, making sure it is evenly distributed.

Pour the cooled syrup over the top of the cake and set aside for 2 hours.

COCONUT SYRUP CAKE

Preparation time: 10 minutes + 2 hours soaking
Total cooking time: 50 minutes
Serves 12

200 g (6½ oz) unsalted butter, softened
1½ cups (375 g/12 oz) caster sugar
6 eggs
1½ cups (185 g/6 oz) self-raising flour
3 cups (270 g/9 oz) desiccated coconut

SYRUP
1 tablespoon lemon zest
1½ cups (375 g/12 oz) sugar

1 Preheat the oven to 180°C (350°F/ Gas 4). Lightly grease and flour a 2-litre (9-cup) fluted baba tin or tube tin, shaking out any excess flour. Using electric beaters, beat the butter and sugar for 5 minutes, or until light and creamy. Add the eggs one at a time, beating well after each addition, until combined. Fold in the flour and coconut and mix well.

2 Spoon the mixture into the prepared tin and bake for 45 minutes, or until a skewer comes out clean when inserted into the centre. Cool slightly in the tin, then turn out onto a wire rack to cool completely.

3 To make the syrup, place the zest, sugar and 1 cup (250 ml/8 fl oz) water in a small saucepan. Stir over medium heat until the sugar has dissolved. Cool to room temperature. Pierce the cake all over with a skewer, pour the syrup over the cake and leave for 2 hours to soak up the syrup. If desired, garnish with shaved coconut.

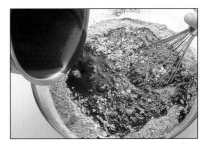

Whisk the chocolate mixture into the well in the dry ingredients.

Pour the cooled chocolate topping over the upside-down cake.

CHOCOLATE MUD CAKE

Preparation time: 30 minutes
Total cooking time: 2 hours
Serves 8

250 g (8 oz) unsalted butter
250 g (8 oz) dark chocolate, chopped
2 tablespoons instant coffee powder
150 g (5 oz) self-raising flour
150 g (5 oz) plain flour
½ teaspoon bicarbonate of soda
½ cup (60 g/2 oz) cocoa powder
2¼ cups (550 g/1 lb 2 oz) caster sugar
4 eggs, lightly beaten
2 tablespoons oil
½ cup (125 ml/4 fl oz) buttermilk

ICING
150 g (5 oz) unsalted butter, chopped
150 g (5 oz) dark chocolate, chopped

1 Preheat the oven to 160°C (315°F/ Gas 2–3). Lightly grease a deep 22 cm (9 inch) round cake tin and line with baking paper, making sure the paper around the side extends at least 5 cm (2 inches) above the top edge.
2 Put the butter, chocolate and coffee in a saucepan with ¾ cup (185 ml/ 6 oz) hot water and stir over low heat until smooth. Remove from the heat.
3 Sift the flours, bicarbonate of soda and cocoa powder into a mixing bowl. Stir in the sugar and make a well in the centre. Place the eggs, oil and buttermilk in a separate mixing bowl and mix until combined. Pour into the dry ingredients and mix together with a whisk. Gradually add the chocolate mixture, whisking well after each addition.
4 Pour the mixture (it will be quite wet) into the tin and bake for 1¾ hours. Test the centre with a skewer—the skewer may be slightly wetter than normal. Remove the cake from the oven. If the top looks raw, bake for another 5–10 minutes, then remove from oven. Leave in the tin until completely cold, then turn out and wrap in plastic wrap.

5 For the icing, combine the butter and chocolate in a saucepan and stir over low heat until the butter and chocolate are melted. Remove and cool slightly. Pour over the cake and allow it to run down the side.

Spread mixture into tins and smooth the surface with a flat-bladed knife.

Once you have put the sponge together, generously dust with icing sugar.

JAM AND CREAM SPONGE

Preparation time: 20 minutes
Total cooking time: 20 minutes
Makes one 20 cm round cake

¹/₂ cup (60 g/2 oz) plain flour
¹/₂ cup (60 g/2 oz) self-raising flour
4 eggs, separated
²/₃ cup (160 g/5¹/₂ oz) caster sugar
4 tablespoons jam
¹/₂ cup (125 ml/4 fl oz) cream, whipped
icing sugar, to dust

1 Preheat the oven to 180°C (350°F/ Gas 4). Grease two shallow 20 cm (8 inch) sandwich tins. Sift the flours three times onto baking paper. Place the egg whites in a large mixing bowl. Using electric beaters, beat the egg whites until stiff peaks form. Add the sugar gradually, beating constantly until the sugar has dissolved and mixture is thick and glossy.

2 Add the egg yolks and beat for another 20 seconds. Using a metal spoon, fold in the flour quickly and lightly. Spread the mixture evenly into the prepared tins and smooth the surface. Bake for 20 minutes, until lightly golden and springy to the touch. Leave cakes in the tins for 5 minutes before turning onto wire racks to cool completely.

3 Spread the jam evenly onto one of the sponges. Spread whipped cream over the jam. Top with the second sponge and dust with sifted icing sugar before serving.

STORAGE: Unfilled sponges can be frozen for up to a month. Thaw cakes at room temperature for 20 minutes. Serve filled sponges immediately.

Once all the ingredients have been added, stir well to combine.

Try any decorative pattern you like when placing the remaining pecans on top of the cake.

FRUIT MINCE AND NUT CAKE

Preparation time: 40 minutes + 3 hours standing
Total cooking time: 3–3¹/₂ hours
Makes one 20 cm round cake

1¹/₂ cups (185 g/6 oz) plain flour
¹/₂ cup (60 g/2 oz) self-raising flour
1 teaspoon mixed spice
³/₄ cup (140 g/4¹/₂ oz) lightly packed soft brown sugar
1 cup (170 g/5¹/₂ oz) raisins
1 cup (160 g/5¹/₂ oz) sultanas
2 cups (200 g/6¹/₂ oz) pecans
100 g (3¹/₂ oz) mixed raw nuts, chopped
250 g (8 oz) butter, melted and cooled
425 g (14 oz) ready-made fruit mince
1 green apple, peeled and grated
2 tablespoons orange marmalade
2 tablespoons rum
2 eggs, lightly beaten

1 Preheat the oven to 160°C (315°F/ Gas 2–3). Lightly grease a 20 cm (8 inch) round cake tin and line base and side with baking paper. Line outside of tin with a double thickness of brown paper and secure with string.

2 Sift the flours and mixed spice into a large bowl. Add the sugar, raisins, sultanas and nuts, reserving half of the pecans. Make a well in the centre of the dry ingredients. Add the butter, fruit mince, grated apple, marmalade, rum and egg and stir until well combined.

3 Spoon the mixture evenly into the prepared tin and smooth the surface. Decorate with the reserved pecans. Bake for 3–3¹/₂ hours or until a skewer comes out clean when inserted in the centre of the cake. Allow the cake to cool in the tin several hours or overnight before turning out.

Gradually add the olive oil to the cake mixture, making sure it is well combined.

Gently stir the mixture then pour into the prepared cake tin and bake for 45 minutes.

ZESTY OLIVE OIL CAKE

Preparation time: 10 minutes
Total cooking time: 45 minutes
Serves 8

2 eggs
$^2/_3$ cup (160 g/5$^1/_2$ oz) caster sugar
2 teaspoons finely grated orange rind
2 teaspoons finely grated lemon rind
$^1/_2$ cup (125 ml/4 fl oz) olive oil
1$^1/_2$ cups (185 g/6 oz) self-raising flour
$^1/_4$ cup (60 ml/2 fl oz) milk
$^1/_4$ cup (60 ml/2 fl oz) orange juice

1 Preheat the oven to 180°C (350°F/ Gas 4). Lightly grease a shallow 20 cm (8 inch) round cake tin and line the base with baking paper. Whisk the eggs and sugar in a large mixing bowl until well combined. Add the orange and lemon rind, then gradually stir in the olive oil.
2 Stir in the sifted flour alternately with the milk and orange juice. Stir the mixture gently for 30 seconds with a wooden spoon. Pour into the prepared tin. Bake for 45 minutes, or until a skewer comes out clean when inserted into the centre of the cake. Leave to cool in the tin for 5 minutes before turning out onto a wire rack.

NOTE: This cake can be dusted with icing sugar before serving, if desired.

The cake mixture must be thick and creamy before you can stop beating.

Pour the mixture into the tin and smooth the surface with a spoon.

SAND CAKE

Preparation time: 10 minutes
Total cooking time: 50 minutes
Serves 8–10

185 g (6 oz) unsalted butter, softened
2 teaspoons vanilla essence
1 cup (250 g/8 oz) caster sugar
3 eggs
1¹/₂ cups (185 g/6 oz) self-raising flour
¹/₃ cup (60 g/2 oz) rice flour
¹/₃ cup (80 ml/2³/₄ fl oz) milk

1 Preheat the oven to 180°C (350°F/ Gas 4). Lightly grease a 23 cm (9 inch) square cake tin and line the base with baking paper.
2 Beat the butter, vanilla essence, sugar, eggs, flours and milk with electric beaters at low speed until combined, then beat at medium speed for 3 minutes, or until the mixture is thick and creamy.
3 Pour the mixture into the prepared tin and smooth the surface. Bake for 50 minutes, or until a skewer comes out clean when inserted into the centre of the cake. Leave the cake for 10 minutes in the tin then turn out onto a wire rack to cool completely.

COFFEE LIQUEUR GATEAU

**Preparation time: 1 hour + 1 hour
  refrigeration
Total cooking time: 35–40 minutes
Serves 8–10**

125 g (4 oz) brazil nuts
²/₃ cup (100 g/3½ oz) blanched almonds
80 g (2¾ oz) hazelnuts
2 tablespoons plain flour
³/₄ cup (185 g/6 oz) caster sugar
7 egg whites
¼ cup (60 ml/2 fl oz) Tia Maria or Kahlúa
small chocolate buttons, to decorate
sifted icing sugar, to dust

COFFEE CREAM
200 g (6½ oz) butter
1 cup (150 g/5 oz) dark chocolate, melted
2–3 teaspoons icing sugar
2 teaspoons warm water
3–4 teaspoons instant coffee powder

1 Preheat the oven to 180°C (350°F/ Gas 4).
Lightly grease a deep 20 cm (8 inch) round tin
and line base and side with baking paper. Place
the nuts on a baking tray and roast for 5–10
minutes, or until golden. Rub the nuts
vigorously in a clean tea towel to remove
hazelnut skins. Place in a food processor and
process until finely ground.

2 Transfer the ground nuts to a large bowl. Add
the flour and 125 g (4 oz) of the sugar and mix
well. Using electric beaters, beat the egg whites
in a large mixing bowl until soft peaks form.
Gradually add the remaining sugar, beating until
the mixture is thick and glossy and the sugar is
dissolved. Using a metal spoon, fold the nut
mixture into the egg mixture a third at a time.
Spoon into the prepared tin and smooth the
surface. Bake for 35–40 minutes, or until
springy to the touch. Leave in the tin to cool.
3 To make the coffee cream, beat the butter in a
small mixing bowl with electric beaters until
light and creamy. Gradually pour in the melted
chocolate, beating until well combined. Add the
icing sugar and combined water and coffee.
Beat until smooth.
4 To assemble the gateau, turn the cake onto a
flat working surface. Using a sharp serrated
knife, carefully cut the cake horizontally into
three layers. (Use the top layer of cake as the
base of gateau.) Brush the first layer with half
the liqueur. Spread with one fifth of the coffee
cream.
5 Place the second cake layer on top. Brush
with the remaining liqueur and spread with a
quarter of the remaining coffee cream. Place the
remaining layer on top. Spread top and sides
with the remaining coffee cream.
6 Decorate with the chocolate buttons and dust
with the icing sugar. Refrigerate for 1 hour or
until firm.

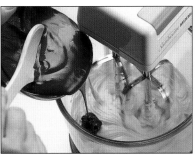

Add the melted chocolate, while beating continuously, to the butter.

Decorate the top of the cake with chocolate
buttons and dust with icing sugar.

Gently fold the chopped figs and half the ginger into the mixture with a metal spoon.

Scatter the chopped ginger over the top after you have smoothed the surface of the mixture.

CHOCOLATE GINGER AND FIG CAKE

Preparation time: 15 minutes
Total cooking time: 1 hour
Serves 8

125 g (4 oz) unsalted butter, softened
1 cup (230 g/7¹/₂ oz) firmly packed soft
   brown sugar
2 eggs, lightly beaten
1¹/₂ cups (185 g/6 oz) self-raising flour
¹/₃ cup (40 g/1¹/₄ oz) cocoa powder
³/₄ cup (185 ml/6 fl oz) milk
²/₃ cup (125 g/4 oz) dried figs, chopped
¹/₃ cup (75 g/2¹/₂ oz) glacé ginger, chopped

1 Preheat the oven to 180°C (350°F/ Gas 4). Lightly grease a 22 x 12 cm (8.5 x 4.5 inch) loaf tin and line the base with baking paper. Using electric beaters, beat the butter and sugar in a mixing bowl until pale and creamy.
2 Gradually add the egg, beating well after each addition. Stir in the sifted flour and cocoa alternately with the milk to make a smooth batter. Fold in the figs and half the ginger.
3 Spoon the mixture into the prepared tin and smooth the surface. Scatter the remaining ginger over the top. Bake for 1 hour, or until a skewer comes out clean when inserted into the centre of the cake. Leave to cool in the tin for 5 minutes before turning out onto a wire rack to cool completely.

Fold in the sifted flour, sultanas and beer into the cake mixture.

Mould the topping into small balls then crumble over the top of the cake.

BEER CAKE

Preparation time: 15 minutes
Total cooking time: 1 hour
50 minutes
Serves 12

1 cup (125 g/4 oz) plain flour
1/2 teaspoon ground cinnamon
3 cups (750 g/11/2 lb) caster sugar
275 g (9 oz) unsalted butter, chopped
3 eggs
4 cups (500 g/1 lb) self-raising flour
3/4 cup (120 g/4 oz) sultanas
2 cups (500 ml/16 fl oz) beer
cream, to serve

1 Preheat the oven to 180°C (350°F/ Gas 4). Lightly grease a deep 25 cm (10 inch) round cake tin and line the base with baking paper. To make the topping, mix together the plain flour, cinnamon and 1 cup (250 g/8 oz) of the sugar. Place in a food processor with 125 g (4 oz) of the butter and process until combined.

2 Place the remaining butter in a large mixing bowl with the remaining sugar and beat with electric beaters until pale and creamy. Gradually add the eggs, beating well after each addition. (The mixture may look curdled but once you add the flour, it will bring it back together.) Fold in the sifted self-raising flour, sultanas and beer.

3 Pour the mixture into the prepared tin and clump the topping together in your hands to form small balls, then sprinkle over the cake. Bake for 1 hour 50 minutes, or until a skewer comes out clean when inserted into the centre of the cake. Leave the cake to cool in the tin before turning out onto a wire rack. If desired, serve with cream.

Spoon the mixture into the prepared tin and then smooth the surface with a metal spoon.

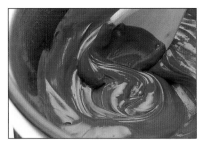

Melt the chocolate by placing in a heatproof bowl and sitting over a saucepan of simmering water.

WALNUT CAKE WITH CHOCOLATE ICING

Preparation time: 15 minutes
Total cooking time: 40 minutes
Serves 6

185 g (6 oz) unsalted butter, softened
$^1/_2$ cup (95 g/3 oz) lightly packed soft brown sugar
2 eggs
1$^1/_2$ cups (185 g/6 oz) self-raising flour
$^3/_4$ cup (90 g/3 oz) chopped walnuts
$^1/_4$ cup (60 ml/2 fl oz) milk

CHOCOLATE ICING
20 g ($^3/_4$ oz) unsalted butter
125 g (4 oz) good-quality dark chocolate, chopped

1 Preheat the oven to 180°C (350°F/ Gas 4). Lightly grease a 20 cm (8 inch) springform tin and line the base with baking paper. Using electric beaters, beat the butter and sugar in a large mixing bowl for 5 minutes, or until thick and creamy. Add the eggs one at a time, beating well after each addition. Using a metal spoon, fold in the sifted flour and $^1/_2$ cup (60 g/2 oz) of the walnuts alternately with the milk until just combined. Spoon the mixture into the prepared tin and smooth the surface. Bake for 35 minutes, or until a skewer comes out clean when inserted into the centre of the cake. Remove from the oven and leave the cake in the tin for 5 minutes before turning out onto a wire rack to completely cool.

2 To make the icing, place the butter and chocolate in a heatproof bowl. Bring a saucepan of water to the boil, then reduce the heat to a gentle simmer. Sit the bowl over the saucepan, making sure the base of the bowl does not touch the water. Stir occasionally until melted and smooth. Remove from the heat and leave to cool slightly. Spread the icing over the cake with a flat-bladed knife. Sprinkle with the remaining walnuts.

Beat the mixture on low speed until combined then increase to medium speed.

Make the icing by combining the melted butter. icing sugar, rind and boiling water.

ORANGE POPPY SEED CAKE WITH CITRUS ICING

Preparation time: 15 minutes + 15 minutes soaking
Total cooking time: 50 minutes
Serves 8

⅓ cup (50 g/1¾ oz) poppy seeds
¾ cup (185 ml/6 fl oz) warm milk
1 cup (250 g/8 oz) caster sugar
3 eggs
2 cups (250 g/8 oz) self-raising flour
210 g (7 oz) unsalted butter, softened
1½ tablespoons finely grated orange rind
2 cups (250 g/8 oz) icing sugar

1 Preheat the oven to 180°C (350°F/ Gas 4). Lightly grease a 23 cm (9 inch) fluted baba tin. Combine the poppy seeds and milk in a mixing bowl and set aside for at least 15 minutes.

2 Place the caster sugar, eggs, sifted flour, 185 g (6 oz) of the butter and 3 teaspoons of the grated orange rind in a large mixing bowl. Add the poppy seed mixture and beat with electric beaters on low speed until just combined. Increase to medium speed and beat for another 3 minutes, or until the mixture is thick and pale. Pour evenly into the prepared tin. Bake for 50 minutes, or until a skewer comes out clean when inserted into the centre of the cake. Leave in the tin for 5 minutes then turn out onto a wire rack to cool completely.

3 To make the icing, melt the remaining butter, then place in a bowl with the icing sugar, remaining rind and 3 tablespoons boiling water. Mix to make a soft icing, then spread over the warm cake.

Pour the egg mixture into the sifted flour then combine with electric beaters.

Test to see if the cake is cooked by inserting a skewer into the centre.

BROWNED BUTTER AND CINNAMON TEACAKE

Preparation time: 30 minutes + 15 minutes cooling
Total cooking time: 35 minutes
Serves 9–12

150g (5 oz) unsalted butter
1½ cups (185 g/6 oz) self-raising flour
¼ cup (30 g/1 oz) cornflour
1 teaspoon ground cinnamon
¾ cup (185 g/6 oz) caster sugar
3 eggs, lightly beaten
1 teaspoon vanilla essence
¼ cup (60 ml/2 fl oz) orange juice
¼ cup (60 ml/2 fl oz) milk
extra ground cinnamon, optional, to decorate

BROWNED CINNAMON ICING
80g (2¾ oz) unsalted butter
½ teaspoon ground cinnamon

1 Preheat the oven to 180°C (350°F/ Gas 4). Lightly grease a 20 cm (8 inch) square cake tin and line with baking paper. Grease the paper. In a small saucepan, stir the butter over low heat until melted. Continue to heat the butter until it turns golden brown. This should take about 6 minutes. Skim fat solids from the surface. Remove from the heat.
2 Sift the flours and cinnamon into a large mixing bowl. Add the sugar and stir. Place the eggs, vanilla essence, juice, milk and the browned butter in a separate bowl and stir until well combined. Make a well in the centre of the dry ingredients and pour the egg mixture in. Using electric mixers, beat the mixture on low speed for 3 minutes, or until just moistened. Beat on high speed for 5 minutes, or until the mixture is free of lumps and increased in volume.
3 Pour the mixture into the prepared tin and smooth the surface. Bake for 40 minutes, or until a skewer comes out clean when inserted into the centre of the cake. Remove from the oven and leave the cake in the tin for 10 minutes before turning out onto a wire rack to cool completely.

4 To make the icing, brown 30 g (1 oz) of the butter using the same method as in step 1. Leave the browned butter to cool to room temperature. Using electric beaters, beat the remaining butter and sifted icing sugar in a small mixing bowl until light and creamy. Add the cinnamon and browned butter, beating for 2 minutes, or until the mixture is smooth and fluffy. Spread the icing over the cake with a flat-bladed knife. Sprinkle with extra ground cinnamon, if desired.

STORAGE: This cake can be stored for up to 4 days in an airtight container or frozen for up to 3 months without icing.
VARIATION: Make the icing without the browned butter, if preferred.

Using a flat-bladed knife, spread the meringue mixture evenly into the prepared tin.

Pipe the whipped cream into rosettes then top each one with a chocolate coffee bean.

COFFEE HAZELNUT MERINGUE TORTE

Preparation time: 1 hour 15 minutes + 2 hours refrigeration
Total cooking time: 1 hour
Serves 12–16

1½ cups (150 g/5 oz) roasted hazelnuts
4 large egg whites
¾ cup (185 g/6 oz) caster sugar
⅓ cup (40 g/1¼ oz) plain flour
1¼ cups (315 ml/10 fl oz) cream
2 tablespoons sugar
1 tablespoon Tia Maria liqueur
chocolate-covered coffee beans, to decorate

COFFEE FILLING
½ cup (125 g/4 oz) caster sugar
2 tablespoons instant coffee granules
4 large egg yolks, lightly beaten
250 g (8 oz) unsalted butter, chopped

1 Preheat the oven to 160°C (315°F/ Gas 2–3). Lightly grease two 20 cm (8 inch) round cake tins and line with baking paper. Grease the baking paper. Place the hazelnuts in a food processor and process until finely ground. Place the egg whites in a clean, dry mixing bowl. Using electric beaters, beat until soft peaks form. Add the sugar gradually, beating constantly until dissolved and the mixture is thick. Transfer to a large mixing bowl and fold in the nuts and sifted flour. Stir until just combined.

2 Divide the meringue into four portions and place two in the refrigerator. Spread one portion into each prepared tin and smooth the surface. Bake for 25 minutes, or until lightly golden and crisp. Leave to cool in tins for 3 minutes, then lift onto wire racks to cool. Repeat with the remaining meringue portions.

3 To make the filling, combine the sugar, coffee powder and ¼ cup (60 ml/2 fl oz) of water in a small pan. Stir constantly over low heat until the mixture boils and sugar dissolves. Simmer, uncovered, without stirring, for 5 minutes. Remove from the heat and cool for 5 minutes.

Using electric beaters, beat the egg yolks in a small mixing bowl on high speed for 10 minutes.Gradually pour the warm coffee syrup into the bowl and beat until glossy and thick. When mixture has cooled, add the butter, a piece at a time, beating well after each addition. Place first meringue layer on a serving plate and spread with one-third of the filling. Repeat with remaining meringue and filling, ending with meringue on top.

4 Using electric beaters, beat the cream, sugar and liqueur in a mixing bowl until stiff peaks form. Spread two-thirds of the whipped cream mixture over top and side of the torte. Using a piping bag fitted with large star nozzle, pipe remaining whipped cream around the top edge of the cake. Decorate with chocolate-covered coffee beans, if using. Chill for at least 2 hours. Remove from the refrigerator and stand for 10 minutes before serving.

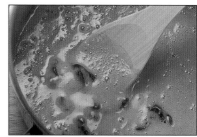

Constantly stir over a low heat until the butter has melted and the sugar dissolved.

Pour butter mixture and the eggs into the well then stir until combined with a wooden spoon.

DATE AND WALNUT LOAF

Preparation time: 25 minutes
Total cooking time: 1 hour
Serves 9–12

125 g (4 oz) unsalted butter
¹/₂ cup (350 g/11 oz) honey (see HINT)
¹/₄ cup (55 g/2 oz) firmly packed light brown
   sugar
2 tablespoons milk
1¹/₂ cups (280 g/9 oz) chopped pitted dates
¹/₄ teaspoon bicarbonate of soda
2 cups (250 g/8 oz) plain flour
¹/₂ teaspoon ground nutmeg
1 cup (125 g/4 oz) chopped walnuts
2 eggs, lightly beaten

1 Preheat the oven to 180°C (350°F/ Gas 4). Lightly grease one 21 x 14 x 8 cm (9 x 5 x 3 inch) loaf tin and line with baking paper. Grease the baking paper.
2 Combine the butter, honey, brown sugar and milk in a medium saucepan. Stir over low heat until the butter has melted and the sugar has dissolved. Remove from the heat. Stir in the dates and soda then set aside to cool. Sift the flour and nutmeg into a large mixing bowl. Add the chopped walnuts and stir. Make a well in the centre of the dry ingredients.
3 Pour the butter mixture and the eggs into the dry ingredients. Using a wooden spoon, stir until well combined but do not overbeat. Spoon evenly into the prepared pan and smooth the surface. Bake for 55 minutes, or until a skewer inserted in the centre of the cake comes out clean. Leave the cake in the tin for 15 minutes, then turn out onto a wire rack. Remove the baking paper. Serve the loaf with extra butter, if desired.

STORAGE: This cake is best eaten on the day it is made.
HINT: Cakes that are made with honey will stay moist for longer than those made with sugar.

Alternate folding in the milk with adding the sifted flour and spices.

Test to see if the cake is cooked by inserting a skewer into the centre.

HONEY AND COCONUT CAKE

Preparation time: 40 minutes
Total baking time: 30 minutes
Serves 18–20

125 g (4 oz) unsalted butter, softened
²⁄₃ cup (140 g/4¹⁄₂ oz) raw sugar
2 large eggs, lightly beaten
1 teaspoon vanilla essence
¹⁄₄ cup (90 g/3 oz) honey
¹⁄₂ cup (45 g/1¹⁄₂ oz) desiccated coconut
1³⁄₄ cups (220 g/7 oz) self-raising flour
1 teaspoon ground nutmeg
¹⁄₄ teaspoon ground cinnamon
¹⁄₄ teaspoon ground allspice
¹⁄₂ cup (125 ml/4 fl oz) milk
extra ground nutmeg, to decorate

HONEY AND CREAM CHEESE ICING
125 g (4 oz) cream cheese, softened
¹⁄₂ cup (60 g/2 oz) icing sugar
1 tablespoon honey

1 Preheat the oven to 180°C (350°F/ Gas 4). Lightly grease a 28 x 18 x 3 cm (11 x 7 x 1¹⁄₄ inch) cake tin. Line with lightly greased baking paper. Using electric beaters, beat the butter and sugar in a small mixing bowl until light and creamy. Add the eggs gradually, beating thoroughly after each addition. Add the vanilla essence and honey. Beat until well combined.

2 Transfer the mixture to a large mixing bowl and add the desiccated coconut. Using a metal spoon, fold in sifted flour and spices alternating with milk. Stir until just combined and the mixture is almost smooth. Spoon into the prepared pan and smooth surface.

3 Bake for 30–35 minutes, or until the skewer comes out clean when inserted in the centre. Leave the cake in the tin for 10 minutes before turning out onto a wire rack to cool completely. Remove the baking paper from the cake. To make the icing, beat the softened cream cheese with electric beaters in a small mixing bowl until creamy. Add the sifted icing sugar and honey, beating for 3 minutes, or until the mixture is smooth and fluffy. Spread the icing evenly over the cake using a flat-bladed knife. Sprinkle the extra nutmeg over the top.

STORAGE: The cake can be stored for 4 days in an airtight container.

Turn the cake out onto baking paper sprinkled with sugar and roll up. Set aside for 5 minutes.

Using a flat-bladed knife, spread with the strawberry jam before re-rolling.

CLASSIC SWISS ROLL

Preparation time: 25 minutes
Total cooking time: 12 minutes
Serves 10

³/₄ cup (90 g/3 oz) self-raising flour
3 eggs, lightly beaten
³/₄ cup (185 g/6 oz) caster sugar
¹/₂ cup (160 g/5¹/₂ oz) strawberry jam (see HINT)

1 Preheat the oven to 210°C (415°F/ Gas 6–7). Lightly grease a 30 x 25 x 2 cm (12 x 10 x ³/₄ inch) Swiss roll tin. Line the base with baking paper, extending over the two long sides. Sift the flour three times onto the baking paper.
2 Using electric beaters, beat the eggs in a small mixing bowl for 5 minutes, or until thick and pale. Add ¹/₂ cup of the sugar gradually, beating constantly until the mixture is pale and glossy.
3 Transfer to a large mixing bowl. Using a metal spoon, fold in the flour quickly and lightly. Spread into the tin and smooth the surface. Bake for 10–12 minutes, or until lightly golden and springy to touch. Meanwhile, place a clean tea towel on a work surface, cover with baking paper and lightly sprinkle with the remaining caster sugar. When the cake is cooked, turn it out immediately onto the sugar.
4 Using the tea towel as a guide, carefully roll the cake up from the short side, rolling the paper inside the roll. Stand the rolled cake on a wire rack for 5 minutes, then carefully unroll and allow the cake to cool to room temperature. Spread with the jam and re-roll. Trim the ends.

HINT: Beat the jam with a spatula for 30 seconds before applying to cake. This softens it and makes it easier to spread. Any type of jam can be used.

Add mashed banana then fold the sifted flour into the mixture with a metal spoon.

Bake for 1 hour and test to see if the cake is cooked by inserting a skewer into the middle.

BANANA PEANUT BUTTER CAKE

Preparation time: 10 minutes
Total cooking time: 1 hour
Serves 9–12

125 g (4 oz) unsalted butter
¹/₂ cup (115 g/4 oz) firmly packed brown sugar
¹/₄ cup (90 g/3 oz) honey
2 large eggs, lightly beaten
¹/₃ cup (90 g/3 oz) crunchy peanut butter
1 cup (240 g/7¹/₂ oz) mashed banana (see HINT)
2 cups (110 g/3¹/₂ oz) wholemeal self-raising flour

1 Preheat the oven to 180°C (350°F/ Gas 4). Lightly grease one 21 x 14 x 7 cm (9 x 6 x 3 inch) loaf tin. Line with greased baking paper. Using electric beaters, beat the butter, sugar and honey in a small mixing bowl until light and creamy. Add the eggs gradually, beating thoroughly after each addition. Add the peanut butter and beat until well combined.

2 Transfer the mixture to a large mixing bowl and stir in banana. Using a metal spoon, fold in the sifted flour including husks. Stir until the mixture is just combined and almost smooth.

3 Spoon the mixture evenly into the prepared tin and smooth surface. Bake for 1 hour or until skewer comes out clean when inserted in centre of cake. Leave the cake in pan for 10 minutes, then turn out onto a wire rack to cool completely. Remove paper. Serve sliced and spread with butter, if desired.

HINT: Use soft, ripe bananas for this recipe. Mash the bananas with a fork; do not blend or process or they will add too much moisture.

Pour the mixture into the prepared tin and bake for 1 hour 30 minutes.

Using a flat-bladed knife, spread the chocolate topping over the cooled cake.

RICH DARK CHOCOLATE CAKE

Preparation time: 15 minutes
Total cooking time: 1 hour 40 minutes
Serves 10–12

185 g (6 oz) unsalted butter, chopped
250 g (8 oz) dark chocolate bits
1³⁄₄ cups (220 g/7 oz) self-raising flour
¹⁄₃ cup (40 g/1¹⁄₄ oz) cocoa powder
1¹⁄₂ cups (375 g/12 oz) caster sugar
3 eggs, lightly beaten

CHOCOLATE TOPPING
20 g (³⁄₄ oz) unsalted butter, chopped
125 g (4 oz) dark chocolate, chopped

1 Preheat the oven to 160°C (315°F/ Gas 2–3). Lightly grease a 22 cm (9 inch) springform tin and line the base with baking paper. Place the butter and chocolate bits in a small heatproof bowl. Place the bowl over a saucepan of simmering water, making sure the base does not touch the water, and stir frequently until melted.
2 Sift the flour and cocoa into a large mixing bowl. Combine the chocolate mixture, sugar and egg, then add 1 cup (250 ml/8 fl oz) of water and mix well. Add to the flour and cocoa and stir until well combined. Pour the mixture into the prepared tin and bake for 1 hour 30 minutes, or until a skewer comes out clean when inserted into the centre of the cake. Leave the cake in the tin for 15 minutes before turning out onto a wire rack to cool completely.
3 To make the topping, place the butter and chocolate pieces in a small heatproof bowl. Place the bowl over a saucepan of simmering water, making sure the base does not touch the water. Spread over the cooled cake in a swirl pattern.

Make a well in the centre of the dry ingredients sifted into a large mixing bowl.

Spoon the mixture into the prepared tin and bake for 35 minutes.

CUSTARD BUTTER CAKE

Preparation time: 15 minutes
Total cooking time: 40 minutes
Serves 8–10

1 cup (125 g/4 oz) self-raising flour
²/₃ cup (85 g/3 oz) custard powder
¹/₂ teaspoon bicarbonate of soda
125 g (4 oz) unsalted butter, chopped
3/4 cup (185 g/6 oz) caster sugar
3 eggs, lightly beaten
¹/₄ cup (60 ml/2 fl oz) buttermilk

ICING
100 g (3¹/₂ oz) white chocolate
¹/₄ cup (60 ml/2 fl oz) cream
200 g (6¹/₂ oz) cream cheese, softened
¹/₃ cup (40 g/1¹/₄ oz) icing sugar
silver cachous and crystallized violets, to
    decorate

1 Preheat the oven to 180°C (350°F/ Gas 4). Lightly grease a deep 20 cm (8 inch) square cake tin and line the base with baking paper. Sift the flour, custard powder and soda into a bowl and make a well in the centre.

2 Melt the butter and sugar in a small saucepan over low heat, stirring until the sugar has dissolved. Remove from the heat. Add the butter mixture and combined egg and buttermilk to the dry ingredients and stir until just combined. Spoon into the prepared tin. Bake for 35 minutes, or until a skewer comes out clean when inserted into the centre. Leave in the tin to cool.

3 To make the icing, melt the chocolate and cream in a saucepan over low heat. Cool and add to the cream cheese and icing sugar. Beat until smooth. Decorate with silver cachous and crystallised violets.

Process in a food processor until the mixture resembles fine breadcrumbs.

Sprinkle the extra sugar over the top then bake for 50 minutes.

BLUEBERRY SHORTCAKE

Preparation time: 15 minutes
Total cooking time: 1 hour
Serves 8–10

³/₄ cup (100 g/4 oz) whole hazelnuts
2¹/₄ cups (280 g/9 oz) self-raising flour
1¹/₂ teaspoons ground cinnamon
³/₄ cup (165 g/5¹/₂ oz) demerara sugar
150 g (5 oz) unsalted butter, chopped
2 eggs
¹/₂ cup (165 g/5¹/₂ oz) blueberry jam
1 tablespoon demarara sugar, extra
fresh blueberries, to serve
cream, to serve

1 Preheat the oven to 180°C (350°F/ Gas 4). Lightly grease a deep 20 cm (8 inch) round cake tin and line the base with baking paper. Spread the hazelnuts on a baking tray and bake for 5–10 minutes. Place in a clean tea towel and rub together to remove the skins, then roughly chop.

2 Process the flour, cinnamon, sugar, butter and half the hazelnuts in a food processor until finely chopped. Add the eggs and process until combined. Press half the mixture onto the base of the prepared tin, then spread the jam evenly over the mixture.

3 Lightly knead the remaining hazelnuts into the remaining dough, then press evenly over the jam layer. Sprinkle the extra sugar over the top and bake for 50 minutes, or until a skewer comes out clean when inserted into the centre. Leave in the tin for 15 minutes before turning out onto a wire rack to cool completely. Serve with fresh blueberries and cream.

Spoon the mixture into an ungreased tin then bake for 45 minutes.

Stir the chocolate, cream and butter over low heat until melted.

ANGEL FOOD CAKE WITH CHOCOLATE SAUCE

Preparation time: 15 minutes
Total cooking time: 45 minutes
Serves 8

1 cup (125 g/4 oz) plain flour
1 cup (250 g/8 oz) caster sugar
10 egg whites, at room temperature
1 teaspoon cream of tartar
$^1/_2$ teaspoon vanilla essence

CHOCOLATE SAUCE
250 g (8 oz) dark chocolate, chopped
$^3/_4$ cup (185 ml/6 fl oz) cream
50 g (1$^3/_4$ oz) unsalted butter, chopped
silver cachous, to decorate

1 Preheat the oven to 180°C (350°F/ Gas 4). Sift the flour and $^1/_2$ cup (125 g/4 oz) of the sugar four times into a large mixing bowl. Set aside. Beat the egg whites, cream of tartar and $^1/_4$ teaspoon salt in a clean, dry large mixing bowl with electric beaters until soft peaks form. Gradually add the remaining sugar and beat until thick and glossy.

2 Add the vanilla essence. Sift half the flour and sugar mixture over the meringue mixture and gently fold in with a metal spoon. Repeat with the remaining flour and sugar. Spoon into an ungreased angel cake tin and bake for 45 minutes, or until a skewer comes out clean when inserted into the centre of the cake. Gently loosen around the side of the cake with a spatula, then turn the cake out onto a wire rack to cool completely.

3 To make the sauce, place the chocolate, cream and butter in a saucepan. Stir over low heat until the chocolate has melted and the mixture is smooth. Drizzle over the cake and decorate with silver cachous. Serve.

NOTE: The tin must be very clean and not greased or the cake will not rise and will slip down the side of the tin.

Don't worry if the mixture looks curdled. Once the flour is added, it will come together.

Spoon the mixture into the prepared pan and bake for 1 hour 20 minutes.

APRICOT PINE NUT CAKE

Preparation time: 15 minutes
Total cooking time: 1 hour 30 minutes
Serves 10

²/₃ cup (100 g/3¹/₂ oz) pine nuts, roughly
   chopped
250 g (8 oz) unsalted butter, softened
1 cup (250 g/8 oz) sugar
3 teaspoons finely grated orange rind
3 eggs, lightly beaten
2¹/₂ cups (310 g/10 oz) self-raising flour,
   sifted
1 cup (200 g/6¹/₂ oz) glacé apricots, finely
   chopped (see NOTE)
1 cup (250 ml/8 fl oz) orange juice
icing sugar, to dust
cream or yoghurt, to serve

1 Preheat the oven to 180°C (350°F/ Gas 4). Lightly grease a 26 cm (10¹/₂ inch) round cake tin and line the base with baking paper. Spread the pine nuts on a baking tray and bake for 5–10 minutes, or until lightly golden. Set aside to cool.
2 Beat the butter, sugar and orange rind with electric beaters until pale and creamy. Add the egg gradually, beating well after each addition. (The mixture may look curdled but once you add the flour, it will bring it back together.) Fold in the flour, pine nuts, apricots and orange juice in two batches.
3 Spoon the mixture into the prepared tin and smooth the surface. Bake for 1 hour 20 minutes, or until a skewer comes out clean when inserted into the centre of the cake. Leave the cake in the tin for 10 minutes before turning out onto a wire rack to cool completely. If desired, dust with the icing sugar and serve with the cream or yoghurt.

NOTE: The chopped apricots may clump together, so flour your hands and rub through to separate.
VARIATION: For a little extra flavor, add 2 tablespoons brandy to the cake mixture with the flour, pine nuts, apricots and orange juice.

Add the chocolate mixture and the eggs into a food processor with the flour and the coconut.

Leave the cake in the tin before turning out onto a wire rack to cool.

CHOCOLATE CHERRY CAKE

Preparation time: 15 minutes
Total cooking time: 1 hour 10 minutes
Serves 8

200 g (6¹/₂ oz) dark chocolate, chopped
250 g (8 oz) unsalted butter, chopped
1 cup (230 g/7¹/₂ oz) firmly packed soft
    brown sugar
1 teaspoon vanilla essence
1¹/₄ cups (155 g/5 oz) self-raising flour
¹/₂ cup (45 g/1¹/₂ oz) desiccated coconut
2 eggs
1 cup (180 g/6 oz) pitted sour cherries,
    drained
icing sugar, to dust
fresh cherries, to garnish

1 Preheat the oven to 160°C (315°F/ Gas 2–3). Lightly grease a 23 cm (9 inch) round cake tin and line the base with baking paper. Grease the paper. Place the chocolate, butter, sugar and vanilla essence in a heatproof bowl. Sit the bowl, making sure the base does not touch the water, over a saucepan of simmering water. Stir occasionally until the chocolate has melted and the mixture is smooth. Remove the saucepan from the heat and sit the bowl in a sink of cold water until cooled.

2 Combine the flour and coconut in a food processor. Add the chocolate mixture and eggs and process in short bursts until the mixture is just combined. Add the pitted sour cherries to the food processor and process until they are just chopped.

3 Pour the mixture into the prepared tin and bake for 1 hour 10 minutes, or until a skewer comes out clean when inserted into the centre of the cake. Leave the cake in the tin for 15 minutes before carefully turning out onto a wire rack to cool completely. If desired, dust with icing sugar and decorate with fresh cherries.

Place the apricots around the base of the tin then sprinkle the pecan mixture over the top.

The cake is cooked if a skewer comes out clean when inserted in the centre.

GINGERBREAD APRICOT UPSIDE-DOWN CAKE

Preparation time: 15 minutes
Total cooking time: 45 minutes
Serves 6

200 g (6½ oz) glacé apricots
175 g (6 oz) unsalted butter
30 g (1 oz) pecans, finely chopped
¾ cup (165 g/5½ oz) firmly packed soft
   brown sugar
¼ cup (90 g/3 oz) golden syrup
1½ cups (185 g/6 oz) self-raising flour
3 teaspoons ground ginger
½ teaspoon ground nutmeg

1 Preheat the oven to 180°C (350°F/ Gas 4). Lightly grease and flour the base of a deep 20 cm (8 inch) round cake tin, shaking out the excess flour. Arrange the apricots around the base, cut-side up. Melt the butter in a small saucepan over low heat. Transfer 1 tablespoon of the melted butter to a bowl. Add the pecans and ¼ cup (55 g/2 oz) of the sugar and mix well. Sprinkle the mixture over the apricots.
2 Add the golden syrup and ½ cup (125 ml/4 fl oz) water to the saucepan and stir over medium heat until well combined. Sift the flour and spices in a mixing bowl, then stir in the remaining sugar. Pour in the golden syrup mixture and mix well. Spoon the mixture over the apricots. Bake for 35–40 minutes, or until a skewer comes out clean when inserted into the centre of the cake. Leave in the tin for 15 minutes before turning out onto a wire rack to cool completely.

STORAGE: The cake will keep for 4 days in an airtight container.

Using a wooden spoon, stir the mixture until all the ingredients are just combined.

The cake is cooked if a skewer inserted into the centre comes out clean.

RUM AND RAISIN CAKE

Preparation time: 15 minutes + 10 minutes soaking
Total cooking time: 45 minutes
Serves 8

1 cup (160 g/5½ oz) raisins
¼ cup (60 ml/2 fl oz) dark rum
1½ cups (185 g/6 oz) self-raising flour
150 g (5 oz) unsalted butter, chopped
¾ cup (140 g/4½ oz) lightly packed soft brown sugar
3 eggs, lightly beaten
ice-cream, to serve

1 Preheat the oven to 180°C (350°F/ Gas 4). Lightly grease a deep 20 cm (8 inch) round cake tin and line the base with baking paper. Soak the raisins and rum in a small bowl for 10 minutes. Sift the flour into a large mixing bowl and make a well in the centre.

2 Melt the butter and sugar in a small saucepan over low heat, stirring until the sugar has dissolved. Remove from the heat. Combine with the rum and raisin mixture and add to the flour with the egg. Stir, making sure not to overbeat, with a wooden spoon until just combined.

3 Spoon the mixture into the prepared tin and smooth the surface. Bake for 40 minutes, or until a skewer comes out clean when inserted into the centre of the cake. Serve with ice-cream.

Leave the cakes to stand in the tins before turning out onto a wire rack to cool.

Beat the cream and lemon butter with electric beaters until soft peaks form.

LEMON CREAM CAKE

Preparation time: 20 minutes
Total cooking time: 20 minutes
Makes 1

¹/₃ cup (40 g/1¹/₄ oz) cornflour
¹/₃ cup (40 g/1¹/₄ oz) plain flour
¹/₃ cup (40 g/1¹/₄ oz) self-raising flour
4 eggs
²/₃ cup (160 g/5¹/₂ oz) caster sugar
2 teaspoons grated lemon rind

LEMON CREAM
1¹/₂ cups (375 ml/12 fl oz) cream
¹/₃ cup lemon butter
¹/₂ cup (60 g/2 oz) halved pecans

1 Preheat the oven to 180°C (350°F/ Gas 4). Lightly grease two shallow 20 cm (8 inch) round cake tins and line bases with baking paper. Grease the baking paper. Dust tins lightly with flour and shake off excess. Sift the combined flours three times onto baking paper.
2 Using electric beaters, beat the eggs in a large mixing bowl for 5 minutes, or until thick and pale. Add the sugar gradually, beating constantly until dissolved. Using a metal spoon, fold in the lemon rind and sifted flours quickly and lightly.
3 Spoon the mixture evenly into the prepared tins and smooth the tops. Bake for 20 minutes, or until lightly golden. Leave the cakes for 2 minutes in the tins before turning out onto a wire rack to cool completely.

4 To make the lemon cream, place the cream and lemon butter in a small mixing bowl. Using electric beaters, beat until soft peaks form. Cut each cake in half horizontally and place one layer on a serving plate. Using a flat-bladed knife, spread the cake layer with a quarter of the lemon cream. Continue layering with the remaining cake and lemon cream, icing the top of the cake with lemon cream as well. Sprinkle with pecans and serve.

STORAGE: This cake is best eaten on the day of baking. It can be assembled several hours ahead and chilled.

Heat half of the passionfruit pulp until nearly boiling then add the gelatine mixture.

Make sure you leave enough filling to cover the side and top of the cake.

LAYERED PASSIONFRUIT TORTE

Preparation time: 45 minutes + chilling
Total cooking time: 25 minutes
Makes 1

6 eggs, separated
³/₄ cup (90 g/3 oz) icing sugar
¹/₂ cup (125 g/4 oz) sugar
¹/₂ teaspoon vanilla essence
¹/₂ cup (60 g/2 oz) cornflour
1¹/₂ teaspoons baking powder
¹/₄ cup (30 g/1 oz) plain flour

FILLING
1 tablespoon lemon juice
1 tablespoon gelatine
pulp of 10 passionfruit
500 g (1 lb) cream cheese
1¹/₂ cups (185 g/6 oz) icing sugar, sifted
³/₄ cup (185 ml/6 fl oz) cream, lightly whipped

¹/₂ cup (125 ml/4 fl oz) cream, extra, whipped
   to stiff peaks
pulp of 2 passionfruit, extra
¹/₄ cup (40 g/1¹/₄ oz) roasted almonds or
   pistachios, chopped

1 Preheat the oven to 180°C (350°F/ Gas 4). Lightly grease two shallow 23 cm (9 inch) round cake tins and line the bases with baking paper. Place the egg whites in a large dry mixing bowl. Beat with electric beaters until stiff peaks form. Add the sugar gradually, beating until all the sugar has dissolved and mixture is thick and glossy. Fold in the yolks and vanilla essence. Sift dry ingredients into the mixture and gently fold in until smooth. Spoon mixture evenly into the prepared tins. Bake for 20 minutes, or until the cakes shrink away from the sides of the tins. Leave the cakes in the tins for 5 minutes before turning out onto wire racks to cool completely.
2 To make the filling, combine the juice, gelatine and water in a small mixing bowl. Heat half the passionfruit pulp in a small saucepan until it boils. Add the gelatine mixture and stir

over medium heat until dissolved. Strain the mixture through a sieve and add to remaining passionfruit pulp. Leave to cool slightly. Beat the cream cheese and sugar with electric beaters until the mixture is smooth and creamy. Add the passionfruit mixture. Fold in the lightly whipped cream.
3 To assemble the cake, cut each cake in half horizontally with a serrated knife. Place one layer on a serving plate and spread with one-fifth of filling. Continue layering, leaving enough filling to spread evenly over the top and side of the cake. Place extra whipped cream in a piping bag and pipe rosettes on top of the cake. Spread extra passionfruit pulp over top. Sprinkle the nuts over the rosettes. Refrigerate for several hours.

STORAGE: Assemble up to 3 days in advance but add the rosettes and pulp just before serving.

Cake Toppings

Your favorite carrot cake just isn't the same without that delicious cream cheese icing, chocolate cake loses a little of its allure without its rich chocolate topping and a simple butter cake gains five-star standing when partnered with coffee buttercream. The icing on the cake can make all the difference.

GINGER AND LEMON GLACE ICING

Sift ⅓ cup (40 g/1¼ oz) icing sugar into a small heatproof bowl. Add ½ teaspoon ginger, 20 g (¾ oz) melted unsalted butter, 2 teaspoons milk and 1 teaspoon lemon juice and mix to form a paste. Place the bowl over a saucepan of simmering water, making sure the base does not touch the water, and stir until the icing is smooth and glossy. Remove the bowl from the heat. Drizzle the icing over the cake or spread with a knife dipped in hot water for even covering. Do not reheat.

LEMON CREAM CHEESE ICING

Place 60 g (2 oz) softened cream cheese and 30 g (1 oz) unsalted butter in a small mixing bowl. Using electric beaters, beat until

combined. Add 1 tablespoon lemon juice and 1½ cups (185 g/6 oz) sifted icing sugar and beat until smooth.

BUTTERSCOTCH FROSTING

Chop 20 g (¾ oz) unsalted butter into small pieces and place in a saucepan with ½ cup

(95 g/3 oz) lightly packed brown sugar. Stir constantly over low heat until mixture boils and the sugar dissolves. Simmer for 3 minutes. Remove from the heat, add ⅓ cup (90 g/3 oz) sour cream and stir. Leave to cool. Place 100 g (3½ oz) softened cream cheese in a mixing bowl and beat with electric beaters until light and creamy. Gradually add the cooled butterscotch mixture, beating well after each addition.

CHOCOLATE GANACHE

Combine ¼ cup (60 ml/2 fl oz) cream and 150 g (5 oz) dark chocolate in a small saucepan. Stir over low heat until the chocolate has melted and the mixture is smooth. Remove from the heat and allow to cool. Pour the ganache on to the cake, then smooth the top and around the side with a flat-bladed knife.

butter and 1½ cups (185 g/6 oz) icing sugar in a mixing bowl. Using electric beaters, beat until pale and creamy. Add ½ teaspoon vanilla, coffee mixture and 2 teaspoons milk and beat for 2 minutes, or until smooth and fluffy.

CARAMEL ICING

Place 1½ cups (185 g/6 oz) icing sugar, 1 tablespoon milk, 2 tablespoons golden syrup and 30 g (1 oz) softened unsalted butter in a bowl and beat with a wooden spoon until smooth. Spread over the cake with a flat-bladed knife.

COFFEE BUTTERCREAM

Dissolve 3 teaspoons instant coffee powder in 2 tablespoons boiling water. Place 125 g (4 oz)

LIME ICING

Place 2 cups (250 g/8 oz) sifted icing sugar, 80 g (2¾ oz) softened unsalted butter and 2 tablespoons lime juice in a mixing bowl and beat with a wooden spoon until smooth, adding 1–2 tablespoons water, if necessary. Spread over the cake with a flat-bladed knife.

CHOCOLATE FUDGE ICING

Coarsely chop 150 g (5 oz) of dark chocolate and place in a small saucepan with 90 g (3 oz) unsalted butter and ½ cup (160 g/5½ oz) condensed milk. Stir over low heat until the chocolate and butter have melted and the mixture is smooth. Remove from the heat. Allow to cool until thick and spreadable.

ORANGE GLACE ICING

Sift 1 cup (125 g/4 oz) icing sugar into a heatproof bowl. Add 10 g (¼ oz) softened unsalted butter, 1 teaspoon grated orange rind and enough orange juice to make a soft pouring consistency. Place the bowl, making sure the base does not touch the water, over a saucepan of simmering water and stir until the icing is smooth and glossy. Remove from the heat. Drizzle over the cake and let it run down the sides.

Little Cakes & Muffins

SACHER SQUARES

Preparation time: 1 hour
Total cooking time: 40 minutes
Makes 24

BASE
1 cup (125 g/4 oz) plain flour
60 g (2 oz) unsalted butter, chopped
$\frac{1}{4}$ cup (60 g/2 oz) sugar
2 egg yolks, lightly beaten
2 teaspoons iced water

CAKE
1 cup (125 g/4 oz) plain flour
$\frac{1}{3}$ cup (40 g/1$\frac{1}{4}$ oz) cocoa powder
1 cup (250 g/ 8 oz) caster sugar
100 g (3$\frac{1}{2}$ oz) unsalted butter
2 tablespoons apricot jam
4 eggs, separated
1 cup (315 g/10 oz) apricot jam, extra

TOPPING
250 g (8 oz) dark chocolate
$\frac{3}{4}$ cup (185 ml/6 fl oz) cream

1 Preheat the oven to 180°C (350°F/ Gas 4). Cut an 18 x 28 cm (7 x 11 inch) rectangle of baking paper. To make the base, sift the flour into a bowl and add the butter. Using fingertips, rub butter into the flour until fine and crumbly. Stir in sugar. Add the yolks and almost all the water, and mix to a dough, adding more liquid if necessary. Knead for 30 seconds or until smooth. Roll out and cut to fit baking paper. Place on a baking tray. Bake for 10 minutes or until golden. Cool.

2 To make the cake, preheat the oven to 180°C (350°F/Gas 4). Lightly grease an 18 x 28 cm (7 x 11 inch) shallow rectangular tin and line with baking paper. Sift the flour and cocoa into a mixing bowl. Combine the sugar, butter and jam in a small pan. Stir over a low heat until butter has melted and sugar dissolved. Add the butter mixture to the dry ingredients. Stir until just combined. Add the egg yolks and mix well.

3 Place the egg whites in a clean, dry mixing bowl. Using electric beaters, beat until soft peaks form. Using a metal spoon, fold into the mixture. Pour into the prepared tin and bake for 30 minutes. Leave in the tin for 15 minutes before turning out onto a wire rack to cool completely.

4 Warm the extra jam over a saucepan of simmering water and push through a fine sieve. Brush the base with $\frac{1}{4}$ cup jam. Place cake on the base. Trim each side evenly, cutting 'crust' from cake and base. Using a sharp knife, cut into 24 squares. Brush with jam. Place on a wire rack, over baking paper, leaving 4 cm (1$\frac{1}{2}$ inch) between each.

5 To make the topping, break the chocolate into pieces and place in a small bowl. Place cream in a small saucepan and bring to the boil. Pour over chocolate and stir until melted. Cool slightly. Pour topping over each square and use a flat-bladed knife to cover completely. Scrape excess from the paper and spoon, with remaining topping, into a small paper piping bag. Pipe an 'S' onto each square.

Make a well in the centre of the dry ingredients and pour in the liquid ingredients.

BANANA MUFFINS

Preparation time: 15 minutes
Total cooking time: 15 minutes
Makes 12

2 cups (250 g/8 oz) self-raising flour
1 cup (75 g/2½ oz) oat bran
¾ cup (185 g/6 oz) caster sugar
60 g (2 oz) butter, melted
¾ cup (185 ml/6 fl oz) milk
2 eggs, lightly beaten
1 cup (240 g/7½ oz) mashed, ripe banana
(2 medium bananas)

1 Preheat the oven to 210°C (415°F/ Gas 6–7). Lightly grease a 12-hole muffin tin. Sift the flour into a large bowl and add the oat bran and the sugar. Make a well in the centre of the dry ingredients.

2 Combine the butter, milk, eggs and banana in a separate mixing bowl and add to the flour mixture all at once. Using a wooden spoon, stir until just mixed. (Do not overbeat; the batter should remain lumpy.)

3 Spoon the mixture into the prepared tin. Bake for 15 minutes, or until puffed and brown. Transfer the muffins to a wire rack to cool completely.

TOPPING SUGGESTION: For muffins with a difference, beat 100 g (3½ oz) cream cheese, 2 tablespoons icing sugar and 2 teaspoons lemon juice with electric beaters until light and creamy. Spread over the muffins and top with dried banana slices.

Stir in the ground almonds and cream with a flat-bladed knife.

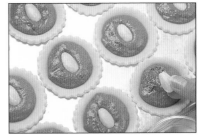

Gently press a blanched almond into the centre of each tart.

CHOCOLATE ALMOND TARTS

Preparation time: 40 minutes
Total cooking time: 20 minutes
Makes 18

1 cup (125 g/4 oz) plain flour
pinch salt
60 g (2 oz) butter, chopped
1 tablespoon icing sugar
1 tablespoon lemon juice

FILLING
1 egg
$1/_3$ cup (90 g/3 oz) caster sugar
2 tablespoons cocoa
$1/_2$ cup (90 g/3 oz) ground almonds
3 tablespoons cream
$1/_4$ cup (80 g/2$3/_4$ oz) apricot jam
18 blanched almonds

1 Preheat the oven to 180°C (350°F/ Gas 4). Lightly grease two flat-bottomed 9-hole cupcake trays. Process the flour, salt, butter and icing sugar in a food processor for 10 seconds, or until the mixture resembles fine breadcrumbs. Add juice and process until the mixture forms a ball. Roll between sheets of baking paper to 5 mm ($1/_4$ inch) thickness. Cut into 7 cm (2$3/_4$ inch) rounds with fluted cutter. Place in the prepared tins and chill for 20 minutes.

2 To make the filling, place the egg and sugar in a mixing bowl. Using electric beaters, beat until thick and pale. Sift the cocoa on top. Stir in the almonds and cream.

3 Place a dab of jam in each tart. Spoon the filling in and place an almond in the centre. Bake for 15 minutes, or until the top is puffed and set. Leave in the tins for 5 minutes then turn out onto wire racks to cool.

Chop the dates and the glacé ginger to the desired size.

HONEY, DATE AND GINGER SCONES

Preparation time: 25 minutes
Total cooking time: 15 minutes
Makes 12

¹/₂ cup (90 g/3 oz) fresh dates
¹/₄ cup (55 g/2 oz) glacé ginger
2 cups (250 g/8 oz) self-raising flour
¹/₂ teaspoon ground ginger
pinch salt
1 tablespoon honey
¹/₂ cup (125 ml/4 fl oz) milk
¹/₄ cup (60 ml/2 fl oz) cream

HONEY GLAZE
1 tablespoon milk
1 teaspoon honey

1 Preheat the oven to 210°C (415°F/ Gas 6–7). Lightly grease a baking tray. Chop the dates and the glacé ginger into small chunks. Sift the flour, ground ginger and salt into a mixing bowl. Add the dates and glacé ginger. Stir to combine.

2 Combine the honey, milk and cream in a small saucepan and stir over low heat until combined. Add to the flour and mix lightly, with a flat-bladed knife, to form a soft dough, adding more milk if necessary. (The dough should have just lost its stickiness but not become dried or tough.)

3 Knead the dough briefly on a lightly floured surface until smooth and press out to 2 cm (³/₄ inch) thickness. Cut rounds with a floured plain 5 cm (2 inch) cutter. Place the rounds on the prepared tray and brush with the honey glaze. Cook for 12–15 minutes, or until lightly golden.

4 To make the honey glaze, gently warm the milk and honey in a pan, stirring until well combined.

NOTE: Use self-raising flour on your hands and work surfaces.

Spoon the topping over the tops of the muffins before baking for 20–25 minutes.

MUESLI MUFFINS

Preparation time: 15 minutes + 20 minutes standing
Total cooking time: 25 minutes
Makes 6 large muffins

$^1/_2$ cup (95 g/3 oz) dried apricots, chopped
$^1/_2$ cup (125 ml/4 fl oz) orange juice
2 teaspoons finely grated orange rind
1 cup (150 g/5 oz) wholemeal self-raising flour
$^1/_2$ cup (60 g/2 oz) self-raising flour
$^1/_2$ teaspoon baking powder
$^1/_4$ cup (45 g/1$^1/_2$ oz) lightly packed soft brown sugar
$^3/_4$ cup (75 g/2$^1/_2$ oz) toasted muesli
1 cup (250 ml/8 fl oz) milk
60 g (2 oz) butter, melted

TOPPING
1 tablespoon plain flour
$^1/_2$ teaspoon cinnamon
$^1/_4$ cup (45 g/1$^1/_2$ oz) lightly packed soft brown sugar
$^1/_3$ cup (35 g/1$^1/_4$ oz) toasted muesli
20 g ($^3/_4$ oz) butter, melted

1 Preheat the oven to 210°C (415°F/ Gas 6–7). Lightly grease a 6-hole large muffin tin. Combine the apricots, orange juice and rind in a bowl. Set mixture aside for 20 minutes.
2 Sift the flours and baking powder into a mixing bowl. Add the sugar and muesli and stir through.
3 Add the combined milk, melted butter and undrained apricot mixture all at once. Mix quickly with a fork until all ingredients are just moistened.
4 Spoon the mixture evenly into the prepared tin. Sprinkle with topping. Bake the muffins for 20–25 minutes, or until golden brown. Loosen muffins with a flat-bladed knife and turn out onto a wire rack to cool completely.

5 To make the topping, place the flour, cinnamon, sugar, muesli and butter in a bowl. Stir to combine.

STORAGE: The muffins can be frozen for up to 3 months. Reheat in a 180°C (350°F/ Gas 4) oven for 10 minutes.

Cook the butter until it turns a deep golden color and then strain and discard any dark solids.

Spoon the mixture into the greased tins until three-quarters filled.

CHOCOLATE HAZELNUT FRIANDS

Preparation time: 20 minutes
Total cooking time: 40 minutes
Makes 12

200 g (6½ oz) whole hazelnuts
185 g (6 oz) butter
6 egg whites
1¼ cups (155 g/5 oz) plain flour
¼ cup (30 g/1 oz) cocoa powder
2 cups (250 g/8 oz) icing sugar
icing sugar, extra, to dust

1 Preheat the oven to 200°C (400°F/ Gas 6). Lightly grease twelve ½-cup (125 ml/4 fl oz) friand or muffin tins. Spread the hazelnuts out on a baking tray. Bake for 8–10 minutes, or until fragrant, taking care not to burn the hazelnuts. Place in a clean tea towel and rub vigorously to loosen the skins. Cool, then process in a food processor until finely ground.

2 Place the butter in a small pan and melt over medium heat, then cook for 3–4 minutes, or until butter turns a deep golden color. Strain any dark solids and set aside to cool (the color will become deeper on standing).

3 Lightly whisk the egg whites in a bowl until frothy but not firm. Sift the flour, cocoa powder and icing sugar into a large mixing bowl and stir in the ground hazelnuts. Make a well in the centre and add the egg whites and butter and mix until combined.

4 Spoon the mixture into the prepared tins until three-quarters filled. Bake for 20–25 minutes, or until a skewer inserted into the centre comes out clean. Leave in the tin for a few minutes, then cool on a wire rack. Dust with icing sugar, to serve.

Lightly fold the blueberries into the mixture, making sure they are well incorporated.

Spoon the batter into the prepared muffin tins and bake until golden brown.

BLUEBERRY MUFFINS

Preparation time: 20 minutes
Total cooking time: 20 minutes
Makes 12

3 cups (375 g/12 oz) plain flour
1 tablespoon baking powder
³/₄ cup (165 g/5¹/₂ oz) firmly packed soft
  brown sugar
125 g (4 oz) butter, melted
2 eggs, lightly beaten
1 cup (250 ml/8 fl oz) milk
1¹/₃ cups (185 g/6 oz) fresh or thawed
  frozen blueberries

1 Preheat the oven to 210°C (415°F/ Gas 6–7). Lightly grease two 6-hole muffin tins. Sift the flour and baking powder into a large mixing bowl. Stir in the sugar and make a well in the centre of the dry ingredients.
2 In a separate mixing bowl, add the melted butter, eggs and milk and stir to combine. Add all at once to the flour mixture and fold until just combined. (Do not overmix, the batter should look quite lumpy.)
3 Fold in the blueberries. Spoon the batter into the prepared tin. Bake for 20 minutes, or until golden brown. Turn out onto a wire rack to cool.

Place a portion of cream cheese in the centre of each muffin.

BERRY CHEESECAKE MUFFINS

Preparation time: 15 minutes
Total cooking time: 30 minutes
Makes 6 large muffins

1¾ cups (215 g/7 oz) self-raising flour
2 eggs, lightly beaten
¼ cup (60 ml/2 fl oz) oil
2 tablespoons raspberry jam
¼ cup (60 g/2 oz) mixed berry yoghurt
½ cup (125 g/4 oz) caster sugar
50 g (1¾ oz) cream cheese (see NOTE)
1 tablespoon raspberry jam, extra, for filling
icing sugar, sifted, to dust

1 Preheat the oven to 180°C (350°F/ Gas 4). Lightly grease a 6-hole muffin tin. Sift the flour into a large bowl and make a well in the centre. Place the eggs, oil, jam, yoghurt and sugar in a separate bowl and combine. Add all at once to the sifted flour. Mix the batter until just combined. (Do not overmix as the batter should look quite lumpy.)

2 Spoon three-quarters of the mixture into the prepared tin. Cut the cream cheese into six equal portions and place a portion on the centre of each muffin. Spread tops with jam and cover with remaining muffin batter.

3 Bake for 30 minutes, or until the muffins are golden. Loosen the muffins with a flat-bladed knife then turn out onto a wire rack to cool completely. Dust with icing sugar and serve.

NOTE: These muffins are best eaten as soon as they are cool enough. The cream cheese filling will melt slightly as the muffins cook and provide a delicious 'surprise' centre.

Once you have spread the jam, roll up the dough from the long side as you would for a Swiss roll.

JAM PINWHEELS

Preparation time: 10 minutes
Total cooking time: 20 minutes
Makes about 12

2¹/₂ cups (310 g/10 oz) self-raising flour
pinch salt
30 g (1 oz) butter, cut into small pieces
¹/₃ cup (90 g/3 oz) caster sugar
²/₃ cup (170 ml/5¹/₂ fl oz) milk
1 egg, lightly beaten
¹/₃ cup (105 g/3¹/₂ oz) strawberry jam (see
   VARIATION)
milk, to glaze
butter or cream, to serve

1 Preheat the oven to 210°C (415°F/ Gas 6–7). Lightly grease an 18 x 28 cm (7 x 11 inch) shallow tin. Sift the flour and salt into a large mixing bowl. Add the butter and rub in with your fingertips until the mixture resembles fine breadcrumbs. Add the sugar and stir it through. Make a well in the centre of the flour mixture. Combine the milk and egg in a separate bowl and add nearly all to the flour mixture. Mix lightly, with a flat-bladed knife, to a soft dough, adding more liquid if necessary. (Dough should have just lost its stickiness, but not become dried or tough.) Knead briefly on a lightly floured surface. Roll out to form a rectangle about 1 cm (¹/₂ inch) thick.

2 Warm the jam in microwave or in a saucepan over low heat. Spread over the dough. Roll up from long side as for a Swiss roll. Cut the roll into 2 cm (³/₄ inch) lengths.

3 Place dough cut-side up in the prepared tin and brush with milk. Bake for 15–20 minutes or until golden brown. Turn onto a wire rack to cool completely. Serve warm or cool with butter or cream.

VARIATION: Spread dough with fruit mince instead of jam, if you prefer.

PLAIN SCONES

Preparation time: 20 minutes
Total cooking time: 12 minutes
Makes 12

2 cups (250 g/8 oz) self-raising flour
pinch salt, optional (see NOTE)
30 g (1 oz) butter, cut into small pieces
1/2 cup (125 ml/4 fl oz) milk
1/3 cup (80 ml/2³/₄ fl oz) water
milk, extra, to glaze
jam and whipped cream, to serve

1 Preheat the oven to 210°C (415°F/ Gas 6–7). Lightly grease a baking tray. Sift the flour and salt, if using, into a large mixing bowl. Add the butter and rub in lightly using your fingertips.
2 Make a well in the centre of the flour. Add almost all of the combined milk and water. Mix with a flat-bladed knife to a soft dough, adding more liquid if necessary.
3 Turn the dough onto a lightly floured surface (use self-raising flour). Knead the dough briefly and lightly until smooth. Press or roll out the dough to form a round about 1–2 cm (1/2–3/4 inch) thick.
4 Cut the dough into rounds using a floured round 5 cm (2 inch) cutter. Place the rounds on the prepared tray and glaze with the milk. Bake for 10–12 minutes, or until golden brown. Serve with jam and whipped cream.

NOTE: Add a pinch of salt to your scones, even the sweet ones. Salt acts as a flavor enhancer and will not be tasted in the cooked product.

WHITE CHOCOLATE MANGO MUFFINS

Preparation time: 10 minutes
Total cooking time: 20 minutes
Makes 12

2¹/₂ cups (310 g/10 oz) self-raising flour
¹/₂ cup (95 g/3 oz) soft brown sugar
³/₄ cup (130 g/4¹/₂ oz) white choc bits (see
    VARIATION)
1 cup chopped fresh mango flesh (2 medium)
    or 440 g (14 oz) can mango pieces, well
    drained
¹/₂ cup (125 ml/4 fl oz) milk
¹/₄ cup (60 ml/2 fl oz) cream
90 g (3 oz) butter, melted
1 egg, lightly beaten

1 Preheat the oven to 180°C (350°F/ Gas 4). Lightly grease a 12-hole muffin tin. Sift the flour into a large mixing bowl. Stir in the sugar and choc bits and mix well. Fold in the chopped mango gently. Make a well in the centre of the mixture.

2 Add the combined milk, cream, butter and egg all at once. Mix with a fork or rubber spatu until just combined. (Do not overmix, the batter should look quite lumpy.) Spoon the mixture into the prepared tin.

3 Bake for 20 minutes, or until lightly golden. Loosen the muffins with a flat-bladed knife and turn out onto a wire rack to cool completely.

NOTE: Serve these muffins warm with whipped cream. They also make an unusual, but delicious, dessert, topped with large shavings of white chocolate or served split with stewed apples.

VARIATION: Dark or milk choc bits can also be used in these muffins.

FRUIT SCROLLS

Preparation time: 20 minutes + 1 hour 20 minutes standing
Total cooking time: 20 minutes
Makes 20

7 g (¼ oz) sachet dried yeast
1 teaspoon sugar
1 tablespoon plain flour
½ cup (125 ml/4 fl oz) milk, warmed
2½ cups (310 g/10 oz) plain flour, extra, sifted
1 tablespoon caster sugar
185 g (6 oz) butter, chopped
1 teaspoon mixed spice
1 egg, lightly beaten
2 teaspoons grated lemon rind
¼ cup (55 g/2 oz) firmly packed soft brown sugar
1⅓ cups (235 g/7½ oz) mixed dried fruit

GLAZE
1 tablespoon milk
2 tablespoons sugar

1 Lightly grease a baking tray and line with baking paper. Combine the yeast, sugar and flour in a small bowl. Gradually add the milk and mix until smooth. Stand the mixture, covered with plastic wrap, in a warm place for 10 minutes or until foamy.

2 Combine the extra flour, caster sugar, 125 g (4 oz) of the butter and ½ teaspoon of the spice in a food processor. Process for 30 seconds or until the mixture is fine and crumbly. Add the egg, rind and yeast mixture. Process for another 15 seconds or until the mixture just comes together.

3 Turn the mixture onto a lightly floured surface and knead for about 2 minutes or until smooth. Shape into a ball. Place in a lightly oiled bowl. Cover with plastic wrap and leave in a warm place for 1 hour, or until well risen. Knead again for 2 minutes, or until smooth.

4 Preheat the oven to 210°C (415°F/ Gas 6–7). Using electric beaters, beat remaining butter and the brown sugar in a bowl until light and creamy. Roll the dough out to a 40 x 35 cm (16 x 14 inch) rectangle. Spread the butter mixture over the dough, leaving a 2 cm (¾ inch) border along the top. Spread with the combined fruit and remaining spice. Roll the dough into a log. Using a sharp knife, cut the roll into 2 cm (¾ inch) thick slices.

5 Arrange the slices evenly apart on the prepared tray. Cover with plastic wrap and leave in a warm place for 10 minutes, or until well risen. Bake for 20 minutes, or until well browned and cooked through.

6 To make the glaze, combine the milk and sugar in a saucepan. Stir over low heat until the sugar dissolves and the mixture has almost come to the boil. Remove from heat and brush liberally over the scrolls while they are still hot. Place on a wire rack to cool.

Sprinkle the dough evenly with combined chopped fruit and spice.

Arrange the scrolls on the prepared baking tray, making sure they are well spaced.

Spoon the mixture into the paper patty cases and bake until lightly golden.

Use a flat-bladed knife to spread the icing over the cupcakes.

COFFEE CUPCAKES

Preparation time: 15 minutes
Total cooking time: 30 minutes
Makes 24

195 g (6½ oz) unsalted butter, softened
⅔ cup (125 g/4 oz) lightly packed soft
   brown sugar
2 eggs
1 tablespoon coffee and chicory essence
1¼ cups (155 g/5 oz) self-raising flour
100 ml (3½ fl oz) buttermilk
1 cup (125 g/4 oz) icing sugar
chocolate-coated coffee beans, to decorate

1 Preheat the oven to 150°C (300°F/ Gas 2). Line two 12-hole cupcake trays with paper patty cake cases. Beat 185g (6 oz) of the butter and the brown sugar with electric beaters until light and creamy. Add the eggs one at a time, beating well after each addition. Mix in 3 teaspoons of the coffee and chicory essence.

2 Fold the flour and a pinch of salt alternately with the buttermilk into the creamed mixture until combined. Spoon evenly into the patty cake cases and bake for 25–30 minutes, or until just springy to the touch. Leave to cool in the tins.

3 To make the icing, combine the remaining butter, remaining essence, the icing sugar and 1½ tablespoons boiling water in a small mixing bowl. Spread a little icing over each cupcake with a flat-bladed knife until evenly covered. If desired, decorate with chocolate-coated coffee beans.

Use a spoon to fold in the flour, buttermilk and chocolate chips.

Leave the cakes to sit in the tin for 5 minutes then turn out onto a wire rack.

INDIVIDUAL WHITE CHOCOLATE CHIP CAKES

Preparation time: 15 minutes
Total cooking time: 20 minutes
Makes 12

125 g (4 oz) unsalted butter, softened
³/₄ cup (185 g/6 oz) caster sugar
2 eggs, lightly beaten
1 teaspoon vanilla essence
2 cups (250 g/8 oz) self-raising flour, sifted
¹/₂ cup (125 ml/4 fl oz) buttermilk
1¹/₄ cups (280 g/9 oz) white chocolate chips

1 Preheat the oven to 170°C (325°F/ Gas 3). Lightly grease a 12-hole ¹/₂-cup (125 ml/4 fl oz) muffin tin.

2 Place the butter and sugar in a large mixing bowl. Using electric beaters, beat until pale and creamy. Gradually add the beaten eggs, beating well after each addition. Add the vanilla essence and beat until well combined. Fold in the flour alternately with the buttermilk, then fold in the chocolate chips.

3 Fill each muffin hole three-quarters full with the mixture and bake for 20 minutes, or until a skewer comes out clean when inserted into the centre of each cake. Leave in the tin for 5 minutes before turning out onto a wire rack to cool completely. Use a flat-bladed knife to loosen around the edges of the cakes if they stick.

PLAIN MUFFINS

Preparation time: 15 minutes
Total cooking time: 25 minutes
Makes 12

2¹/₂ cups (310 g/10 oz) self-raising flour
¹/₄ cup (60 g/2 oz) caster sugar
2 teaspoons baking powder
2 eggs, lightly beaten
1¹/₂ cups (375 ml/12 fl oz) milk
160 g (5¹/₂ oz) butter, melted

1 Preheat the oven to 210°C (415°F/ Gas 6–7). Lightly grease a 12-hole muffin tin.
2 Sift the flour, sugar and baking powder into a mixing bowl. Make a well in the centre. Place the egg, milk and melted butter in a separate mixing bowl. Combine and add all at once to the flour mixture.
3 Stir gently with a fork or rubber spatula until the mixture is just moistened. (Do not overmix, the batter should look quite lumpy.)
4 Spoon the mixture evenly into the prepared tin. Bake for 20–25 minutes, or until golden brown. Loosen the muffins with a flat-bladed knife and transfer to a wire rack to cool.

TOPPING SUGGESTION: Beat ¹/₃ cup (80 ml/ 2³/₄ fl oz) cream together with 1 tablespoon icing sugar until soft peaks form. Cut a circle from the top of each muffin, about 2 cm (³/₄ inch) deep, and cut these circles in half to make 'wings'. Spoon ¹/₂ teaspoon strawberry jam into each muffin, top with the cream mixture and arrange the 'wings' in cream.

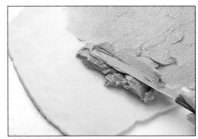

Using a flat-bladed knife, spread the filling evenly over the dough.

Place the scrolls, close together, on the prepared tray and bake until golden brown.

CINNAMON SCROLLS

Preparation time: 25 minutes
Total cooking time: 12 minutes
Makes 12

2 cups (250 g/8 oz) self-raising flour
pinch salt
90 g (3 oz) butter, chopped
$2/3$ cup (170 ml/$5^1/2$ fl oz) milk

FILLING
60 g (2 oz) butter, softened
2 tablespoons soft brown sugar
1 teaspoon cinnamon

ICING
1 cup (125 g/4 oz) icing sugar, sifted
1 tablespoon boiling water.

1 Preheat the oven to 210°C (415°F/ Gas 6–7). Lightly grease a baking tray. Sift the flour and salt into a mixing bowl. Using your fingertips, rub the butter into the flour. Make a well in the centre and add almost all the milk. Mix lightly, with a flat-bladed knife, until a soft dough forms, adding more liquid if necessary.

2 Knead the dough briefly on a lightly floured surface until smooth. Roll out to a 25 x 40 cm (10 x 16 inch) rectangle of 5 mm ($1/4$ inch) thickness.

3 To make the filling, place the butter, sugar and cinnamon in a mixing bowl. Using electric beaters, beat until light and fluffy. Spread the filling evenly over the dough rectangle and roll up from the long side. Using a sharp knife, slice the dough into 3 cm ($1^1/4$ inch) pieces. Place the dough pieces close together, cut-side up, on the prepared tray. Bake for 12 minutes, or until golden brown. Remove from the oven and leave to cool slightly. Drizzle the icing over the top.

4 To make the icing, combine the icing sugar and boiling water in a small bowl. Beat the mixture until smooth and well combined.

VARIATION: Add chopped sultanas to the filling, if desired.

Add the sugar and sultanas and stir to combine with a wooden spoon.

SULTANA SCONES

Preparation time: 20 minutes
Total cooking time: 12 minutes
Makes 12

2 cups (250 g/8 oz) self-raising flour
pinch salt
30 g (1 oz) butter, cut into small pieces
⅓ cup (90 g/3 oz) caster sugar
¼ cup (30 g/1 oz) sultanas (see VARIATION)
1 egg, lightly beaten
¾ cup (185 ml/6 fl oz) milk
extra milk, to glaze
butter, to serve

1 Preheat the oven to 210°C (415°F/ Gas 6–7). Lightly grease a baking tray. Sift the flour and salt into a large mixing bowl. Add the butter and rub in lightly with fingertips.

2 Add the sugar and sultanas and stir to combine. Make a well in the centre of the mixture. Add the egg and almost all the milk. Mix quickly, with a flat-bladed knife, to a soft dough, adding more milk if necessary. Turn out onto a lightly floured surface and knead briefly until smooth. Press or roll out to form a round about 2 cm (3/4 inch) thick.

3 Cut the dough into rounds using a floured plain 5 cm (2 inch) cutter or cut into squares using a floured knife. Place the rounds close together on the prepared tray and brush with extra milk. Bake for 10–12 minutes, or until golden brown. Serve with butter.

VARIATION: Use any type of dried fruit in this recipe, for example, currants, raisins, or chopped and pitted dates or prunes.

Make a small hole in the top of the muffin to accommodate the topping.

ORANGE POPPY SEED MUFFINS

Preparation time: 20 minutes
Total cooking time: 12 minutes
Makes 12

1³/₄ cups (215 g/7 oz) self-raising flour
1 tablespoon caster sugar
1 teaspoon baking powder
¹/₄ teaspoon bicarbonate of soda
1 tablespoon poppyseeds
90 g (3 oz) butter
¹/₂ cup (160 g/5¹/₂ oz) orange marmalade
1 egg, lightly beaten
³/₄ cup (185 ml/6 fl oz) milk
icing sugar, to dust

1 Preheat the oven to 210°C (415°F/ Gas 6–7). Lightly grease a 12-hole muffin tin. Sift the flour, sugar, baking powder and soda into a mixing bowl. Add the poppy seeds and stir. Make a well in the centre.

2 Combine the butter and marmalade in a small saucepan and stir over low heat until marmalade becomes runny and butter has melted. Add the butter mixture and combined egg and milk to flour mixture; stir until just combined. (Do not overmix, the batter should be quite lumpy.)

3 Spoon the batter into the prepared tin and cook for 10–12 minutes or until golden. Loosen the muffins with a flat-bladed knife and transfer to a wire rack. Dust with the icing sugar.

TOPPING SUGGESTION: Beat 60 g (2 oz) soft butter, 2 tablespoons icing sugar and 1 teaspoon orange rind until light and creamy. Cut a small section from the top of the muffin, fill with mixture and replace the tops.

Make the syrup by combining sugar, water and honey in a saucepan over low heat.

Set the wire rack over a baking tray to catch any excess syrup.

BAKLAVA FINGERS

Preparation time: 30 minutes
Total cooking time: 20 minutes
Makes 24

FILLING
³/₄ cup (90 g/3 oz) finely chopped walnuts
1 tablespoon brown sugar
1 teaspoon cinnamon
20 g (³/₄ oz) butter, melted

8 sheets filo pastry
50 g (1³/₄ oz) butter, melted

SYRUP
1 cup (250 g/8 oz) sugar
¹/₂ cup (125 ml/4 fl oz) water
2 tablespoons honey
2 teaspoons orange flower water, optional

1 Preheat the oven to 210°C (415°F/ Gas 6–7). Lightly grease a baking tray. To make the filling, place the walnuts, sugar, cinnamon and butter in a small bowl and stir until combined.

2 Working with one at a time, lay a sheet of filo pastry on the workbench. Brush the pastry with melted butter and fold it in half. Cut the sheet into three strips and place a heaped teaspoon of filling close to the front edge of the pastry. Roll up, tucking in the edges. Place on the prepared tray and brush with melted butter.

3 Repeat with the remaining pastry sheets. Bake for 15 minutes until fingers are golden brown. Transfer to a wire rack over a baking tray and spoon the syrup over the pastries while both the pastries and syrup are still warm.

4 To make the syrup, combine the sugar, water and honey in a small pan. Stir over low heat without boiling until sugar has completely dissolved. Bring to boil, reduce heat and simmer for 5 minutes. Remove from heat and add the orange flower water, if desired.

STORAGE: Store in an airtight container for up to 2 days.
NOTE: Baklava Fingers are very sweet. They are best served with small cups of strong black coffee.

STRAWBERRY AND PASSIONFRUIT MUFFINS

Preparation time: 20 minutes
Total cooking time: 15 minutes
Makes 12

1³/₄ cup (215 g/7 oz) self-raising flour
pinch salt
1 teaspoon baking powder
¹/₂ teaspoon bicarbonate of soda
¹/₄ cup (60 g/2 oz) caster sugar
1 cup (175 g/6 oz) fresh strawberries, chopped
¹/₂ cup (125 g/4 oz) passionfruit pulp, canned or fresh
1 egg
³/₄ cup (185 ml/6 fl oz) milk
60 g (2 oz) butter, melted
whipped cream, to serve
fresh strawberries, halved, extra
icing sugar, to dust

1 Preheat the oven to 210°C (415°F/ Gas 6–7). Lightly grease a 12-hole muffin tin.
2 Sift the flour, salt, baking powder, soda and sugar into a mixing bowl. Add the strawberries and stir to combine. Make a well in the centre.
3 Place the egg and milk in a separate mixing bowl and stir to combine. Add the passionfruit pulp and egg mixture to the flour mixture. Pour the melted butter all at once and lightly stir with a fork until just combined. (Do not overmix, the batter should look quite lumpy.)
4 Spoon the mixture into prepared tins and bake 10–15 minutes, or until golden brown. Loosen muffins with a flat-bladed knife and turn out onto a wire rack to cool. Top with whipped cream and fresh strawberry halves and sprinkle with icing sugar, if desired.

NOTE: Folding the fruit through the dry mixture helps it to be evenly distributed throughout.

Spoon the mixture into paper patty cases and bake until golden.

Cut a circle from the top of each cake then cut it in half to form the 'wings'.

BUTTERFLY CUPCAKES

Preparation time: 10 minutes
Total cooking time: 30 minutes
Makes 12

125 g (4 oz) unsalted butter, softened
$^2/_3$ cup (160 g/5$^1/_2$ oz) caster sugar
1$^1/_2$ cups (185 g/6 oz) self-raising flour
$^1/_2$ cup (125 ml/4 fl oz) milk
2 eggs
$^1/_2$ cup (125 ml/4 fl oz) thick cream
$^1/_4$ cup (80 g/2$^3/_4$ oz) strawberry jam
icing sugar, to dust

1 Preheat the oven to 180°C (350°F/ Gas 4). Line a flat-bottomed 12-hole cupcake tray with paper patty cases. Place the butter, sugar, flour, milk and eggs in a large mixing bowl. Using electric beaters, beat on low speed then increase the speed and beat until the mixture is smooth and pale. Divide the mixture evenly among the cases and bake for 30 minutes, or until cooked and golden. Transfer to a wire rack to cool.

2 Cut shallow rounds from the centre of each cake using the point of a sharp knife, then cut in half. Spoon 2 teaspoons cream into each cavity, top with 1 teaspoon jam and position two halves of the cake tops in the jam to resemble butterfly wings. Dust with icing sugar.

NOTE: If using foil patty cases instead of the standard paper cases as suggested, the size and number of butterfly cakes may vary.

Bring the dates and water to the boil then stir in the bicarbonate of soda and butter.

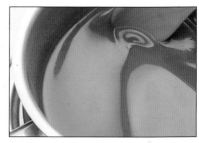

Combine the golden syrup, cream, butter and sugar in a saucepan over low heat.

INDIVIDUAL STICKY DATE CAKES

Preparation time: 10 minutes
Total cooking time: 25 minutes
Makes 6

1½ cups (270 g/9 oz) pitted dates, chopped
1 teaspoon bicarbonate of soda
150 g (5 oz) unsalted butter, chopped
1½ cups (185 g/6 oz) self-raising flour
265 g (8½ oz) firmly packed soft brown
    sugar
2 eggs, lightly beaten
2 tablespoons golden syrup
¾ cup (185 ml/6 fl oz) cream

1 Preheat the oven to 180°C (350°F/ Gas 4). Grease six 1-cup (250 ml/8 fl oz) muffin holes. Place the dates and 1 cup (250 ml/8 fl oz) water in a saucepan, bring to the boil, then remove from the heat and stir in the bicarbonate of soda. Add 60 g (2 oz) of the butter and stir until dissolved. Sift the flour into a large bowl, add ⅔ cup (125 g/4 oz) of the sugar and stir. Make a well in the centre, add the date mixture and egg and stir until just combined. Spoon the mixture evenly into the prepared holes and bake for 20 minutes, or until a skewer comes out clean when inserted into the centre of the cake.

2 To make the sauce, place the golden syrup and cream with the remaining butter and sugar in a small saucepan and stir over low heat for 3–4 minutes, or until the sugar has dissolved. Bring to the boil, then reduce the heat and simmer, stirring the sauce occasionally, for 2 minutes. To serve, turn the cakes out onto serving plates, pierce the tops a few times with a skewer and drizzle with the sauce.

Add the sugar, pecans and cinnamon to the topping mixture.

COFFEE PECAN STREUSEL MUFFINS

Preparation time: 20 minutes
Total cooking time: 12 minutes
Makes 9

1³/₄ cups (215 g/7 oz) self-raising flour
1 teaspoon baking powder
¹/₄ cup (60 g/2 oz) caster sugar
¹/₂ cup (60 g/2 oz) finely chopped pecans
1 tablespoon instant coffee powder
1 tablespoon boiling water
1 egg
³/₄ cup (185 ml/6 fl oz) milk
¹/₃ cup (80 ml/2³/₄ fl oz) oil
icing sugar, to dust

STREUSEL TOPPING
30 g (1 oz) butter
¹/₄ cup (30 g/1 oz) self-raising flour
2 tablespoons soft brown sugar
1 teaspoon cinnamon
2 tablespoons finely chopped pecans

1 Preheat the oven to 210°C (415°F/ Gas 6–7). Lightly grease nine holes of a 12-hole muffin tin. Sift the flour and baking powder into a mixing bowl. Add the caster sugar and pecans. Make a well in the centre.

2 Combine the coffee powder with boiling water and stir until dissolved. Cool and add to the flour mixture. In a separate bowl, combine the egg, milk and oil. Add to flour mixture and stir until just combined. (Do not overmix, the batter should look quite lumpy.)

3 Spoon into the prepared tin. Sprinkle with the topping and bake for 10–12 minutes, or until golden brown. Loosen the muffins with a flat-bladed knife and turn out onto a wire rack to cool completely. Sprinkle with icing sugar, if desired.

4 To make the topping, place the flour into a mixing bowl. Rub the butter into the flour until the mixture resembles coarse breadcrumbs. Add the sugar, cinnamon and pecans and mix until well combined.

Cream the butter and sugar with electric beaters then add the egg.

STRAWBERRY SHORTCAKES

Preparation time: 20 minutes
Total cooking time: 12 minutes
Makes 12

30 g (1 oz) butter
2 tablespoons caster sugar
1 egg
1¹/₂ cups (185 g/6 oz) self-raising flour
pinch salt
¹/₂ cup (125 ml/4 fl oz) milk
1 tablespoon milk, extra
1 tablespoon caster sugar, extra
strawberries, halved, to serve
whipped cream, to serve

1 Preheat the oven to 210°C (415°F/ Gas 6–7). Lightly grease a baking tray. Place the butter and sugar in a mixing bowl. Using electric beaters, beat the butter and sugar until light and fluffy. Add the egg and mix well.

2 Sift the flour and salt into a mixing bowl. Make a well in the centre of the dry ingredients. Add the butter, sugar and egg mixture and almost all of the milk. Using a flat-bladed knife, lightly mix until a soft dough forms, adding more milk if necessary. Knead the dough briefly on a lightly floured surface until smooth. Press out dough to 2 cm (³/₄ inch) thickness. Using a floured plain 5 cm (2 inch) cutter, cut rounds from the dough and place on the prepared tray.

3 Brush the rounds with extra milk and top with a sprinkling of caster sugar. Bake for 10–12 minutes, or until lightly golden. Remove and place on a wire rack. When the scones are cool, split and serve with strawberries and whipped cream.

RUM BABA WITH FIGS

Preparation time: 40 minutes + 2 hours standing
Total cooking time: 35 minutes
Makes 10
Serves 4–6

1½ cups (185 g/6 oz) plain flour
2 teaspoons dried yeast (see NOTE)
¼ teaspoon salt
2 teaspoons sugar
⅓ cup (80 ml/2¾ fl oz) lukewarm milk
80 g (2¾ oz) butter
3 eggs, lightly beaten
2 cups (500 ml/16 fl oz) water
1½ cups (375 g/12 oz) caster sugar
⅓ cup (80 ml/2¾ fl oz) dark rum
¾ cup (240 g/7½ oz) apricot jam
2 tablespoons dark rum, extra
4–6 figs

1 Lightly brush ten ½-cup (125 ml/ 4 fl oz) dariole moulds with oil. Place 1 tablespoon of the flour and the yeast, salt, sugar and milk in a small bowl. Cover with plastic wrap and leave in a warm place for 10 minutes, or until the mixture is foamy. Using your fingertips, rub butter into the remaining flour in a large mixing bowl, until it resembles fine breadcrumbs.

2 Add the yeast mixture and eggs to the flour mixture. Beat with a spoon for 2 minutes, until smooth and glossy. Scrape the mixture down the side of the bowl. Cover and leave in a warm place for 1½ hours, until well risen.

3 Preheat the oven to 210°C (415°F/ Gas 6–7). Using a wooden spoon, beat the mixture again for 2 minutes. Divide the mixture evenly between prepared tins. Set aside, covered with plastic wrap, for another 30 minutes, until the dough is well risen.

4 Bake for 20 minutes, or until golden brown. Meanwhile, combine the water and sugar in a medium saucepan. Stir over medium heat without boiling until the sugar has dissolved. Bring to the boil then reduce heat slightly and simmer, without stirring, for 15 minutes. Remove from heat, cool slightly and add the rum.

5 Turn out onto a wire rack placed over a shallow oven tray. Brush the warm babas liberally with warm rum syrup until they are well soaked. Strain excess syrup to remove any crumbs if necessary and reserve syrup.

6 Heat the jam in a small saucepan or in the microwave and strain through a fine sieve. Add the extra rum, stir to combine and brush the warm jam all over the babas to glaze. To serve, place one or two babas on each plate, drizzle a pool of reserved syrup around them. Cut the figs in half and place on the plate beside babas.

STORAGE: Rum Babas are best served on the day they are made.
HINT: If you do not have dariole or baba moulds, use empty baked bean tins. The 130 g (4½ oz) size is best. Wash and dry the tins thoroughly and prepare as directed.
NOTE: It is very important when working with a yeast dough that the temperature of the liquid used, as well as the surrounding temperature during rising, is neither too cold nor too hot. Measure ingredients accurately as they must be in the correct proportions. The yeast must not be stale. Oven temperature is also particularly important. If you have any reason to doubt the accuracy of your oven temperature readings, test with an oven thermometer so that you can make adjustments if needed.

Brush the babas liberally with the rum syrup while they are still warm.

Add the pumpkin, egg and milk and stir well with a wooden spoon.

PUMPKIN SCONES

Preparation time: 35 minutes
Total cooking time: 12 minutes
Makes 12

30 g (1 oz) butter, chopped
2 tablespoons caster sugar
$\frac{1}{2}$ cup (125 g/4 oz) mashed cooked
     pumpkin (see NOTE)
1 egg, lightly beaten
$\frac{1}{2}$ cup (125 ml/4 fl oz) milk
$2\frac{1}{2}$ cups (310 g/10 oz) self-raising flour
pinch salt
milk, to glaze
butter, to serve

1 Preheat the oven to 210°C (415°F/ Gas 6–7). Lightly grease a baking tray. Using electric beaters, beat the butter and sugar in a small mixing bowl until the mixture is light and creamy. Add the pumpkin, egg and milk. Mix until well combined.
2 Sift the flour and salt into a large mixing bowl. Make a well in the centre and add almost all of the mashed pumpkin. Mix lightly, using a flat-bladed knife, to form a soft dough, adding more liquid if necessary.
3 Knead the dough briefly on a lightly floured surface. Roll the dough out to 2 cm ($\frac{3}{4}$ inch) thickness.
4 Cut into rounds using a floured plain 5 cm (2 inch) cutter. Place the rounds, close together, on the prepared tray and brush with a little milk. Bake for 10–12 minutes, or until golden brown. Serve warm with butter.

NOTE: To make $\frac{1}{2}$ cup of mashed pumpkin you will need around 250 g (4 oz) of raw pumpkin.

The muffins can be topped with a chocolate and cream mixture.

DOUBLE CHOC MUFFINS

Preparation time: 15 minutes
Total cooking time: 12–15 minutes
Makes 6 large muffins

2 cups (250 g/8 oz) plain flour
2¹/₂ teaspoons baking powder
¹/₄ cup (30 g/1 oz) cocoa powder
2 tablespoons caster sugar
1 cup (175 g/6 oz) dark choc bits
1 egg, lightly beaten
¹/₂ cup (125 g/4 oz) sour cream
³/₄ cup (185 ml/6 fl oz) milk
90 g (3 oz) butter, melted
icing sugar, to dust

1 Preheat the oven to 180°C (350°F/ Gas 4). Brush a 6-hole large muffin tin with melted butter or oil. Sift the flour, baking powder and cocoa into a large mixing bowl. Add the sugar and ³/₄ cup (130 g/4¹/₂ oz) choc bits and mix. Make a well in the centre.

2 Add the combined egg, sour cream, milk and melted butter all at once and stir with a fork until just combined. (Do not overbeat, the batter should look quite lumpy.)

3 Spoon the batter into the prepared tin and scatter with remaining choc bits. Bake for 12–15 minutes, or until firm. Loosen muffins with a flat-bladed knife and turn out onto a wire rack to cool completely.

TOPPING SUGGESTION: Combine 50 g (1³/₄ oz) chocolate, 1 tablespoon cream and 10 g (¹/₄ oz) butter in a pan. Stir over low heat until smooth. Refrigerate until firm, then pipe over the muffins. Dust with icing sugar.

Sift the self-raising flours into a large mixing bowl, returning the husks.

Place the dough squares on the prepared tray, making sure they are well spaced.

WHOLEMEAL DATE SCONES

Preparation time: 20 minutes
Total cooking time: 15 minutes
Makes 12

1½ cups (185 g/6 oz) self-raising flour
1½ cups (225 g/7 oz) wholemeal self-raising flour
½ teaspoon baking powder
¼ teaspoon salt
60 g (2 oz) butter, cut into small pieces
2 tablespoons caster sugar
1 cup (185 g/6 oz) chopped dates
1¼ cups (315 ml/10 fl oz) buttermilk
½ cup (125 ml/4 fl oz) water
buttermilk, extra, to glaze
butter or whipped cream, to serve

1 Preheat the oven to 210°C (415°F/ Gas 6–7). Lightly grease a baking tray. Sift the flours, baking powder and salt into a large mixing bowl, returning the husks. Add the chopped butter and rub in lightly using your fingertips. Stir in the sugar and the chopped dates.

2 Make a well in the centre of the flour mixture. Add the buttermilk and almost all of the water. Mix quickly, using a flat-bladed knife, to form a soft dough, adding more water if necessary. (The dough should have lost its stickiness but not become too dry or tough.)

3 Knead dough briefly on a lightly floured surface until smooth. Press out the dough with floured hands to form a 2 cm (³/₄ inch) thick square. Cut into 16 smaller squares. Place the squares on the prepared tray, leaving a 2 cm (³/₄ inch) gap between each scone. Brush with extra buttermilk.

4 Bake the scones for 12–15 minutes, or until golden brown. Serve straight from the oven with butter or whipped cream, if desired.

NOTE: These scones are more heavily textured than the traditional recipe. Returning the flour husks to the mixture will contribute to this texture, however it is still necessary to sift the flours as this introduces air through the dry ingredients.

Spoon the jam into the indentation, then fold the dough over.

RASPBERRY BUN SCONES

Preparation time: 20 minutes
Total cooking time: 12 minutes
Makes 8

2 cups (250 g/8 oz) self-raising flour
pinch salt
2 tablespoons caster sugar
1/2 cup (125 ml/4 fl oz) milk
30 g (1 oz) butter, melted
1/3 cup (80 ml/2¾ fl oz) water
1 tablespoon raspberry jam
1 tablespoon milk, extra
caster sugar, extra
butter, to serve

1 Preheat the oven to 210°C (415°F/ Gas 6–7). Lightly grease a baking tray. Sift the flour and salt into a large mixing bowl. Add the sugar and stir to combine.

2 Make a well in the centre of the flour. Place milk and melted butter in a separate bowl and combine. Add to the flour mixture all at once, reserving a teaspoonful for glazing. Add almost all of the water. Mix quickly, using a flat-bladed knife, to form a soft dough, adding more water if necessary.

3 Knead the dough briefly on a lightly floured surface until smooth. Cut the dough into 8 rounds using a floured 7 cm (2¾ inch) cutter. Turn each of scones over and make an indentation in the centre with your thumb. Place 1/2 teaspoon of jam in the indentation and fold over dough. Place the rounds, well apart, on the prepared tray and flatten tops. Brush with the milk and sprinkle with the extra caster sugar. Bake for 10–12 minutes, or until golden. Serve warm with butter.

Process remaining ingredients until smooth and thoroughly combined.

Layer walnut and cake mixtures in the prepared tin, finishing with a layer of the walnut mixture.

BABY COFFEE AND WALNUT SOUR CREAM CAKES

Preparation time: 15 minutes
Total cooking time: 20 minutes
Makes 24

³/₄ cup (75 g/2¹/₂ oz) walnuts
²/₃ cup (155 g/5 oz) firmly packed soft
    brown sugar
125 g (4 oz) unsalted butter, softened
2 eggs, lightly beaten
1 cup (125 g/4 oz) self-raising flour
¹/₃ cup (80 g/2³/₄ oz) sour cream
1 tablespoon coffee and chicory essence

1 Preheat the oven to 160°C (315°F/ Gas 2–3). Lightly grease two 12-hole ¹/₄-cup (60 ml/2 fl oz) baby muffin tins. Process the walnuts and ¹/₄ cup (45 g/1¹/₂ oz) of the brown sugar in a food processor until the walnuts are roughly chopped into small pieces. Transfer to a mixing bowl.
2 Cream the butter and remaining sugar together in the food processor until pale and creamy. With the motor running, gradually add the egg and process until smooth. Add the flour and blend until well mixed. Add the sour cream and essence and process until thoroughly mixed.
3 Spoon ¹/₂ teaspoon of the walnut and sugar mixture into the base of each muffin hole, followed by a teaspoon of the cake mixture. Sprinkle a little more walnut mixture over the top, a little more cake mixture and top with the remaining walnut mixture. Bake for 20 minutes, or until risen and springy to the touch. Leave in the tins for 5 minutes. Remove the cakes using a flat-bladed knife to loosen the side and base, then transfer to a wire rack to cool completely.

Line each muffin hole with mango slices then spoon in the mixture.

Drizzle the lime syrup over the cakes while still in the tin. Leave to stand for 5 minutes.

MINI MANGO CAKES WITH LIME SYRUP

Preparation time: 15 minutes
Total cooking time: 35 minutes
Makes 4

425 g (14 oz) can mango slices in syrup, drained
90 g (3 oz) unsalted butter, softened
³/₄ cup (185 g/6 oz) caster sugar
2 eggs, lightly beaten
¹/₂ cup (60 g/2 oz) self-raising flour
2 tablespoons ground almonds
2 tablespoons coconut milk
2 tablespoons lime juice

1 Preheat the oven to 200°C (400°F/ Gas 6). Lightly grease a 4-hole 1-cup (250 ml/8 fl oz) muffin tin and line with mango slices. Beat the butter and ¹/₂ cup (125 g/4 oz) of the sugar in a bowl with electric beaters until light and creamy. Gradually add the egg, beating well after each addition. Fold in the sifted flour, then add the almonds and coconut milk, then spoon into the muffin tin. Bake for 25 minutes, or until a skewer comes out clean when inserted into the centre of the cakes.

2 To make the syrup, place the lime juice, the remaining sugar and ¹/₂ cup (125 ml/4 fl oz) water in a small saucepan and stir over low heat until the sugar dissolves. Increase the heat and simmer for 10 minutes. Pierce holes in each cake with a skewer. Drizzle the syrup over the top and allow to stand for 5 minutes to soak up the liquid. Turn out and serve.

Slices

HAZELNUT TRUFFLE SLICE

Preparation time: 20 minutes + 2 hours
    refrigeration
Total cooking time: 25 minutes
Makes 32 pieces

100 g (3¹/₂ oz) hazelnuts
90 g (3 oz) butter
¹/₃ cup (90 g/3 oz) caster sugar
³/₄ cup (90 g/3 oz) plain flour
1¹/₂ tablespoons cocoa powder

CHOCOLATE BRANDY ICING
200 g (6¹/₂ oz) dark chocolate, chopped (see
    NOTE)
¹/₂ cup (125 ml/4 fl oz) cream
2 teaspoons brandy or rum

1 Preheat the oven to 180°C (350°F/ Gas 4).
Lightly grease an 11 x 21 cm (4¹/₂ x 8¹/₂ inch)
loaf tin and line with baking paper, overhanging
two opposite sides.
2 Spread the hazelnuts on a baking tray and
bake for 7 minutes, or until lightly browned.
Remove from the oven and, while they are still
hot, wrap them in a tea towel and rub away the
skins. Allow to cool and then chop roughly.
3 Beat the butter and sugar with electric
beaters until light and creamy. Sift the flour and
cocoa powder into a bowl, then stir into the
butter mixture. Press evenly over the base of the
tin and bake for 15–20 minutes, or until firm.
Leave to cool completely.
4 To make the chocolate brandy icing, place
the chocolate and cream in a small saucepan.
Stir over low heat until the chocolate has melted
and the mixture is very smooth, being careful
not to overheat. Leave the mixture to cool
slightly, then add the brandy or rum and stir
until well combined.
5 Stir the hazelnuts into the icing, then pour
over the cooled pastry base. Refrigerate for
several hours, or until the topping is firm. The
slice is very rich, so cut into small pieces to
serve.

STORAGE: This slice can be stored for up to a
week in an airtight container but is not suitable
for freezing. Store in the fridge in warm weather.
NOTE: Use the best quality eating or cooking
chocolate you can afford.

Toast the hazelnuts in the oven, then rub with a tea
towel to remove the skins.

Stir the chopped hazelnuts into the icing, then
pour over the base.

Press the dough into the tin and prick all over with a fork before baking.

Beat the eggs and sugar, then stir in the rind, juice, almonds and cream.

LEMON AND ALMOND SLICE

Preparation time: 25 minutes
Total cooking time: 35 minutes
Makes 15 pieces

$^1/_2$ cup (60 g/2 oz) plain flour
$^1/_3$ cup (40 g/11/4 oz) self-raising flour
2 tablespoons icing sugar
60 g (2 oz) butter, chopped
1 egg, lightly beaten
whipped cream, to serve
lemon zest, to garnish

ALMOND CREAM

3 eggs, at room temperature
$^1/_2$ cup (125 g/4 oz) caster sugar
2 teaspoons grated lemon rind
$^1/_2$ cup (125 ml/4 fl oz) lemon juice
$^2/_3$ cup (80 g/2$^3/_4$ oz) ground almonds
1 cup (250 ml/8 fl oz) cream

1 Preheat the oven to 190°C (375°F/ Gas 5). Lightly grease a 23 cm (9 inch) square shallow tin.
2 Put the flours, sugar and butter in a food processor and process until the mixture resembles fine breadcrumbs. Add the egg and process briefly, until the dough just comes together, adding a small amount of water if necessary.
3 Press the dough into the base of the prepared tin and prick well with a fork. Bake for 10–12 minutes, or until pale. Allow to cool. Reduce the oven to 180°C (350°F/ Gas 4).
4 To make the almond cream, beat the eggs and sugar with a wooden spoon. Stir in the lemon rind, juice, almonds and cream. Pour over the pastry and bake for 20–25 minutes, or until lightly set. Leave to cool in the tin. Serve with whipped cream and garnish with zested lemon rind.

Gradually add the sugar to the cream cheese, beating well after each addition.

Smooth the chocolate topping over the vanilla topping with the back of a spoon.

TRIPLE-DECKER FUDGE SLICE

Preparation time: 25 minutes + refrigeration
Total cooking time: 50 minutes
Makes 20 pieces

¹/₂ cup (60 g/2 oz) plain flour
2 tablespoons cocoa powder
2 tablespoons caster sugar
60 g (2 oz) butter, melted
1 tablespoon milk
¹/₂ teaspoon vanilla essence

VANILLA TOPPING

250 g (8 oz) cream cheese, cubed
¹/₃ cup (90 g/3 oz) caster sugar
1 egg
1 teaspoon vanilla essence

CHOCOLATE TOPPING

125 g (4 oz) milk chocolate, chopped
125 g (4 oz) butter, chopped
2 eggs, lightly beaten
¹/₂ cup (125 g/4 oz) caster sugar
¹/₄ cup (30 g/1 oz) plain flour
icing sugar, to dust

1 Lightly grease an 18 x 28 cm (7 x 11 inch) shallow tin and line with baking paper, overhanging two opposite sides.
2 Sift the flour, cocoa and sugar into a bowl. Add the butter, milk and vanilla and mix well to form a dough. Gently knead for 1 minute, adding more flour if sticky. Press into the prepared tin and refrigerate for 20 minutes. Preheat the oven to 190°C (375°F/Gas 5).
3 Cover the pastry with baking paper, fill with baking beads or rice and bake for 10–15 minutes. Remove the paper and rice and reduce the heat to 180°C (350°F/Gas 4). Bake for 5–10 minutes, then leave to cool.

4 To make the vanilla topping, beat the cream cheese in a mixing bowl until smooth. Gradually beat in the sugar, then the egg and vanilla essence. Beat well, pour over the base and refrigerate.
5 To make the chocolate topping, melt the chocolate and butter in a small saucepan, stirring over very low heat until smooth. Mix together the eggs and sugar. Stir in the chocolate mixture and flour until just combined.
6 Pour the chocolate topping over the cold vanilla topping and smooth with a spoon. Reduce the oven to 160°C (315°F/Gas 2–3) and bake for 35–40 minutes, or until just set. Leave to cool completely, then refrigerate for 2 hours, or until firm. Dust with icing sugar before cutting and serving.

Put the flours, sugars, cinnamon, coconut and dates in a large bowl.

Add the butter, peaches and liquid and stir until just combined. Do not overmix.

DATE AND PEACH SLICE

Preparation time: 15 minutes + 30 minutes soaking
Total cooking time: 40 minutes
Makes 24 pieces

200 g (6¹/₂ oz) dried peaches
1 cup (125 g/4 oz) self-raising flour
1 cup (125 g/4 oz) plain flour
¹/₂ cup (90 g/3 oz) lightly packed soft brown sugar
¹/₂ cup (110 g/3¹/₂ oz) raw sugar
1¹/₂ teaspoons ground cinnamon
³/₄ cup (45 g/1¹/₂ oz) shredded coconut
²/₃ cup (125 g/4 oz) dates, chopped
125 g (4 oz) butter, melted

1 Lightly grease a 23 cm (9 inch) shallow square tin and line with baking paper, overhanging two opposite sides.
2 Roughly chop the peaches and place in a bowl. Cover the peaches with boiling water and leave to soak for 30 minutes. Preheat the oven to 180°C (350°F/Gas 4). Drain the peaches, reserving ¹/₂ cup (125 ml/ 4 fl oz) of the liquid.
3 Place the flours, sugars, cinnamon, coconut and dates in a large mixing bowl. Add the melted butter, peaches and reserved liquid and stir gently until only just combined.
4 Spread into the prepared tin and bake for 35–40 minutes, or until golden brown and a skewer inserted into the centre of the slice comes out clean. Cool in the tin for 5 minutes before turning out onto a wire rack to cool completely.

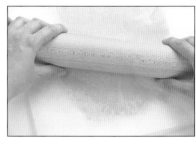

Roll out the pastry between two sheets of baking paper until it is large enough to fit the tin.

Mix all the nuts together and scatter over the pastry base.

MIXED NUT SLICE

Preparation time: 25 minutes
Total cooking time: 50 minutes
Makes 20 pieces

1½ cups (185 g/6 oz) plain flour
2 tablespoons icing sugar
125 g (4 oz) butter, chopped
1–2 tablespoons lemon juice or water
½ cup (80 g/2¾ oz) macadamia nuts
½ cup (80 g/2¾ oz) whole unblanched
   almonds
½ cup (75 g/2½ oz) pistachio nuts
½ cup (70 g/2¼ oz) hazelnuts
2 eggs, lightly beaten
50 g (1¾ oz) butter, melted
⅓ cup (60 g/2 oz) lightly packed soft brown
   sugar
⅓ cup (80 ml/2¾ fl oz) dark corn syrup
1 teaspoon vanilla essence
2 tablespoons cream

1 Preheat the oven to 180°C (350°F/Gas 4). Lightly grease an 18 x 28 cm (7 x 11 inch) shallow tin and line with baking paper, overhanging two opposite sides.
2 Process the flour, icing sugar and butter in a food processor until crumbs form. Add the lemon juice or water and process until the mixture just comes together. Roll the pastry out between two sheets of baking paper to fit the base and sides of the tin. Trim away the excess pastry.
3 Cover the pastry with baking paper and fill with baking beads or uncooked rice. Bake for 10 minutes. Remove the paper and beads and bake the pastry base for 5–10 minutes longer, or until lightly golden. Cool completely.
4 Mix together the nuts and scatter over the pastry base.
5 Whisk together the remaining ingredients, pour over the nuts, then bake the slice for 25–30 minutes, or until set. Cool completely in the tin before lifting out to cut and serve.

Beat together the butter and sugar, then stir in the mashed banana and egg.

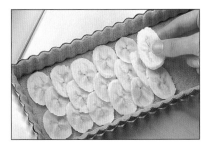

Thinly slice the other banana and arrange over the pastry base.

BANANA HAZEL SLICE

Preparation time: 40 minutes + 30 minutes refrigeration
Total cooking time: 50 minutes
Makes 12 pieces

²/₃ cup (85 g/3 oz) plain flour
1 teaspoon mixed spice
1¹/₂ tablespoons soft brown sugar
40 g (1¹/₄ oz) butter
1 egg yolk
icing sugar, to dust

BANANA FILLING
60 g (2 oz) butter
¹/₄ cup (60 g/2 oz) soft brown sugar
2 bananas
1 egg
¹/₂ cup (60 g/2 oz) ground hazelnuts
¹/₄ cup (30 g/1 oz) plain flour
¹/₄ cup (35 g/1¹/₄ oz) hazelnuts, halved

1 Lightly grease the base and sides of an 11 x 35 cm (4¹/₂ x 14 inch) loose-bottomed flan tin.
2 Place the flour, mixed spice and sugar in a food processor, add the butter, and process in short bursts until crumbly. Add the egg yolk and enough water to make the dough just come together. Wrap in plastic wrap and refrigerate for 30 minutes. Preheat the oven to 200°C (400°F/Gas 6).
3 Roll the pastry out between two sheets of baking paper to fit the tin and trim away the excess. Line with baking paper, fill with baking beads or rice, then bake for 8 minutes. Remove the beads and paper and bake the pastry for 8 minutes, or until lightly browned. Cool. Reduce the oven to 180°C (350°F/Gas 4).

4 To make the banana filling, beat the butter and sugar. Mash one of the bananas and stir into the beaten mixture with the egg. Stir in the ground hazelnuts and flour. Thinly slice the other banana and arrange over the pastry. Top with the banana filling and decorate with hazelnuts.
5 Bake for 30 minutes, or until golden brown and firm. Cool in the tin for 5 minutes, then on a wire rack. Dust lightly with icing sugar to serve.

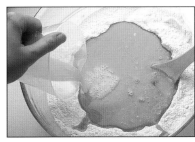

Make a well in the centre and add the melted butter, milk and eggs.

Smooth the surface and then brush lightly with the beaten egg white.

TIPSY CURRANT SLICE

Preparation time: 20 minutes + 15 minutes standing
Total cooking time: 25 minutes
Makes 20 pieces

$^1/_2$ cup (75 g/2$^1/_2$ oz) currants
$^1/_4$ cup (60 ml/2 fl oz) brandy
1 cup (125 g/4 oz) plain flour
1 cup (175 g/6 oz) rice flour
1 teaspoon baking powder
1 teaspoon mixed spice
$^3/_4$ cup (185 g/6 oz) caster sugar, plus extra to sprinkle
125 g (4 oz) butter, melted
$^2/_3$ cup (170 ml/5$^1/_2$ fl oz) milk
2 eggs, lightly beaten
1 egg white, lightly beaten

1 Preheat the oven to 180°C (350°F/ Gas 4). Lightly grease an 18 x 28 cm (7 x 11 inch) shallow tin and line with baking paper, overhanging two opposite sides. Soak the currants in the brandy, covered, for 15 minutes.
2 Sift the flours, baking powder and mixed spice into a large bowl. Stir in the sugar. Make a well in the centre, add the melted butter, milk and eggs. Add the currants and mix gently.
3 Spoon into the tin and smooth the surface. Brush with the egg white and sprinkle with sugar. Bake for 25 minutes, or until a skewer inserted into the slice comes out clean. Leave to cool in the tin, then lift out. Sprinkle again with sugar and serve.

Using a metal spoon, fold the beaten egg white into the topping mixture.

Bake the slice for 40–45 minutes, or until it is golden and then leave to cool in the tin.

FRUIT AND OAT SLICE

Preparation time: 20 minutes + 10 minutes standing
Total cooking time: 1 hour
Serves 8

125 g (4 oz) butter
$^1/_2$ cup (95 g/3 oz) lightly packed soft brown sugar
2 eggs, separated
1 cup (160 g/5$^1/_2$ oz) wholemeal self-raising flour
$^1/_4$ cup (25 g/$^3/_4$ oz) wheatgerm
$^1/_4$ cup (35 g/1$^1/_4$ oz) dried apricots, chopped
$^1/_4$ cup (60 ml/2 fl oz) boiling water

425 g (14 oz) can pie apple (see NOTE)
1 small zucchini, grated
$^1/_2$ cup (45 g/1$^1/_2$ oz) rolled oats
$^1/_2$ cup (45 g/1$^1/_2$ oz) desiccated coconut
2 tablespoons honey

1 Preheat the oven to 180°C (350°F/ Gas 4). Lightly grease a 20 x 30 cm (8 x 12 inch) shallow tin. Line the base and sides with baking paper. Using electric beaters, beat the butter and sugar in a large bowl until light and creamy. Add the egg yolks and beat until combined. Sift the flour into mixture, return husks, and mix with a flat-bladed knife. Add the wheatgerm and mix until a soft dough forms. Press the mixture over the base of the prepared tin and smooth the surface. Bake for 12–15 minutes, or until golden.
2 Soak the apricots in a saucepan of boiling water for 10 minutes, or until almost all the liquid is absorbed. Spread the apple over the base. Combine undrained apricots with zucchini, oats, coconut and honey in a mixing bowl.
3 Using electric beaters, beat the egg whites in a clean, dry mixing bowl until stiff peaks form and gently fold into the mixture.
4 Spoon mixture over the base. Bake for 40–45 minutes, or until golden. Leave to cool in the tin, then cut into slices to serve.

NOTE: Freshly cooked apples may be used instead.

Add the sugar, milk and vanilla to the melted butter, constantly stirring with a wooden spoon.

Remove the slice from the baking tin and cut into squares while it is still warm.

CHERRY SLICE

Preparation time: 15 minutes
Total cooking time: 35 minutes
Makes about 24

2 cups (250 g/8 oz) plain flour
$^1/_2$ cup (60 g/2 oz) icing sugar
250 g (8 oz) butter, chopped

TOPPING
30 g (1 oz) butter
$^1/_3$ cup (90 g/3 oz) caster sugar
1 tablespoon milk

2 teaspoons vanilla essence
$^3/_4$ cup (90 g/3 oz) chopped hazelnuts
$^3/_4$ cup (150 g/5 oz) sliced red glacé cherries

1 Preheat the oven to 210°C (415°F/ Gas 6–7). Lightly grease an 18 x 28 cm (7 x 11 inch) shallow tin. Line the base with baking paper, overhanging two opposite sides. Sift the flour and icing sugar into a mixing bowl. Add the butter and, using your fingertips, rub in until the mixture forms a dough. Press into a prepared tin. Bake for 15 minutes, or until light golden brown.
2 To make the topping, melt the butter in a small saucepan and add the sugar, milk and vanilla. Stir, without boiling, until the sugar dissolves then bring to the boil. Remove from heat. Add the hazelnuts and cherries to the mixture and stir.
3 Spread the topping over the base. Bake for 15–20 minutes, or until golden. Cut the slice into squares while still warm and allow to cool before serving.

VARIATION: Melt dark chocolate and drizzle over the cooled slice.

Spread pear mixture over the base and spoon over the cheese filling.

Sprinkle the pecan mixture over the top and bake until golden and set.

PEAR, PECAN AND CHEESE SLICE

Preparation time: 25 minutes
Total cooking time: 45 minutes
Makes 12 pieces

$^1/_4$ cup (30 g/1 oz) sultanas
1 tablespoon marsala or brandy
$1^2/_3$ cups (200 g/6$^1/_2$ oz) self-raising flour
$^1/_3$ cup (90 g/3 oz) caster sugar
80 g (2$^3/_4$ oz) butter
1 egg
2 tablespoons chopped pecans
825 g (1 lb 11 oz) can pears, well drained and cubed
1 teaspoon vanilla essence
$^1/_4$ teaspoon ground cinnamon

CHEESE FILLING
250 g (8 oz) cottage cheese
2 tablespoons sugar
2 eggs
2 tablespoons grated lemon rind
$^1/_2$ teaspoon vanilla essence
2 tablespoons plain flour

1 Preheat the oven to 180°C (350°F/ Gas 4). Lightly grease a 23 cm (9 inch) square shallow tin and line with baking paper, overhanging two opposite sides.
2 Put the sultanas and marsala in a bowl and set aside to soak.
3 Place the flour, sugar and butter in a food processor and process for 15 seconds, or until the mixture resembles fine breadcrumbs. Add the egg and process again.
4 Transfer a third of the mixture to a bowl, stir in the pecans and set aside. Spread the remaining mixture into the tin, pressing firmly and evenly.

5 Put the pear cubes in a bowl, add the vanilla essence and cinnamon and mix well. Spread over the pastry base.
6 To make the cheese filling, blend the cottage cheese and sugar in a food processor until just smooth. Add the remaining ingredients and process until smooth. Stir in the sultanas and marsala, then spoon over the pears.
7 Sprinkle the remaining base mixture over the top. Bake for 40–45 minutes, or until golden and set. Leave to cool before cutting.

Mix together the peaches, honey and sultanas and spread over the base.

Sprinkle the remaining crumble mixture over the top and bake until golden.

PEACH CRUMBLE SLICE

Preparation time: 30 minutes
Total cooking time: 1 hour
Makes 9 pieces

$^1\!/_2$ cup (60 g/2 oz) self-raising flour
$^3\!/_4$ cup (90 g/3 oz) plain flour
1 cup (60 g/2 oz) shredded coconut
$^1\!/_2$ cup (50 g/1$^3\!/_4$ oz) rolled oats
$^1\!/_2$ cup (95 g/3 oz) lightly packed soft brown sugar
160 g (5$^1\!/_2$ oz) butter, melted
1 teaspoon vanilla essence
2 x 415 g (13 oz) cans pie peaches
2 tablespoons honey
$^1\!/_2$ cup (60 g/2 oz) sultanas
$^1\!/_4$ teaspoon ground cinnamon
icing sugar, to dust
cream, to serve

1 Preheat the oven to 180°C (350°F/ Gas 4). Lightly grease an 18 x 28 cm (7 x 11 inch) shallow tin and line with baking paper, overhanging two opposite sides.

2 Sift the flours into a mixing bowl. Stir in the coconut, rolled oats and brown sugar. Mix in the butter and vanilla essence.

3 Set aside a third of the mixture and press the rest into the prepared tin. Smooth the surface and bake for 15–20 minutes. Leave to cool in the tin.

4 Mix the peaches, honey and sultanas in a bowl and spread over the base. Mix the cinnamon into the reserved crumble mixture and sprinkle over the top. Bake for 35–40 minutes, or until golden. Dust with icing sugar and serve warm with cream.

Add the chocolate mixture and the lightly beaten egg and stir with a wooden spoon.

After the slice has set, place a chocolate-dipped pecan on top of each piece.

CHOCOLATE HEDGEHOG SLICE

Preparation time: 30 minutes
Total cooking time: 5–10 minutes + 30 minutes refrigeration
Makes 50

250 g (8 oz) chocolate cream biscuits, finely crushed
$\frac{1}{2}$ cup (45 g/1$\frac{1}{2}$ oz) desiccated coconut
1 cup (125 g/4 oz) chopped pecans
1 tablespoon cocoa powder, sifted
100 g (3$\frac{1}{2}$ oz) dark chocolate, chopped
80 g (2$\frac{3}{4}$ oz) unsalted butter
1 tablespoon golden syrup
1 egg, lightly beaten
extra pecans, for decoration
60 g (2 oz) dark chocolate melts, extra

ICING
100 g (3$\frac{1}{2}$ oz) dark chocolate, chopped
40 g (1$\frac{1}{4}$ oz) unsalted butter

1 Line the base and sides of a shallow 30 x 20 cm (12 x 8 inch) rectangular tin with foil. Combine the biscuit crumbs, coconut, pecans and cocoa in a medium mixing bowl. Make a well in the centre of the ingredients.

2 Combine the chocolate, butter and syrup in a small heavy-based pan. Stir over low heat until chocolate and butter have melted and mixture is smooth. Remove from heat. Pour chocolate mixture and egg into dry ingredients. Using a wooden spoon, stir until well combined. Press the mixture evenly into prepared tin. Refrigerate for 30 minutes, or until set.

3 To make the icing, place the chocolate and butter in a small heatproof bowl. Stand over a saucepan of simmering water. Stir until the chocolate and butter have melted and mixture is smooth. Cool slightly. Spread the mixture evenly over the slice base. Refrigerate until set. Remove from the tin and cut into small squares. Decorate with the pecans dipped in the extra melted chocolate.

Using a metal spoon, fold the sifted flour and ground ginger into the creamed butter and sugar.

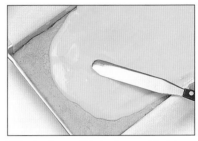

While the slice is still in the tin, spread the icing over the top with a flat-bladed knife.

GINGER AND PISTACHIO SQUARES

Preparation time: 20 minutes
Total cooking time: 35 minutes
Makes 28

125 g (4 oz) unsalted butter
1 cup (185 g/6 oz) lightly packed soft brown sugar
2 eggs, lightly beaten
1 1/4 cups (175 g/6 oz) self-raising flour
6 teaspoons ground ginger

WHITE CHOCOLATE ICING
150 g (5 oz) white chocolate, chopped
1/4 cup (60 ml/2 fl oz) cream
2 tablespoons chopped glacé ginger
2 tablespoons chopped pistachio nuts (see VARIATION)

1 Preheat the oven to 180°C (350°F/ Gas 4). Grease a shallow 27 x 18 cm (11 x 7 inch) rectangular cake tin. Cover the base with baking paper, overhanging over opposite two sides, and grease the paper.

2 Using electric beaters, beat the butter and sugar in a small mixing bowl until light and creamy. Add the eggs gradually, beating thoroughly after each addition. Transfer the mixture to a large mixing bowl. Using a metal spoon, fold in the the sifted flour and ginger and stir until just combined.

3 Spread the mixture into the prepared tin. Bake for 30 minutes, or until golden and firm in the centre. Leave to cool in the tin.

4 To make the white chocolate icing, combine the chocolate and cream in a small saucepan. Stir over low heat until the chocolate has melted and the mixture is smooth. Leave to cool. Using a flat-bladed knife, spread the icing evenly over slice. Sprinkle with the glacé ginger and pistachio nuts. Allow the icing to set and then cut into squares to serve.

STORAGE: Slice may be stored for up to 3 days in an airtight container or up to 2 months in the freezer un-iced.
VARIATION: Any chopped nuts, such as walnuts, pecans or toasted almonds are suitable for this recipe. If preferred, ice with lemon icing.

Stir the ground almonds and flour into the filling mixture until well combined.

Boil the almond topping gently until it starts to come away from the side of the saucepan.

FRANGIPANE SLICE

Preparation time: 40 minutes
Total cooking time: 50 minutes
Makes 15 pieces

90 g (3 oz) butter
⅓ cup (90 g/3 oz) caster sugar
1 teaspoon vanilla essence
1 egg, lightly beaten
⅔ cup (90 g/3 oz) plain flour
⅓ cup (40 g/1¼ oz) self-raising flour

ALMOND FILLING
90 g (3 oz) butter
⅓ cup (90 g/3 oz) caster sugar
2 eggs, lightly beaten
1½ cups (180 g/6 oz) ground almonds
¼ cup (30 g/1 oz) plain flour

ALMOND TOPPING
60 g (2 oz) butter
¼ cup (60 g/2 oz) caster sugar
1 tablespoon honey
⅔ cup (60 g/2 oz) flaked almonds

1 Preheat the oven to180°C (350°F/ Gas 4). Lightly grease an 18 x 28 cm (7 x 11 inch) shallow tin and line with baking paper, overhanging two opposite sides.
2 Using electric beaters, beat the butter, sugar and vanilla in a mixing bowl until light and creamy. Add the egg a little at a time, beating well after each addition.
3 Sift the flours together and fold into the mixture with a metal spoon. Spread evenly into the prepared tin.
4 To make the almond filling, beat the butter and sugar with electric beaters until light and creamy. Gradually beat in the egg–the mixture will look curdled–mixing well after each addition. Stir in the ground almonds and flour then spread over the base. Bake for 25–30 minutes, or until firm and golden. Leave in the tin to cool.

5 Put the almond topping ingredients in a small saucepan. Bring slowly to the boil, stirring to dissolve the sugar. Boil gently for 2 minutes, or until the mixture starts to come away from the side of the saucepan. Quickly spread over the slice with a metal spatula. Bake for 10–15 minutes, or until golden brown, taking care not to burn the topping. Cool in the tin, then lift out and cut into pieces to serve.

After chilling the dough, roll it out between two sheets of baking paper.

Stir the cake, jam, flour, cocoa and spices into the creamed mixture with a metal spoon.

SPICY FRUIT CAKE SLICE

Preparation time: 25 minutes + 20 minutes refrigeration
Total cooking time: 30 minutes
Makes 32 pieces

¹/₂ cup (60 g/2 oz) plain flour
1 tablespoon cornflour
1 tablespoon self-raising flour
50 g (1³/₄ oz) butter
2 tablespoons caster sugar
1 egg yolk

FRUITY TOPPING
125 g (4 oz) butter
¹/₂ cup (125 g/4 oz) caster sugar
1 egg
2 cups (440 g/14 oz) crumbled dark fruit cake or pudding
2 tablespoons raspberry jam
¹/₂ cup (60 g/2 oz) self-raising flour

1 tablespoon cocoa powder
1 teaspoon ground cinnamon
1 teaspoon mixed spice
icing sugar, to dust

1 Preheat the oven to 180°C (350°F/ Gas 4). Lightly grease a 20 x 30 cm (8 x 12 inch) shallow tin and line with baking paper, overhanging two opposite sides.
2 Put the flours, butter and sugar in a food processor and process until the mixture resembles fine breadcrumbs. Add the egg yolk and 1–2 teaspoons of water, or enough to make the dough just come together. Gather into a smooth ball and wrap in plastic wrap. Chill for 20 minutes, then roll the dough out between two sheets of baking paper to fit the base of the tin.
3 To make the fruity topping, beat the butter and sugar with electric beaters until light and fluffy. Add the egg and beat until well incorporated. Stir in the crumbled cake, jam, flour, cocoa and spices and mix well. Spread the topping over the pastry base and bake for about 30 minutes, or until a skewer inserted into the centre comes out clean. Cool in the tin for 5 minutes before turning out on a wire rack to cool completely. Dust lightly with icing sugar and serve.

Strain mixture into the hot milk and stir until thick enough to cling to the back of a spoon.

Pour the chocolate custard over the baked biscuit base and then chill until set.

CHOCOLATE DESSERT SLICE

Preparation time: 30 minutes
Total cooking time: 20 minutes + 2 hours
refrigeration
Makes 16

200 g (6½ oz) dark chocolate cream
   biscuits
50 g (1¾ oz) unsalted butter, melted
1 cup (250 ml/8 fl oz) milk
3 egg yolks
⅓ cup (90 g/3 oz) caster sugar
2 tablespoons cornflour
¼ cup (30 g/1 oz) cocoa powder
1 tablespoon marsala
1 cup (250 g/8 oz) mascarpone cheese
1 tablespoon boiling water
2½ teaspoons gelatine
50 g (1¾ oz) white chocolate shavings

1 Preheat the oven to 180°C (350°F/ Gas 4). Lightly grease a 20 cm (8 inch) shallow square cake tin. Line base and sides with baking paper, overhanging two opposite sides.
2 Place the biscuits in a food processor and process until finely crushed. Add the butter and process until combined. Press the mixture firmly into the base of prepared tin. Bake for 10 minutes, and leave to cool completely.
3 Heat the milk in a small saucepan until almost boiling. Remove from heat. Whisk the egg yolks, sugar, cornflour, cocoa and 2 tablespoons of the milk in a small mixing bowl until creamy. Add the remaining milk gradually, beating constantly. Strain the mixture into the pan. Stir over a low heat for 3 minutes until the mixture thickens slightly and coats the back of a wooden spoon. Remove from the heat and stir in marsala. Pour into a mixing bowl and cover with plastic wrap. Cool to lukewarm and fold in mascarpone until combined.

4 Dissolve the gelatine in boiling water then add to the custard. Stir until combined. Pour the custard onto the biscuit base, cover with plastic wrap and refrigerate for 2 hours.
5 When set, carefully lift the slice from the tin. Cut into squares and decorate with chocolate shavings.

Place the plastic wrap on the surface of the custard and it will prevent a skin forming.

Finish the slice off with a layer of passionfruit icing before chilling for several hours.

VANILLA AND PASSIONFRUIT SLICE

Preparation time: 35 minutes + 2 hours refrigeration
Total cooking time: 20–25 minutes
Makes 12

2 sheets puff pastry

CUSTARD
1/4 cup (30 g/1 oz) custard powder
1/4 cup (60 g/2 oz) caster sugar
1 cup (250 ml/8 fl oz) cream
1 1/2 cups (375 ml/12 fl oz) milk
1/2 teaspoon vanilla essence

ICING
1/4 cup passionfruit pulp
25 g (3/4 oz) unsalted butter
1 1/2 cups (185 g/6 oz) icing sugar

1 Preheat the oven to 210°C (415°F/ Gas 6–7). Line two baking trays with baking paper. Place the puff pastry sheets on the prepared trays and prick all over with a fork. Bake for 10–15 minutes, or until golden and crisp. Cool on a wire rack.
2 To make the custard, combine the custard powder, sugar and cream in a medium heavy-based saucepan. Gradually stir in the milk and stir constantly over medium heat until the custard boils and thickens. Remove from heat. Stir in vanilla essence. Place plastic wrap onto the surface of the custard to prevent a skin forming. Cool.
3 Place one sheet of pastry onto a board. Spread the custard evenly over surface. Top with the remaining pastry sheet upside down.
4 To make the icing, combine the pulp, butter and icing sugar in a medium heatproof bowl. Stand over a saucepan of simmering water and stir until the icing is smooth and glossy. Remove from heat. Spread the icing evenly over the pastry sheet, using a flat-bladed knife. Refrigerate for several hours or until the pastry softens slightly. Cut the slice into squares using a serrated knife.

STORAGE: The slice can be stored in an airtight container in the refrigerator for up to 2 days.

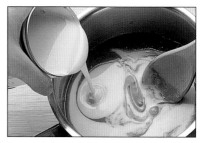

Remove the butter and sugar from the heat and stir in the condensed milk.

Trim the crusty edges off the slice before cutting into squares to serve.

CARAMEL PECAN SQUARES

Preparation time: 15 minutes + 3 hours refrigeration
Total cooking time: 35 minutes
Makes 16 pieces

250 g (8 oz) plain chocolate biscuits
1 tablespoon drinking chocolate
1¹/₂ cups (150 g/5 oz) pecans
185 g (6 oz) butter, melted

CARAMEL TOPPING
¹/₂ cup (90 g/3 oz) lightly packed soft brown sugar
60 g (2 oz) butter
400 g (13 oz) can sweetened condensed milk
icing sugar, to dust
drinking chocolate, to dust

1 Preheat the oven to 180°C (350°F/ Gas 4). Lightly grease an 18 x 28 cm (7 x 11 inch) shallow tin and line with baking paper, overhanging two opposite sides.

2 Finely crush the biscuits, drinking chocolate and a third of the pecans in a food processor. Transfer to a mixing bowl and add the melted butter. Mix well and press firmly into the prepared tin. Press the rest of the pecans gently over the top.

3 To make the caramel topping, place the brown sugar and butter in a saucepan over low heat. Stir until the butter melts and the sugar dissolves. Remove from the heat, stir in the condensed milk, then pour over the biscuit base.

4 Bake for 25–30 minutes, or until the caramel is firm and golden–the edges will bubble and darken. Cool, then refrigerate for at least 3 hours.

5 Trim off the crusty edges and cut the slice into squares. Before serving, hold a piece of paper over one half of each piece and sprinkle the other half with icing sugar. Sprinkle the other side with drinking chocolate.

Arrange the plum halves on top, pressing gently into the filling mixture.

Scatter the flaked almonds over the top, then drizzle with the honey.

PLUM AND ALMOND SLICE

Preparation time: 30 minutes
Total cooking time: 1 hour 10 minutes
Makes 9 pieces

160 g (5¹/₂ oz) butter
²/₃ cup (160 g/5¹/₂ oz) caster sugar
2 eggs
¹/₂ cup (60 g/2 oz) plain flour
¹/₃ cup (40 g/1¹/₄ oz) cornflour
2 tablespoons rice flour
1¹/₂ tablespoons thinly sliced glacé ginger
825 g (1 lb 11 oz) can plums in syrup,
    drained and halved (see NOTE)
1 cup (100 g/3¹/₂ oz) flaked almonds
1 tablespoon warmed honey

1 Preheat the oven to 180°C (350°F/ Gas 4). Lightly grease a 20 cm (8 inch) square tin and line with baking paper, extending over the top edge of the tin on all sides.
2 Using electric beaters, beat the butter and sugar in a mixing bowl until light and creamy. Add the eggs one at a time, beating well. Fold the sifted flours into the mixture with the ginger. Spread into the tin. Arrange the plums on top, pressing them in. Scatter with the almonds, pressing in gently, then drizzle with the honey.
3 Bake for 1 hour 10 minutes, or until firm and golden (cover with foil if over-browning). Cool before cutting.

NOTE: If in season, use 7 ripe blood plums instead of canned. They may bleed more than the canned.

STREUSEL KUCHEN

Preparation time: 40 minutes + 2 hours standing
Total cooking time: 55 minutes
Serves 6–8

7 g (¼ oz) sachet dried yeast
2 tablespoons lukewarm water
½ cup (125 ml/4 fl oz) milk
¼ cup (60 g/2 oz) caster sugar
50 g (1¾ oz) butter
½ teaspoon salt
2¾ cups (340 g/11 oz) plain flour
1 egg, lightly beaten
½ cup (160 g/5½ oz) apricot jam
2 tablespoons water or lemon juice
2 x 410 g (13 oz) cans pie apple (see VARIATIONS)

CRUMBLE TOPPING
½ cup (95 g/3 oz) lightly packed soft brown sugar
⅓ cup (40 g/1¼ oz) plain flour
1 teaspoon cinnamon
60 g (2 oz) butter, cubed
1 cup (125 g/4 oz) walnuts, roughly chopped (see VARIATIONS)

1 Lightly grease a 30 x 25 cm (12 x 10 inch) Swiss roll tin. Dissolve the yeast in warm water and set aside for 5 minutes, or until frothy. Combine the milk, sugar and butter in a saucepan. Stir over medium heat until the butter has melted.

2 Sift 2½ cups (310 g/10 oz) of the flour and the salt into a large mixing bowl. Make a well in the centre and add the yeast, milk mixture and egg. Beat until well combined.

3 Add enough of the remaining flour to form a soft dough. Turn the dough onto a lightly floured surface and knead for 10 minutes, or until smooth and elastic. Place the dough in a lightly oiled bowl. Cover with lightly oiled plastic wrap and leave in a warm place for 1 hour or until dough is well risen. Knead the dough again for 1 minute.

4 Divide the dough in two, making one portion larger than the other. Roll out the larger portion to fit into the prepared tin. Place the dough in the tin, pressing up the sides of the tin.

5 Combine the jam and water in a small saucepan and stir over low heat until the jam is warm and slightly liquefied. Spread half of the warmed jam over the dough in the tin. Top with the pie apple and remaining jam. Roll out the remaining dough to make a lid and place on apple mixture. Scatter the crumble topping thickly over the dough. Cover and leave in a warm place for about 1 hour or until well risen. Preheat the oven to 210°C (415°F/Gas 6–7). Bake the dough for 5 minutes. Reduce the oven temperature to 180°C (350°F/Gas 4). Bake for another 40–50 minutes, or until the dough is cooked and the top is golden.

6 To make the crumble topping, combine the sugar, flour and cinnamon in small bowl. Using your fingertips, rub the butter in until the mixture resembles coarse breadcrumbs. Stir in the walnuts.

STORAGE: Store in an airtight container for up to 4 days. To freeze, wrap tightly in foil, place in a freezer bag and store for up to a month. Reheat in a 180°C (350°F/Gas 4) oven for 20 minutes.
VARIATIONS: Use an 825 g (1 lb 11 oz) can of apricot halves, making sure they are well drained, instead of pie apple. You can also replace the walnuts in the topping with shredded coconut.

Fold the flour and buttermilk into the mixture, then add the chocolate.

Brush the syrup over the slice as soon as it comes out of the oven.

WHITE CHOCOLATE AND MANGO SLICE

Preparation time: 25 minutes
Total cooking time: 45 minutes
Makes 10 pieces

100 g (3½ oz) butter
½ cup (125 g/4 oz) caster sugar
2 eggs, lightly beaten
1 teaspoon vanilla essence
1½ cups (185 g/6 oz) self-raising flour
½ cup (125 ml/4 fl oz) buttermilk
100 g (3½ oz) white chocolate, grated
2 x 425 g (14 oz) cans mango slices,
    drained, or 2 large fresh mangos, sliced
¼ cup (60 g/2 oz) caster sugar, extra

1 Preheat the oven to 180°C (350°F/ Gas 4). Lightly grease an 18 x 28 cm (7 x 11 inch) shallow tin and line with baking paper, overhanging two opposite sides.

2 Using electric beaters, beat the butter and sugar in a mixing bowl until light and creamy. Gradually add the egg and vanilla essence, beating until well combined.

3 Using a metal spoon, alternately fold the sifted flour and buttermilk into the mixture, stirring until just combined. Add grated chocolate. Pour into the prepared tin and smooth the surface. Arrange the mango over the top. Place the tin on an oven tray to catch any drips. Bake for 35–40 minutes, or until golden brown.

4 Put the extra sugar in a small saucepan with 1 tablespoon of water and stir over low heat until dissolved. Bring to the boil, then simmer for 1–2 minutes. Brush the syrup over the slice as soon as it comes out of the oven. Cut into pieces and serve hot.

Fold in the flour, custard powder, baking powder, cake crumbs and hazelnuts.

Spread the mixture over the base and bake for 45 minutes.

RASPBERRY LINZER SLICE

Preparation time: 30 minutes
Total cooking time: 45 minutes
Makes 24 pieces

90 g (3 oz) butter
1/2 cup (125 g/4 oz) caster sugar
1 teaspoon vanilla essence
1 egg, lightly beaten
2/3 cup (85 g/3 oz) plain flour
1/3 cup (40 g/1 1/4 oz) self-raising flour
3/4 cup (240 g/7 1/2 oz) raspberry jam, warmed

HAZELNUT TOPPING
125 g (4 oz) butter
1/3 cup (90 g/3 oz) caster sugar
1 egg, lightly beaten
1/2 cup (60 g/2 oz) plain flour
1 tablespoon custard powder
1 teaspoon baking powder

1 cup (120 g/4 oz) firmly packed plain cake crumbs
1/2 cup (60 g/2 oz) ground hazelnuts
1/3 cup (80 ml/2 3/4 fl oz) milk

1 Preheat the oven to 180°C (350°F/ Gas 4). Lightly grease a 20 x 30 cm (8 x 12 inch) shallow tin and line with baking paper, overhanging two opposite sides.
2 Using electric beaters, beat the butter, sugar and vanilla essence in a mixing bowl until light and creamy. Add the egg to the mixture gradually, beating well after each addition.
3 Sift the flours and fold into the mixture with a metal spoon. Spread into the tin and spread evenly with the raspberry jam.

4 To make the hazelnut topping, beat the butter and sugar with electric beaters until light and creamy. Add the egg gradually, beating well after each addition. Sift the flour, custard powder and baking powder and fold into the mixture with the cake crumbs and ground hazelnuts. Fold in the milk and spread over the base.
5 Bake for 45 minutes, or until firm and golden brown. Leave to cool in the tin before cutting to serve.

Place mixture into the prepared tin, pressing firmly with the back of a spoon.

After the base has cooled, spread the pie apple over the top and sprinkle crumble mixture over.

APPLE CRUMBLE SLICE

Preparation time: 20 minutes
Total cooking time: 40 minutes
Makes 24 squares

³/₄ cup (90 g/3 oz) self-raising flour
³/₄ cup (90 g/3 oz) plain flour
1 cup (90 g/3 oz) desiccated coconut
250 g (8 oz) unsalted butter
³/₄ cup (140 g/4¹/₂ oz) lightly packed soft
   brown sugar
410 g (13 oz) can pie apple (see
   VARIATION)
¹/₃ cup (35 g/1¹/₄ oz) rolled oats
¹/₄ cup (35 g/1¹/₄ oz) currants
¹/₄ teaspoon ground cinnamon

1 Preheat the oven to 180°C (350°F/ Gas 4). Lightly grease an 18 x 27 cm (7 x 11 inch) shallow rectangular tin and line with baking paper, overhanging two opposite sides. Sift the flours into a large mixing bowl and add the coconut. Combine 200 g (6¹/₂ oz) of the butter and sugar in a small saucepan. Stir over low heat until the butter has melted and sugar has dissolved. Remove from heat and pour the butter mixture into the dry ingredients. Using a wooden spoon, stir until well combined.

2 Reserve one cup of mixture. Press the remaining mixture into the prepared tin. Bake for 15 minutes and leave to cool completely.

3 Spread the pie apple over the cooled base. Combine reserved mixture, remaining butter, oats and currants. Using fingertips, crumble mixture over the apple. Dust with the cinnamon. Bake for 35 minutes. Cool, lift from tin and cut into squares.

STORAGE: The slice can be stored for up to 2 days in an airtight container.
VARIATION: Pie apricots can be used instead of the apple.

Use a rubber spatula to spread the mixture evenly around the prepared tin.

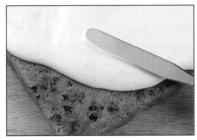

After the slice has cooled, use a flat-bladed knife to spread the frosting over the top.

CHOCOLATE CARROT SLICE

Preparation time: 15 minutes
Total cooking time: 30 minutes
Makes 32

1 cup (125 g/4 oz) self-raising flour
1 teaspoon ground cinnamon
3/4 cup (185 g/6 oz) caster sugar
1/2 cup finely grated carrot
1 cup (190 g/6 1/2 oz) mixed dried fruit
1/2 cup (95 g/3 oz) choc bits
1/3 cup (30 g/1 oz) desiccated coconut
2 eggs, lightly beaten
90 g (3 oz) unsalted butter, melted
1/3 cup (40 g/1 1/4 oz) chopped walnuts
Cream Cheese Frosting
125 g (4 oz) cream cheese
30 g (1 oz) unsalted butter
1 1/2 cups (185 g/6 oz) icing sugar, sifted
1 teaspoon hot water

1 Preheat the oven to 180°C (350°F/ Gas 4). Lightly grease a 23 cm (9 inch) square shallow cake tin and line with baking paper, overhanging two opposite sides. Sift the flour and cinnamon into a large mixing bowl. Add the sugar, grated carrot, mixed fruit, choc bits and coconut and stir until just combined. Add the beaten eggs and butter. Stir until the mixture is just combined.

2 Spread the mixture evenly into the prepared tin and smooth the surface. Bake for 30 minutes, or until golden. Leave to cool in tin and then turn out.

3 To make the cream cheese frosting, beat the cream cheese and butter with electric beaters in a small bowl until smooth. Add the icing sugar and beat for 2 minutes or until the mixture is light and fluffy. Add the water and beat until combined. Using a flat-bladed knife, spread the frosting on top of the slice and sprinkle with walnuts. Cut into 16 squares, then cut each square into triangles.

STORAGE: Slice may be stored for up to 2 days in an airtight container or up to 2 months in the freezer, without icing.

HINT: Sprinkle the frosting with grated chocolate if desired.

Using your fingertips, press the mixture firmly and evenly into the slice tin.

Spread the chocolate icing over the base with a flat-bladed knife.

CHOC-NUT TRIANGLES

Preparation time: 25 minutes
Total cooking time: 20 minutes
Makes 16 pieces

1 cup (125 g/4 oz) self-raising flour
2 tablespoons cocoa powder
½ cup (125 g/4 oz) caster sugar
⅔ cup (60 g/2 oz) desiccated coconut
125 g (4 oz) butter, melted
1 teaspoon vanilla essence
1 cup (125 g/4 oz) chopped pecans or
    walnuts

CHOCOLATE ICING
1 cup (125 g/4 oz) icing sugar
1 tablespoon cocoa powder
15 g (½ oz) butter, melted
½–1 tablespoon milk
½ cup (60 g/2 oz) chopped walnuts or
    pecans

1 Preheat the oven to 180°C (350°F/ Gas 4). Lightly grease an 18 x 28 cm (7 x 11 inch) shallow tin and line with baking paper, overhanging two opposite sides.
2 Sift the flour and cocoa into a large mixing bowl. Stir in the sugar and coconut. Add the melted butter, vanilla essence and the nuts and stir until well combined. Press the mixture firmly and evenly into the prepared tin. Bake for 20 minutes, or until golden brown. Allow the slice to cool completely before removing from the tin.
3 To make the chocolate icing, sift the icing sugar and cocoa powder into a mixing bowl. Add the butter and enough milk to make a smooth, spreadable icing. Mix until well combined. Spread evenly over the cooled base, using a flat-bladed knife. Sprinkle with the nuts and leave to set for about 1 hour. Cut into triangles using a sharp knife.

Remove the saucepan from the heat and add the vanilla, pears, choc bits and nuts.

Spread the mixture over the pastry base and bake for 30 minutes.

CHUNKY PEAR AND MACADAMIA FINGERS

Preparation time: 25 minutes + 30 minutes refrigeration
Total cooking time: 50 minutes
Makes 20 pieces

³/₄ cup (90 g /3 oz) plain flour
25 g (³/₄ oz) butter, chopped
1¹/₂ tablespoons ground almonds
1¹/₂ tablespoons icing sugar
1 egg yolk
¹/₄ teaspoon vanilla essence

MACADAMIA TOPPING
³/₄ cup (100 g/3¹/₂ oz) macadamia nuts, roughly chopped
1 cup (185 g/6 oz) lightly packed soft brown sugar
150 g (5 oz) butter, chopped
1 teaspoon vanilla essence

100 g (3¹/₂ oz) dried pears, chopped
¹/₃ cup (50 g/1³/₄ oz) choc bits

1 Place the flour, butter, ground almonds and icing sugar in a food processor and process until the mixture is crumbly. Add the egg yolk, vanilla and enough cold water to make the dough just come together. Turn out, gather into a ball and wrap in plastic wrap. Chill for 30 minutes.
2 Preheat the oven to 180°C (350°F/ Gas 4). Lightly grease a 20 cm (8 inch) square cake tin and line base and sides with baking paper. Roll out the dough to fit the base of the tin. Bake for 15 minutes, or until lightly browned. Leave to cool.
3 Spread the macadamias on a baking tray and roast for 7 minutes, or until golden brown.
4 Put the sugar and butter in a saucepan and stir over low heat until the butter melts and the sugar dissolves. Bring to the boil, reduce the heat and simmer for 1 minute, stirring. Remove from the heat and add the vanilla, pears, choc bits and macadamias.
5 Spread the mixture over the pastry and bake for 30 minutes, or until bubbling all over. Leave the slice to cool completely in the tin before cutting into fingers to serve.

Fold the almonds and flour into the beaten mixture and spread over the base.

Frozen berries can be used instead, simply make sure they are thawed and drained.

BERRY ALMOND SLICE

Preparation time: 25 minutes
Total cooking time: 1 hour 15 minutes
Makes 15 pieces

1 sheet puff pastry
150 g (5 oz) unsalted butter
³/₄ cup (185 g/6 oz) caster sugar
3 eggs, lightly beaten
2 tablespoons grated lemon rind
²/₃ cup (125 g/4 oz) ground almonds
2 tablespoons plain flour
150 g (5 oz) raspberries
150 g (5 oz) blackberries
icing sugar, to dust

1 Preheat the oven to 200°C (400°F/ Gas 6). Lightly grease a 23 cm (9 inch) square shallow tin and line with baking paper, overhanging two opposite sides.

2 Place the pastry on a baking tray lined with baking paper. Prick all over with a fork and bake for 15 minutes, or until golden. Ease pastry into the tin, trimming the edges if necessary. Reduce the oven to 180°C (350°F/Gas 4).

3 Using electric beaters, beat the butter and sugar in a mixing bowl until light and fluffy. Gradually add the egg, beating after every addition, then the lemon rind. Fold in the almonds and flour. Spread over the pastry base.

4 Scatter the fruit on top and bake for 1 hour, or until lightly golden. Cool in the tin before lifting out to cut. Dust with icing sugar and serve.

Sift the dry ingredients into a bowl, then add the melted butter and egg.

Using a flat-bladed knife spread the peppermint filling evenly over the cooled base.

CHOCOLATE PEPPERMINT SLICE

Preparation time: 25 minutes + 30 minutes refrigeration
Total cooking time: 20 minutes
Makes 24 pieces

²/₃ cup (85 g/3 oz) self-raising flour
¹/₄ cup (30 g/1 oz) cocoa powder
¹/₂ cup (45 g/1¹/₂ oz) desiccated coconut
¹/₄ cup (60 g/2 oz) sugar
140 g (4¹/₂ oz) unsalted butter, melted
1 egg, lightly beaten

PEPPERMINT FILLING

1¹/₂ cups (185 g/6 oz) icing sugar, sifted
30 g (1 oz) copha (white vegetable shortening), melted
2 tablespoons milk
¹/₂ teaspoon peppermint essence

CHOCOLATE TOPPING

185 g (6 oz) dark chocolate, chopped
30 g (1 oz) copha

1 Preheat the oven to 180°C (350°F/ Gas 4). Lightly grease a shallow tin measuring 18 x 28 cm (7 x 11 inches) and line with baking paper, leaving the paper hanging over on the two long sides. This makes it easy to lift the cooked slice out of the tin.

2 Sift the flour and cocoa into a bowl. Stir in the coconut and sugar, then add the butter and egg and mix well. Press the mixture firmly into the tin. Bake for 15 minutes, then press down with the back of a spoon and leave to cool.

3 For the peppermint filling, sift the icing sugar into a bowl. Stir in the copha, milk and peppermint essence. Spread over the base and refrigerate for 5–10 minutes, or until firm.

4 For the chocolate topping, put the chocolate and copha in a heatproof bowl. Half fill a saucepan with water, bring to the boil, then remove from the heat. Sit the bowl over the saucepan, making sure the base of the bowl does not touch the water. Stir occasionally until the chocolate and copha have melted and combined. Spread evenly over the filling. Refrigerate the slice for 20 minutes, or until the chocolate topping is firm. Carefully lift the slice from the tin, using the paper as handles. Cut into pieces with a warm knife to give clean edges. Store in an airtight container in the refrigerator.

Fold the sifted flour and milk into the mixture until well combined.

Spread the pineapple topping over the shortbread base and then grill for 5 minutes.

PINEAPPLE SHORTBREAD

Preparation time: 15 minutes + 15 minutes cooling
Total cooking time: 30 minutes
Makes 20 pieces

150 g (5 oz) butter
1/2 cup (125 g/4 oz) caster sugar
2 eggs, lightly beaten
1 1/4 cups (155 g/5 oz) plain flour
1/2 teaspoon baking powder
2 tablespoons milk

PINEAPPLE CRISP
60 g (2 oz) butter, softened
1/2 cup (95 g/3 oz) lightly packed soft brown sugar
440 g (14 oz) can crushed pineapple, very well drained (see NOTE)
1/2 cup (60 g/2 oz) chopped walnuts

1 Preheat the oven to 180°C (350°F/ Gas 4). Line a lightly greased 18 x 28 cm (11 x 7 inch) shallow tin with baking paper, overhanging two opposite sides.

2 Using electric beaters, beat the butter and sugar in a mixing bowl until light and creamy. Gradually add the egg, beating thoroughly after each addition.

3 Sift the flour and baking powder with a pinch of salt and gently fold into the creamed mixture. Fold in the milk. Spread evenly into the tin and bake for 25 minutes, or until lightly golden. Cool for 15 minutes. Preheat the grill to high.

4 To make the pineapple crisp, beat the butter and sugar until just combined, then stir in the pineapple and walnuts. Spread gently over the shortbread base, then place under the hot grill for about 5 minutes, or until the topping bubbles and caramelizes.

5 Leave to cool for a few minutes before cutting.

STORAGE: Will keep for up to 3 days in an airtight container.
NOTE: Make sure the pineapple is drained thoroughly or it will make the shortbread base soggy.

Fold the flour and baking powder into the mixture with a metal spoon.

Add enough lemon juice to the mixture until it is easy to spread.

FRUITY CHEWS

Preparation time: 25 minutes + cooling
Total cooking time: 30 minutes
Makes 12 pieces

2 eggs
1 cup (230 g/7½ oz) firmly packed soft
   brown sugar
90 g (3 oz) butter, melted
1 teaspoon vanilla essence
1½ cups (185 g/6 oz) plain flour
1 teaspoon baking powder
¾ cup (140 g/4½ oz) chopped dates
¾ cup (90 g/3 oz) chopped walnuts or
   pecans
½ cup (110 g/3½ oz) chopped glacé ginger
½ cup (50 g/1¾ oz) rolled oats

LEMON FROSTING
60 g (2 oz) butter
1 teaspoon grated lemon rind
1 cup (125 g/4 oz) icing sugar
2 teaspoons lemon juice
⅓ cup (75 g/2½ oz) finely chopped glacé
   ginger

1 Preheat the oven to 180°C (350°F/ Gas 4). Lightly grease an 18 x 28 cm (7 x 11 inch) shallow tin and line with baking paper, overhanging two opposite sides.

2 Using electric beaters, beat the eggs and brown sugar in a large mixing bowl for 1 minute, or until well combined. Stir in the melted butter and vanilla essence. Sift the flour and baking powder and fold into the mixture with a metal spoon until just combined. Do not overmix.

3 Stir in the remaining ingredients until well combined. Spread into the prepared tin and smooth the surface. Bake for 25 minutes, or until lightly browned. Leave to cool in the tin.

4 To make the lemon frosting, place the butter and lemon rind in a small bowl and beat with electric beaters until creamy. Gradually add the sifted icing sugar, beating well between each addition. Add enough lemon juice to make a spreadable icing. Spread the lemon frosting over the cold slice, sprinkle with the ginger and cut into pieces to serve.

To make the caramel, heat the condensed milk, butter, sugar and syrup until thick.

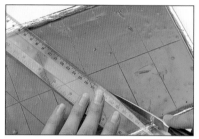

Using a sharp knife, mark out the 24 triangles before chilling and then cutting.

CHOCOLATE CARAMEL SLICE

**Preparation time: 15 minutes +
refrigeration**
Total cooking time: 20 minutes
Makes 24 triangles

125 g (4 oz) plain sweet biscuits, crushed
80 g (2³/₄ oz) unsalted butter, melted
2 tablespoons desiccated coconut
400 g (13 oz) can sweetened condensed
   milk
125 g (4 oz) butter
¹/₃ cup (90 g/3 oz) caster sugar
¹/₃ cup golden syrup
250 g (8 oz) milk chocolate melts (see
   VARIATION)
1 tablespoon vegetable oil

1 Lightly grease a shallow 30 x 20 cm (12 x 8 inch) rectangular cake tin and line with aluminium foil. Grease the foil. Combine the biscuits, melted butter and coconut together in a medium mixing bowl. Press the mixture evenly into the prepared tin and smooth the surface.
2 Combine the condensed milk, butter, sugar and syrup in a small pan. Stir over low heat for 15 minutes or until the sugar has dissolved and the mixture is smooth, thick and lightly browned. Remove from heat and leave to cool slightly. Pour over the biscuit base and smooth the surface.
3 Place the milk chocolate melts and oil in a small heatproof bowl. Stand over a pan of simmering water, stir until melted. Spread the chocolate mixture over caramel. Allow to partially set before marking into 24 triangles. Refrigerate until firm.

STORAGE: Slice may be stored in an airtight container for up to 2 days.
VARIATION: Use dark chocolate melts in place of milk chocolate.

To make the base, combine the melted chocolate and butter with the crushed biscuits.

Add the chocolate, brandy and liqueur to the light and creamy mixture.

BRANDY ALEXANDER SLICE

Preparation time: 20 minutes + overnight refrigeration
Total cooking time: 5 minutes
Makes 12 bars

80 g (2¾ oz) unsalted butter, chopped
60 g (2 oz) dark cooking chocolate, chopped
250 g (8 oz) packet plain chocolate biscuits, crushed
300 g (10 oz) ricotta cheese
¼ cup (60 ml/2 fl oz) cream
⅓ cup (40 g/1¼ oz) icing sugar, sifted
½ cup grated milk chocolate
1 tablespoon brandy
1 tablespoon crème de cacao liqueur (see VARIATION)
½ teaspoon ground nutmeg
60 g (2 oz) dark chocolate melts

1 Lightly grease a shallow 30 x 20 cm (12 x 8 inch) rectangular tin and line with baking paper. Place the butter and chocolate in a small heatproof bowl. Stand over a pan of simmering water. Stir until the chocolate is melted and mixture is smooth. Remove from heat. Using a flat-bladed knife, mix chocolate mixture with the biscuit crumbs in a small mixing bowl.

2 Press the biscuit mixture evenly over the base of the prepared tin and set aside.

3 Using electric beaters, beat the cheese, cream and sugar in a small mixing bowl on medium speed for 3 minutes, or until mixture is light and creamy. Add the chocolate, brandy and liqueur and beat until combined.

4 Spread the cheese mixture over the prepared base and sprinkle with the nutmeg. Refrigerate for several hours or overnight. Cut into 12 bars before serving. Place the chocolate melts in a small heatproof bowl and stand over simmering water until melted. Place in a small piping bag and pipe the design on top of each bar.

STORAGE: Store in the refrigerator for up to 2 days.
VARIATION: Use Tia Maria in place of the crème de cacao.

APPLE CUSTARD STREUSEL SLICE

Preparation time: 30 minutes + 20 minutes refrigeration
Total cooking time: 1 hour
Makes 16 pieces

PASTRY
1¼ cups (155 g/5 oz) plain flour
1 tablespoon caster sugar
80 g (2¾ oz) butter, melted and cooled
1 egg yolk

APPLE CUSTARD TOPPING
3 green apples
20 g (¾ oz) butter
4 tablespoons caster sugar
2 eggs
¾ cup (185 ml/6 fl oz) thick cream
1 teaspoon vanilla essence

CRUMBLE TOPPING
½ cup (60 g/2 oz) plain flour
2 tablespoons dark brown sugar
⅓ cup (40 g/1¼ oz) finely chopped walnuts (see NOTE)
60 g (2 oz) butter, melted

1 Lightly grease an 18 x 28 cm (7 x 11 inch) shallow tin and line with baking paper, overhanging two opposite sides.

Bake for 15 minutes, then remove the paper and baking beads or rice.

2 To make the pastry, sift the flour and sugar into a large mixing bowl. Add the melted butter, egg yolk and 2–3 tablespoons of water and mix until dough comes together. Roll out the dough between two sheets of baking paper to fit the base of the tin. Refrigerate for 20 minutes. Preheat the oven to 190°C (375°F/Gas 5).

3 Line the pastry base with baking paper and fill with baking beads or uncooked rice or beans. Bake for 15 minutes. Remove the paper and beads, reduce oven temperature to 180°C (350°F/Gas 4) and bake the pastry for 5 minutes, or until golden. Leave to cool.

4 To make the apple custard topping, peel, core and chop the apples and place in a saucepan with the butter, half the sugar and 2 tablespoons of water. Cover and cook over low heat for 15 minutes, or until soft and pulpy. Uncover and simmer for another 5 minutes, to reduce the liquid. Use a wooden spoon to break down the apples until they have a smooth texture. Leave to cool.

5 Whisk together the eggs, cream, remaining sugar and vanilla essence in a mixing bowl. Spread the cooled apple mixture over the pastry base, then carefully pour over the cream mixture. Bake for 20 minutes, or until the custard has half set.

6 To make the crumble topping, mix together the flour, brown sugar and walnuts in a mixing bowl. Stir in the melted butter until the mixture is crumbly. Sprinkle over the custard and bake for 15 minutes. Leave to cool in the tin before slicing.

STORAGE: The slice will keep for up to a week, if refrigerated in an airtight container.
NOTE: To keep walnuts fresh, store them in an airtight container or jar in the fridge or freezer. Lightly toasting them before use will bring out the flavor. If walnuts aren't available, use pecans instead.

Spread the base mixture evenly in the tin and bake until pale golden.

Spread the meringue mixture evenly over the strawberries and sprinkle with almonds.

STRAWBERRY MERINGUE SLICE

Preparation time: 30 minutes +
  refrigeration
Total cooking time: 40 minutes
Makes 12 pieces

375 g (12 oz) strawberries, sliced
1¹/₂ tablespoons grappa (see VARIATION)
2 tablespoons caster sugar

CAKE BASE
125 g (4 oz) butter, softened
¹/₃ cup (90 g/3 oz) caster sugar
1 egg
¹/₂ teaspoon vanilla essence
³/₄ cup (90 g/3 oz) plain flour
¹/₃ cup (40 g/1¹/₄ oz) self-raising flour

MERINGUE
2 egg whites
¹/₂ cup (125 g/4 oz) caster sugar
¹/₃ cup (30 g/1 oz) flaked almonds

1 Preheat the oven to 180°C (350°F/ Gas 4). Lightly grease an 18 x 28 cm (7 x 11 inch) shallow tin and line with baking paper, overhanging two opposite sides.
2 Mix the strawberries, grappa and sugar in a mixing bowl, cover and refrigerate until ready to use.
3 To make the base, beat the butter and sugar in a small mixing bowl with electric beaters until light and fluffy. Add the egg and vanilla essence and mix well. Sift the flours together and gently fold in. Spread the mixture into the tin and bake for 15–20 minutes, or until pale golden. Leave to cool slightly in the tin.
4 Drain the strawberries and spread them over the warm base.

5 To make the meringue, beat the egg whites with electric beaters in a small mixing bowl until stiff peaks form. Gradually add the sugar, beating well after each addition. Spread meringue mixture over the strawberries and sprinkle with the flaked almonds.
6 Bake for 15–20 minutes, or until lightly colored. Slice and serve warm.

VARIATION: Vodka can be used instead of grappa, if preferred.

Cut the cherries in half and scatter evenly over the biscuit base.

Mix the sour cream, sugar and egg together and pour over the cherries.

SOUR CREAM AND CHERRY SLICE

Preparation time: 30 minutes + 1 hour refrigeration
Total cooking time: 30 minutes
Makes 15 pieces

200 g (6 oz) sweet biscuits, crushed
1 teaspoon ground cinnamon
90 g (3 oz) butter, melted
2 x 425 g (14 oz) cans pitted dark cherries
2 x 300 g (10 oz) cartons sour cream
$1/3$ cup (90 g/3 oz) caster sugar
2 eggs, lightly beaten

1 Lightly grease a 20 x 30 cm (8 x 12 inch) shallow tin and line with baking paper, overhanging two opposite sides. Preheat the oven to 160°C (315°F/Gas 2–3).

2 Place the biscuit crumbs, cinnamon and butter in a mixing bowl and mix until well combined. Press the mixture firmly into the prepared tin. Refrigerate for 30 minutes, or until firm.

3 Drain the cherries, rinse well and pat dry with paper towels. Cut the cherries in half and scatter over the biscuit base. Mix together the sour cream, sugar and egg and pour over the cherries.

4 Bake for about 30 minutes, or until the topping has just set. Allow to cool, then refrigerate for 30 minutes, or until firm, before lifting out to cut.

Mix the ginger, flour, sugar, salt, egg and melted butter in a bowl.

Stir the ginger icing until it comes to the boil, then remove from the heat.

GINGER DELIGHTS

Preparation time: 20 minutes + cooling
Total cooking time: 50 minutes
Makes 16 pieces

100 g (3½ oz) glacé ginger
1¾ cups (220 g/7 oz) plain flour
1 cup (220 g/7 oz) raw sugar
160 g (5½ oz) butter, melted
1 egg

GINGER ICING
80 g (2¾ oz) butter
1 tablespoon golden syrup
¾ cup (90 g/3 oz) icing sugar
1 teaspoon ground ginger
¼ cup (40 g/1¼ oz) chopped macadamia
   nuts, toasted

1 Preheat the oven to 180°C (350°F/ Gas 4). Lightly grease a 19 cm (8 inch) square cake tin and line with baking paper, overhanging two sides.

2 Toss the ginger in 1–2 tablespoons of the flour, then chop finely. Put the ginger in a mixing bowl with the remaining flour, sugar, melted butter, egg, pinch of salt and mix well.

3 Press the mixture into the prepared tin and smooth the surface. Bake for 40–45 minutes, or until firm and golden. Cool in the tin for 20 minutes before lifting out.

4 To make the ginger icing, mix the butter, syrup, icing sugar and ginger in a pan over low heat. Stirring often, bring just to the boil then remove from the heat. Spread over the base and sprinkle with macadamias. Leave to cool before cutting.

Press the dough into the tin, smooth the surface and prick with a fork.

Fold the whipped cream into the mixture quickly, so the marshmallow doesn't set.

PASSION MALLOW SLICE

Preparation time: 25 minutes + overnight refrigeration
Total cooking time: 30 minutes
Makes 20 pieces

150 g (5 oz) butter
1/4 cup (60 g/2 oz) caster sugar
1/2 teaspoon vanilla essence
1 cup (125 g/4 oz) plain flour
1/2 cup (60 g/2 oz) self-raising flour

MARSHMALLOW TOPPING

1/2 cup (125 ml/4 fl oz) passionfruit pulp (or 5–6 passionfruit)
250 g (8 oz) white marshmallows
1/2 cup (125 ml/4 fl oz) milk
2 tablespoons caster sugar
2 teaspoons lemon juice
1 1/4 cups (315 ml/10 fl oz) cream, lightly whipped

1 Preheat the oven to 180°C (350°F/ Gas 4). Lightly grease an 18 x 28 cm (7 x 11 inch) shallow tin and line with baking paper, overhanging two opposite sides.
2 Using electric beaters, beat the butter and sugar in a mixing bowl until light and creamy, and the sugar has dissolved. Stir in the vanilla essence. Sift the flours into a bowl, then fold into the butter mixture and mix to a soft dough. Knead gently to bring together.
3 Press the dough into the prepared tin and smooth with the back of a spoon. Lightly prick the dough and bake for 25 minutes, or until golden. Remove from the oven and leave to cool completely.
4 To make the topping, put the passionfruit, marshmallows, milk and sugar in a pan and stir over low heat until the marshmallows have melted.
5 Stir in the lemon juice and transfer to a bowl to cool. Refrigerate, stirring occasionally, for 30 minutes, or until slightly thickened. Quickly fold in the cream so the marshmallow doesn't set, then pour over the slice and refrigerate overnight, or until set. Cut into squares to serve.

Melt the chocolate and shortening in a heatproof bowl set over a pan of simmering water.

Spoon the melted chocolate mixture over the slices then leave to set.

FAMILY STYLE ROCKY ROAD SLICE

Preparation time: 35 minutes + cooling
Total cooking time: 20–30 minutes
Makes 2 slices

150 g (5 oz) unsalted butter
$1/3$ cup (40 g/$1^{1}/_4$ oz) icing sugar
1 cup (125 g/4 oz) self-raising flour
2 tablespoons cocoa powder
250 g (8 oz) colored marshmallows
100 g ($3^{1}/_2$ oz) glacé cherries, halved (see VARIATION)
200 g ($6^{1}/_2$ oz) dark chocolate, chopped
15 g ($^{1}/_2$ oz) copha (white vegetable shortening)

1 Preheat the oven to 160°C (315°F/ Gas 2–3). Lightly grease two 26 x 8 x 4.5 cm ($10^{1}/_2$ x 3 x $1^{3}/_4$ inch) bar tins and line with baking paper. Using electric beaters, beat the butter and sifted icing sugar in a large mixing bowl until light and creamy. Sift in the flour and cocoa and fold in with a metal spoon. Mix until well combined. Divide mixture evenly between both prepared tins. Press the mixture evenly into the tin using fingertips. Bake for 25–30 minutes, or until lightly colored. Leave to cool in the tins.

2 Scatter the marshmallows and cherries on top of the bases.

3 Place the chocolate and shortening in a heatproof bowl. Stand over a saucepan of simmering water, making sure the base does not touch the water, and stir until the chocolate and shortening have melted and the mixture is smooth. Cool slightly.

4 Spoon the chocolate mixture evenly over both slices. Tap tins gently on the bench to distribute the chocolate evenly. Allow the chocolate to set and cut into squares or fingers.

STORAGE: Slice may be stored in an airtight container for up to 4 days.

VARIATION: Sprinkle $1/4$ cup of roughly chopped mixed nuts over the cherries and marshmallows before spooning on the chocolate topping.

HINT: If you have refrigerated the slice to set the chocolate, allow it to come to room temperature before cutting.

Bake for 30 minutes and test to see if the brownie base is cooked by inserting a skewer in the centre.

Spread the icing over the top then slice into diamonds with a sharp knife.

WALNUT BROWNIES

Preparation time: 10 minutes
Total cooking time: 35 minutes
Makes 20 diamonds

100 g (3½ oz) unsalted butter
⅔ cup (125 g/4 oz) lightly packed soft
    brown sugar
¼ cup (40 g/1¼ oz) sultanas, chopped
¾ cup (185 ml/6 fl oz) water
1 cup (125 g/4 oz) self-raising flour
1 cup (125 g/4 oz) plain flour
1 teaspoon ground cinnamon
1 tablespoon cocoa powder
½ cup (60 g/2 oz) chopped walnuts
¼ cup (90 g/3 oz) choc bits
20 walnut halves

ICING
60 g (2 oz) unsalted butter
¾ cup (90 g/3 oz) icing sugar
1 tablespoon cocoa powder
1 tablespoon milk

1 Preheat the oven to 180°C (350°F/ Gas 4). Lightly grease a 27 x 18 cm (11 x 7 inch) shallow rectangular tin. Line the base with baking paper, extending it over the two longer sides. Grease the paper. Combine the butter, sugar, sultanas and water in a small saucepan. Constantly stir over low heat for 5 minutes, or until the butter is melted and the sugar dissolved. Remove from the heat.

2 Sift the dry ingredients into a large mixing bowl and add the nuts and choc bits. Make a well in the centre of the dry ingredients and add the butter mixture. Using a wooden spoon, stir until just combined. Do not overmix.

3 Spoon the mixture evenly into the prepared tin and smooth the surface. Bake for 30 minutes, or until a skewer comes out clean when inserted in the centre of the slice. Leave in the tin for 20 minutes before turning onto a wire rack to cool.

4 To make the icing, beat the butter with electric beaters until light and creamy. Add the sugar, cocoa powder and milk. Beat until smooth. Spread the icing over the brownie. Cut into diamonds and top with walnuts.

Using a wooden spoon, stir the custard mixture over the heat until it boils and thickens.

Remove from the heat, cool slightly and whisk in the butter and egg yolks.

LIME CUSTARD SLICE

Preparation time: 30 minutes + 3 hours refrigeration
Total cooking time: 10 minutes
Makes 12 pieces

250 g (8 oz) plain sweet biscuits, crushed
120 g (4 oz) butter, melted
$1/3$ cup (40 g/$1^1/4$ oz) custard powder
1 cup (250 g/8 oz) caster sugar
$1/2$ cup (60 g/2 oz) cornflour
3 cups (750 ml/24 fl oz) milk
1 cup (250 ml/8 fl oz) lime juice
$3/4$ cup (185 ml/6 fl oz) water
60 g (2 oz) butter
3 egg yolks
whipped cream and chocolate curls, to serve

1 Lightly grease a 20 x 30 cm (8 x 12 inch) shallow tin and line with baking paper, overhanging two sides.

2 Combine the biscuit crumbs and melted butter and press firmly into the prepared tin and refrigerate.

3 Put the custard powder, sugar and cornflour in a saucepan. Mix the milk, lime juice and water in a separate bowl and gradually stir into the custard mixture. Stir over medium heat for 5 minutes, or until the custard thickens. Remove and cool a little. Whisk in the butter and egg yolks.

4 Pour over the base and chill for 2–3 hours. Serve with the whipped cream and chocolate curls.

Sieve the flours into a bowl, returning the husks from the wholemeal flour to the bowl.

Press the mixture into the prepared tin with a spoon then bake for 25–30 minutes.

WHOLEMEAL LEMON AND WALNUT SLICE

Preparation time: 30 minutes
Total cooking time: 30 minutes
Makes 30 pieces

2 teaspoons finely grated lemon rind
$^1/_3$ cup (40 g/1$^1/_4$ oz) icing sugar
$^3/_4$ cup (110 g/3$^1/_2$ oz) wholemeal plain flour
$^1/_4$ cup (30 g/1 oz) plain flour
$^1/_2$ cup (125 g/4 oz) raw sugar
1$^1/_4$ cups (150 g/5 oz) walnuts, roughly chopped
$^1/_2$ cup (90 g/3 oz) mixed peel, finely chopped
$^1/_3$ cup (115 g/4 oz) golden syrup
125 g (4 oz) unsalted butter, chopped

1 Put the lemon rind and icing sugar in a small bowl and rub gently to just combine. Spread out on a plate and leave to dry.
2 Preheat the oven to 180°C (350°F/ Gas 4). Lightly grease a 20 x 30 cm (8 x 12 inch) shallow tin and line with baking paper, overhanging two opposite sides.
3 Sift the flours into a large mixing bowl, returning any husks to the bowl. Stir in the sugar, walnuts and mixed peel.
4 Put the syrup and butter in a saucepan and stir over low heat for 5 minutes, or until melted. Add to the bowl and mix well.
5 Spread into the prepared tin and bake for 25–30 minutes, or until golden brown and a skewer inserted into the centre of the slice comes out clean. Leave to cool completely in the tin. Put the lemon sugar in a sieve and sprinkle over the slice before cutting into fingers or squares to serve.

Pour the chocolate mixture into the processed biscuits and walnuts.

Press firmly into the tin and then refrigerate for 10 minutes before covering with chocolate.

JAFFA FUDGE SLICE

Preparation time: 20 minutes + 40 minutes refrigeration
Total cooking time: 3 minutes
Makes 32 pieces

200 g (6½ oz) plain sweet chocolate biscuits
1 cup (125 g/4 oz) chopped walnuts
125 g (4 oz) dark chocolate, chopped
½ cup (60 g/2 oz) icing sugar
125 g (4 oz) butter
1 tablespoon grated orange rind
125 g (4 oz) dark chocolate, extra, melted

1 Lightly grease an 18 x 28 cm (7 x 11 inch) shallow tin and line with baking paper or foil, overhanging two opposite sides.
2 Place the biscuits and walnuts in a food processor and process until the mixture resembles coarse breadcrumbs. Transfer to a large mixing bowl and make a well in the centre.
3 Put the chopped chocolate, sifted icing sugar and butter in a small saucepan and stir over low heat until melted and smooth. Remove from the heat, stir in the orange rind, then pour into the biscuit mixture and stir until well combined.
4 Press the mixture firmly into the prepared tin. Chill for 10 minutes. Spread the melted chocolate over and chill for 30 minutes to set.

STORAGE: Slice can be kept in an airtight container for up to a week.

Press the mixture firmly into the prepared tin, then bake for 20 minutes.

Stir the chocolate and sour cream in a heatproof bowl over simmering water.

FUDGY COCONUT FINGERS

Preparation time: 20 minutes + cooling
Total cooking time: 25 minutes
Makes 20 pieces

1 cup (125 g/4 oz) plain flour
1 tablespoon cocoa powder
¹/₂ cup (125 g/4 oz) caster sugar
1 cup (90 g/3 oz) desiccated coconut
185 g (6 oz) butter, melted
1 teaspoon vanilla essence
125 g (4 oz) dark chocolate, chopped
2 tablespoons sour cream
¹/₂ cup (30 g/1 oz) flaked coconut, lightly
    toasted

1 Preheat the oven to 180°C (350°F/ Gas 4). Lightly grease an 18 x 28 cm (7 x 11 inch) shallow tin and line with baking paper, overhanging two opposite sides.

2 Sift the flour and cocoa into a large mixing bowl. Add the sugar and desiccated coconut and mix until well combined. Add the butter and vanilla essence and mix until well combined. Press firmly into the prepared tin and bake for 20 minutes, or until firm and golden brown. Leave to cool in the tin.

3 Stir the chocolate and sour cream in a heatproof bowl over a saucepan of simmering water until melted. Spread over the base and sprinkle with the coconut. Leave for 20 minutes before cutting into fingers.

STORAGE: Will keep in an airtight container for up to 4 days.

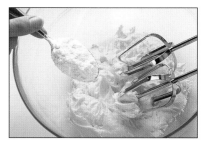

Gradually add the icing sugar to the creamed butter and sugar.

Spread the chocolate topping evenly over the chilled slice base.

CONTINENTAL SLICE

Preparation time: 25 minutes + 4 hours refrigeration
Total cooking time: 10 minutes
Makes about 36

125 g (4 oz) butter
½ cup (125 g/4 oz) caster sugar
¼ cup (30 g/1 oz) cocoa powder
250 g (8 oz) shredded wheat biscuits, crushed
¾ cup (75 g/2½ oz) desiccated coconut
¼ cup (30 g/1 oz) chopped hazelnuts
¼ cup chopped glacé cherries
1 egg, lightly beaten
1 teaspoon vanilla essence

TOPPING
60 g (2 oz) butter
1¾ cups (220 g/7 oz) icing sugar
2 tablespoons custard powder
1 tablespoon hot water
1 tablespoon Grand Marnier
125 g (4 oz) dark chocolate
60 g (2 oz) copha (white vegetable shortening)

1 Line the base and sides of an 18 x 28 cm (7 x 11 inch) shallow tin with foil. Combine the butter, sugar and cocoa in a small saucepan. Stir over low heat until the butter melts and mixture is well combined. Cook, stirring, for 1 minute. Remove from the heat and cool slightly. Combine the biscuit crumbs, coconut, hazelnuts and cherries in a large mixing bowl. Make a well in the centre and add butter mixture, egg and vanilla and stir well. Press the mixture firmly into the prepared tin. Refrigerate until firm.

2 To make the topping, beat the butter with electric beaters until creamy. Gradually add the icing sugar and custard powder, alternately with water and Grand Marnier. Beat mixture until light and fluffy. Spread evenly over base. Refrigerate until set.

3 Place the chocolate and copha in a heatproof bowl and set over a saucepan of simmering water. Stir over low heat until the chocolate melts and mixture is smooth. Spread over the slice. Refrigerate until firm. Cut into small squares to serve.

Add the sour cream to the mixture and stir until well combined.

Arrange the apples over the slice base and sprinkle with the pecan mixture.

APPLE AND CINNAMON SLICE

Preparation time: 15 minutes
Total cooking time: 40 minutes
Makes about 36

125 g (4 oz) butter
1/2 cup (125 g/4 oz) caster sugar
2 eggs
2 cups (250 g/8 oz) self-raising flour, sifted
1 1/4 cups (300 g/10 oz) sour cream
2 green apples, peeled, cored and sliced
1/2 cup (60 g/2 oz) finely chopped pecans
2 tablespoons caster sugar
1 teaspoon ground cinnamon

1 Preheat the oven to 180°C (350°F/ Gas 4). Lightly grease a 20 x 30 cm (8 x 12 inch) shallow tin and line with baking paper, overhanging two opposite sides. Using electric beaters, beat the butter and sugar until light and creamy. Add the eggs one at a time, beating well after each addition. Transfer to a large mixing bowl.

2 Using a metal spoon, fold in the flour. Add the sour cream and stir to combine. Spoon the mixture into the prepared tin.

3 Arrange the apples over the slice base. Sprinkle with the combined pecans, sugar and cinnamon. Bake for 35–40 minutes. Leave to cool in the tin. Cut into squares to serve.

Bake the slice for 20 minutes, or until the top is lightly golden then set aside to cool.

Using electric beaters, beat the icing ingredients until smooth and fluffy

COCONUT PINEAPPLE SQUARES

Preparation time: 20 minutes
Total cooking time: 20 minutes
Makes 24

250 g (8 oz) oatmeal biscuits, crushed
1 cup (90 g/3 oz) shredded coconut
1 cup (250 g) chopped glacé pineapple
1 cup (90 g/3 oz) flaked almonds
200 ml condensed milk
100 g (3^1/$_2$ oz) unsalted butter, melted

COCONUT ICING
60 g (2 oz) butter, softened
few drops coconut essence
^{3}/$_4$ cup (90 g/3 oz) icing sugar, sifted
1 tablespoon milk
1 cup (90 g/3 oz) toasted flaked coconut
   (see HINT)

1 Preheat the oven to 180°C (350°F/ Gas 4). Lightly grease a shallow 27 x 18 cm (11 x 7 inch) rectangular cake tin and line with baking paper. Combine the biscuits, coconut, pineapple and almonds in a large mixing bowl. Make a well in the centre of the ingredients and pour the condensed milk and butter in. Stir until well combined.

2 Press mixture firmly into the prepared tin. Bake for 20 minutes, or until the top is lightly golden and leave to cool in the tin.

3 To make the coconut icing, beat the butter and coconut essence with electric beaters in a mixing bowl until light and creamy. Add the icing sugar and milk. Beat until smooth and fluffy. Spread the icing evenly over the slice and sprinkle with the toasted coconut. Cut into squares to serve.

STORAGE: The slice may be stored for up to 3 days in an airtight container or up to 2 months in the freezer, without icing.
HINT: Toast the coconut by simply spreading it on a baking tray and baking for 5 minutes, or until golden.

After the shortbread has cooled, remove from the tin and cut into wedges.

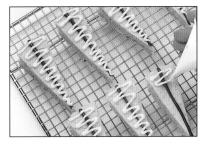

Place wedges on a wire rack and decorate with the melted chocolate.

CHOCOLATE HAZELNUT WEDGES

Preparation time: 30 minutes
Total cooking time: 50 minutes
Makes 16

150 g (5 oz) unsalted butter
1/2 cup (60 g/2 oz) icing sugar
1/3 cup (40 g/1 1/4 oz) ground hazelnuts (see VARIATION)
1 1/4 cups (155 g/5 oz) plain flour
50 g (1 3/4 oz) dark chocolate melts
80 g (2 3/4 oz) white chocolate melts

1 Preheat the oven to 150°C (300°F/ Gas 2). Lightly grease a shallow 21 cm (8 1/2 inch) round, fluted flan tin. Using electric beaters, beat the butter and sugar in a large mixing bowl until light and creamy. Add the nuts and beat until combined. Using a metal spoon, fold in the sifted flour. Mix well.

2 Press the mixture evenly into the prepared tin and smooth surface. Score into 16 wedges, using a sharp knife. Bake for 35–40 minutes, or until pale golden. Stand in tin to cool.

3 Carefully remove the shortbread from tin. Using a sharp knife, cut into scored wedges.

4 Place the dark chocolate in a small heatproof bowl. Stand over a saucepan of simmering water and stir until the chocolate is melted and smooth. Leave to cool slightly. Spoon the chocolate into a small paper icing bag, seal open end. Snip off tip. Pipe a wide strip down the centre of each wedge. Melt the white chocolate melts in the same way as the dark chocolate. Pipe a white zigzag pattern over the dark chocolate stripe. Leave to set.

STORAGE: Store wedges in an airtight container in a cool, dry place for up to 3 days.
VARIATION: Use ground almonds or walnuts instead of hazelnuts.

Stir in the almonds and then pour the mixture over the cooled base.

Dip the bars into the chocolate icing, making sure they are completely coated.

BRANDY MOCHA BARS

Preparation time: 45 minutes + overnight refrigeration
Total cooking time: 12 minutes
Makes 32 pieces

125 g (4 oz) butter
$\frac{1}{4}$ cup (60 g/2 oz) caster sugar
1$\frac{1}{4}$ cups (155 g/5 oz) plain flour
1 tablespoon instant coffee
2$\frac{1}{4}$ cups (280 g/9 oz) icing sugar
1 cup (110 g/3$\frac{1}{2}$ oz) full-cream milk powder
$\frac{1}{2}$ cup (60 g/2 oz) cocoa powder
2 eggs
3 tablespoons brandy
375 g (12 oz) copha (white vegetable shortening), melted
1$\frac{1}{4}$ cups (125 g/4 oz) flaked almonds, toasted

CHOCOLATE ICING
1$\frac{2}{3}$ cups (250 g/8 oz) dark choc melts, chopped
50 g (1$\frac{3}{4}$ oz) copha, chopped
toasted flaked almonds or chocolate curls, to decorate

1 Preheat the oven to 180°C (350°F/ Gas 4). Lightly grease a shallow 23 cm (9 inch) square tin and line with baking paper, overhanging two opposite sides.
2 Using electric beaters, beat the butter and sugar in a mixing bowl until just combined. Stir in the flour, then press into the prepared tin and bake for 10 minutes, or until lightly browned. Leave to cool.
3 Dissolve the coffee in 1 tablespoon of boiling water. Place the icing sugar, milk powder, cocoa, coffee, eggs and brandy in a large mixing bowl. Using electric beaters, beat until well combined. Gradually add the copha and mix until well combined. Stir in the almonds then pour the mixture over the base. Refrigerate overnight, or until the topping is firm. Cut into small pieces.
4 To make the chocolate icing, place the chocolate and copha in a heatproof bowl. Place the bowl over a saucepan of barely simmering water, making sure the base does not touch the water, and stir until the chocolate has melted. Using a fork and a spoon, dip the bars into the icing until well coated and place on a wire rack over baking paper. Leave to set and decorate with toasted flaked almonds, or chocolate curls.

Adjust the electric beaters to low speed when adding the gelatine and chocolate.

Scatter the raspberries over the base, pressing them down a little.

CHOC-RASPBERRY CHEESECAKE SLICE

Preparation time: 1 hour + overnight refrigeration
Total cooking time: 5 minutes
Makes 16 pieces

150 g (5 oz) sweet biscuits, crushed
90 g (3 oz) butter, melted
1/2 teaspoon mixed spice
1 tablespoon gelatine
100 g (3 1/2 oz) white chocolate
125 g (4 oz) cream cheese, softened
1/3 cup (90 g/3 oz) caster sugar
1 egg
1 cup (250 ml/8 fl oz) cream
1 teaspoon vanilla essence
300 g (10 oz) raspberries (see NOTE)
white chocolate curls, to serve

1 Line a 20 cm (8 inch) square cake tin with baking paper, covering the base and overhanging all sides.
2 Mix together the biscuit crumbs, melted butter and mixed spice and press evenly into the prepared tin. Refrigerate until set.
3 Dissolve the tablespoon of gelatine in 2 table-spoons of water, then leave to cool slightly. Place the chocolate in a heatproof bowl. Sit the bowl over a saucepan of barely simmering water, make sure the base of the bowl does not touch the water, and stir the chocolate until melted. Leave to cool.
4 Using electric beaters, beat the cream cheese and sugar in a mixing bowl until light and creamy. Beat in the egg, cream and vanilla essence until just combined. With the beaters running at low speed, add the cooled gelatine and melted chocolate to the mixture and mix until just combined. Do not overmix.
5 Pour the mixture over the set biscuit base, then scatter with the raspberries, pressing them down. Refrigerate overnight. Using a sharp knife dipped in hot water, cut the slice into squares and top with chocolate curls or shavings to serve.

NOTE: If you are using frozen raspberries, defrost and drain them well on paper towels before using.
HINT: It is important to make sure the melted chocolate and gelatine have cooled before beating them into the cream cheese mixture or they'll become lumpy.

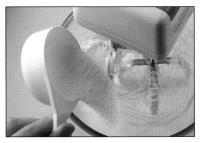

Beat the cream cheese, mascarpone and sour cream with electric beaters.

Pour the filling mixture over the base and bake for 30–35 minutes.

CAPPUCCINO SLICE

Preparation time: 30 minutes + cooling
Total cooking time: 50 minutes
Makes 16 pieces

¹/₃ cup (40 g/1¹/₄ oz) self-raising flour
¹/₄ cup (30 g/1 oz) plain flour
1 tablespoon dark cocoa powder
¹/₄ cup (60 g/2 oz) caster sugar
1 egg, lightly beaten
1 teaspoon vanilla essence
65 g (2¹/₄ oz) butter, melted
¹/₄ cup (60 ml/2 fl oz) milk

CAPPUCCINO FILLING
350 g (11 oz) cream cheese
100 g (3¹/₂ oz) mascarpone cheese
¹/₃ cup (90 g/3 oz) sour cream
¹/₃ cup (90 g/3 oz) caster sugar
3 eggs, lightly beaten
1 tablespoon coffee powder
50 g (1³/₄ oz) dark chocolate, grated

1 Preheat the oven to 180°C (350°F/ Gas 4). Lightly grease a 19 cm (8 inch) square cake tin and line with baking paper, overhanging two opposite sides.
2 Sift the flours and cocoa into a large mixing bowl. Add the sugar and make a well in the centre of the dry ingredients. In a separate bowl, mix the egg, vanilla essence, butter and milk until well combined. Pour the egg mixture into the well and stir until just combined. Spoon into the prepared tin and bake for 10–15 minutes and then cool completely. Reduce the oven to 160°C (315°F/ Gas 2–3).

3 To make the filling, beat the cream cheese, mascarpone and sour cream with electric beaters for 3 minutes, or until smooth. Add the sugar in batches and beat for another 3 minutes. Add the eggs gradually, beating well after each addition.
4 Dissolve the coffee in a little warm water, add to the filling and beat until well combined. Pour over the base. Bake for 30–35 minutes, or until set. Leave in the tin to cool completely. Cut into slices, top with grated chocolate and serve.

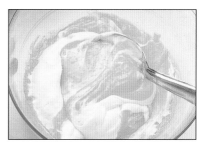

Use a light touch to fold the whipped cream into the lemon mixture.

Leave the lemon slices to drain on a wire rack until they are cooled.

LEMON GINGER SLICE

Preparation time: 40 minutes + 2–3 hours refrigeration
Total cooking time: 30 minutes
Makes 15 pieces

200 g (6¹/₂ oz) gingernut biscuits
90 g (3 oz) butter, melted
1 lemon
¹/₂ cup (125 ml/4 fl oz) water
¹/₂ cup (125 g/4 oz) sugar

LEMON FILLING
100 g (3¹/₂ oz) butter, chopped
6 egg yolks
¹/₂ cup (125 g/4 oz) caster sugar
¹/₃ cup (80 ml/2³/₄ fl oz) lemon juice
2 teaspoons finely grated lemon rind
2 teaspoons gelatine
¹/₂ cup (125 ml/4 fl oz) cream, whipped

1 Lightly grease an 18 x 28 cm (7 x 11 inch) shallow tin and line with baking paper, overhanging two opposite sides. Finely crush the biscuits in a food processor, add the melted butter and process in short bursts. Place into the prepared tin and smooth with the back of a spoon. Refrigerate until ready to use.
2 To make the lemon filling, stir the butter, yolks, sugar, lemon juice and rind in a heatproof bowl set over a saucepan of simmering water for 15 minutes, or until the mixture is smooth and thick. Take care not to overheat or the mixture may curdle. Set aside to cool slightly.
3 Place 1 tablespoon of water in a small mixing bowl and sprinkle with the gelatine. Stand the bowl in hot water to soften the gelatine, then whisk with a fork to dissolve. Stir into the lemon mixture. Leave to cool at room temperature, stirring now and then—do not refrigerate. Gently fold in the whipped cream. Spread over the biscuit base and smooth the surface with the back of the spoon. Refrigerate for 2–3 hours, or until set.

4 Cut 8 thin slices from the lemon. Put the sugar in a small saucepan with the water and stir without boiling for 5 minutes, or until the sugar dissolves completely. Add the lemon slices, bring the sugar syrup to the boil then reduce the heat and simmer for another 10 minutes. Remove the lemon slices, drain and cool on a wire rack, then cut into quarters. Cut the slice into squares and top each one with a lemon quarter.

Refrigerator Slices

Slices are pretty easy to make at the best of times, but the simplest of all are those which don't even need baking. Just pop them into a tin and then into the fridge to set.

NUTTY CHOCOLATE SQUARES

Put 200 g (6½ oz) butter, 200 g (6½ oz) dark chocolate, 2 tablespoons golden syrup and ¼ cup (30 g/1 oz) cocoa powder in a small saucepan and stir until melted. Mix 200 g (6½ oz) crushed plain shortbread biscuits, 60 g (2 oz) toasted slivered almonds and 60 g (2 oz) chopped raisins in a large bowl. Add the chocolate mixture and mix well. Press into a lined 19 cm (8 inch) square cake tin and refrigerate until firm. Dust with icing sugar. Makes 16 pieces.

DATE AND GINGER SLICE

Line an 18 x 28 cm (7 x 11 inch) shallow tin with baking paper, overhanging two opposite sides. Put 175 g (6 oz) chopped dates, 100 g (3½ oz) butter, ¼ cup (45 g/1½ oz) lightly packed soft brown sugar and 3 tablespoons light corn syrup in a saucepan. Stir over gentle heat until dissolved. Simmer for 2 minutes, stirring constantly. Mix together 4 cups (200 g/6½ oz) lightly crushed cornflakes, ½ cup (30 g/1 oz) flaked coconut and 100 g (3½ oz) chopped glacé ginger, then pour in the date mixture and mix well. Press firmly into the tin and refrigerate until firm. Makes 15 pieces.

EASY CHEESECAKE SLICE

Line a 20 x 30 cm (8 x 12 inch) shallow tin with baking paper, overhanging two opposite sides. Mix 250 g (8 oz) crushed plain sweet biscuits with 1 teaspoon ground cinnamon and 60 g (2 oz) melted butter. Press into the tin and refrigerate until smooth. Put 2 tablespoons raspberry jam, without any lumps, in a piping bag and pipe thin strips lengthways over the base. Freeze while preparing the topping. Beat 250 g (8 oz) cream cheese, 250 g (8 oz) sieved ricotta cheese, ½ cup (125 g/4 oz) caster sugar and 1 teaspoon vanilla essence until smooth. Dissolve 3 teaspoons gelatine in 2 tablespoons hot water, then stir into the cheese mixture. Beat ½ cup (125 ml/4 fl oz) cream into soft peaks, fold into the mixture and spread over the jam. Refrigerate for several hours, or until firm. Makes 20 pieces.

COCONUT ICE SLICE

Mix 250 g (8 oz) crushed plain shortbread biscuits with 125 g (4 oz) melted butter. Press firmly into a lined 20 x 30 cm (8 x 12 inch) shallow tin and refrigerate until firm. Mix 2½ cups (310 g/10 oz) icing sugar with 2 cups (180 g/ 6 oz) desiccated coconut. Gently melt 60 g (2 oz) copha in a small saucepan. Add to the coconut mixture with ⅔ cup (210 g/7 oz) condensed milk and 2 egg whites. Mix well. Add enough food coloring to turn the coconut pink. Cut 100 g (3½ oz) white marshmallows into quarters and stir into the coconut ice. Spread over the biscuit base and press down firmly so it sticks—the top will look rough. Refrigerate until firm. Makes 20 pieces.

JELLY SLICE

Mix 100 g (3½ oz) melted butter with 250 g (8 oz) crushed plain biscuits. Press into a lined 18 x 28 cm (7 x 11 inch) shallow tin and refrigerate until firm. Dissolve an 85 g (3 oz) packet raspberry jelly crystals in 1 cup (250 ml/8 fl oz) boiling water, stir in ½ cup (125 ml/4 fl oz) cold water and set aside. Dissolve 2 teaspoons gelatine in 1 tablespoon hot water. Beat 400 g (13 oz) condensed milk and ⅓ cup (80 ml/2¾ fl oz) lemon juice for 1 minute, then beat in the gelatine. Spread over the base and refrigerate with the jelly for 30 minutes—the jelly should be syrupy, not set. Pour the jelly over the slice and refrigerate for 3 hours, or until firm. Makes 15 pieces.

CHERRY RIPE SLICE

Mix 250 g (8 oz) crushed plain biscuits with 2 cups (180 g/ 6 oz) desiccated coconut and 300 g (10 oz) chopped red glacé cherries. Melt 125 g (4 oz) butter and add to the mixture with 400 g (13 oz) condensed milk, ½ teaspoon vanilla essence and ¼ teaspoon red food coloring. Mix well. Press evenly into a lined 18 x 28 cm (7 x 11 inch) shallow tin and refrigerate. Melt 200 g (6½ oz) chopped dark chocolate and 60 g (2 oz) butter together until smooth, then spread over the slice and refrigerate until firm. Makes 15 pieces.

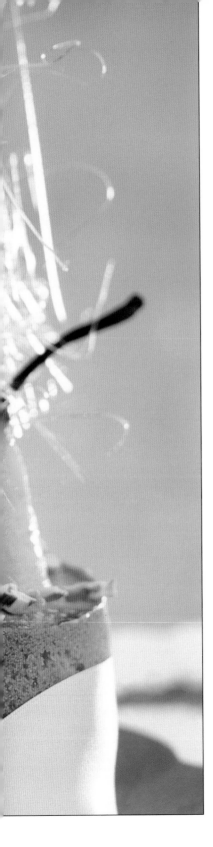

Party Cakes

PEARS WITH A SPUN TOFFEE HALO

Preparation time: 2–2 hours 15 minutes
Total cooking time: 2 hours

one uncooked butter cake mixture. We used the recipe on page 244.

1 cinnamon stick
2 strips lemon rind
1 tablespoon lemon juice
440 g (14 oz) caster sugar
6 beurre bosc or packham pears
3 tablespoons apricot jam
2 tablespoons chopped pecans

1 Put the cinnamon, lemon rind, juice, 1 litre water and half the sugar in a large pan and stir over heat until the sugar has dissolved. Core the pears through the bases with a melon baller, then peel and place in the syrup. Simmer, partly covered, for 10 minutes, or until tender. Remove from heat and leave to cool in the syrup. Drain and leave on paper towel.

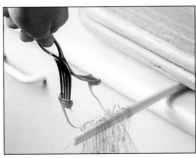

Flick the toffee backwards and forwards over the handle of the wooden spoon.

2 Preheat the oven to 180°C (350°F/ Gas 4). Lightly grease two 23 cm (9 inch) round springform tins and line the bases with baking paper. Divide the mixture between the tins. Arrange pears around the edge of one cake, about 2 cm (1 inch) in from the edge, and press into the mixture. Bake for 40 minutes, or until a skewer inserted into the centre of the plain cake comes out clean. Cook the pear cake for another 40 minutes, or until a skewer inserted in the centre comes out clean. Leave the cakes in their tins for 5 minutes, before removing.

3 Warm the jam, strain and spread some over the plain cake. Sit the pear cake on top, brush with jam and sprinkle with the pecans.

4 For the spun toffee, place sheets of newspaper on the floor where you will be spinning the toffee. Place a wooden spoon on the work surface with its handle over the edge, above the newspaper (weigh the spoon down with a heavy object). Lightly oil the spoon handle. Put a heavy-based pan over medium heat, gradually sprinkle with some of the remaining sugar and, as it melts, sprinkle the rest. Stir to melt lumps and prevent any burning. Meanwhile, run cold water into the sink. When the toffee is golden brown, quickly remove from the heat and place in the water to quickly cool and prevent any burning.

5 Hold two forks back to back and dip in the hot toffee. Carefully flick the toffee backwards and forwards over the handle of the spoon, redipping in the pan as often as necessary—you may need to do this several times. If the toffee gets too thick, warm over low heat. Lift the toffee off the spoon and mould into a large halo shape, about the same width as the top of the pears. Make a couple more halos and place over the pears.

STRIPED CHOCOLATE CURLS

Preparation time: 1 hour 45 minutes
Total cooking time: 20 minutes + cake
   cooking time

one 20 cm (8 inch) round cake. We used the
   chocolate cake recipe on page 247, but
   you could use the butter cake on page
   244 or the mud cake on page 245.

WHITE CHOCOLATE GANACHE
150 g (5 oz) white chocolate melts
130 g (4½ oz) white chocolate
125 ml (4 fl oz) cream
250 g (8 oz) unsalted butter

STRIPED CURLS
150 g (5 oz) each of dark and white
   chocolate melts

CHOCOLATE COLLAR
60 g (2 oz) dark chocolate, chopped
60 g (2 oz) dark chocolate melts

1 To make the ganache, put all the ingredients
in a saucepan. Stir over low heat until melted
and smooth. Transfer to a small bowl, cover the
surface with plastic wrap and cool. Beat the
cooled mixture for 3–5 minutes, or until thick
and creamy.
2 To make the curls, put the dark chocolate
melts in a heatproof bowl. Sit the bowl over a
saucepan of simmering water, making sure the
base does not sit in the water. Stir until the
chocolate has melted. Quickly spread fairly
thinly over a marble board. Drag a fork or a cake
decorating comb through the chocolate. Set at
room temperature unless very warm.

3 Melt the white chocolate melts and spread
over the dark chocolate. Spread firmly to fill all
the gaps. Leave until just set.
4 Using the edge of a sharp knife at a 45°
angle, scrape over the top of the chocolate. The
strips will curl as they come away so don't press
too hard. If the chocolate has set too firmly, the
curls will break: leave in a warm place and try
again.
5 Cut the domed top off the cake to give a flat
surface. Slice the cake horizontally into three
even layers. Sandwich the layers together with
the ganache, leaving enough to spread thinly
over the top and side.
6 To make the collar, measure the height of the
cake and add 5 mm (¼ inch). Cut a strip of
clear contact this wide and long enough to wrap
around the cake with a small overlap. Melt all
the chocolate and spread thinly and evenly over
the shiny side of the contact. Let it set a little,
but you need to be able to bend the paper
without the chocolate cracking. Work quickly:
wrap the contact around the cake with the
chocolate on the inside. Seal the ends and leave
until the chocolate sets completely. Peel away
the contact and pile the chocolate curls on top
of the cake.

STORAGE: The chocolate curls can be stored in
an airtight container for up to 4 days. Don't put
them on the cake until you are ready to serve.
The cake can be iced a day in advance—keep in
the fridge in warm weather, but return to room
temperature before serving.

Drag the comb through the chocolate. If you don't
have a comb, use a fork.

Spread the white chocolate firmly, so that it fills in
the gaps in the dark chocolate.

Use a sharp knife held at an angle to scrape the
curls from the chocolate.

CUSTARD MERINGUE GATEAU

Preparation time: 2 hours 15 minutes
Total cooking time: 15–20 minutes + cake
cooking time

two 23 cm (9 inch) classic sponges. We
used the recipe on page 248.

75 g (2½ oz) caster sugar
300 g (10 oz) raspberries, plus extra to
decorate
90 g (3 oz) flaked almonds, toasted
2 tablespoons apricot jam
fresh raspberries, to serve
icing sugar, to dust

CUSTARD FILLING
2 tablespoons custard powder
2 tablespoons cornflour
55 g (2 oz) caster sugar
1 teaspoon vanilla essence
500 ml (16 fl oz) milk
2 eggs, beaten

MERINGUE TOPPING
4 egg whites
250 g (8 oz) caster sugar

1 Combine the sugar and 160 ml (5½ fl oz)
water in a small saucepan and stir over medium
heat until the sugar has dissolved, then simmer
for 2 minutes. Allow to cool.
2 To make the custard filling, blend the custard
powder, cornflour, sugar and vanilla in a
saucepan with a little of the milk to make a
smooth paste. Stir in the remaining milk and
eggs and mix well. Stir over the heat until the
mixture boils and thickens. Pour into a large
bowl and cover the surface with plastic wrap to
prevent a skin forming. Stir occasionally.

3 Slice the sponges in half horizontally. Place
one layer of sponge on a lined baking tray.
Brush liberally with the cooled sugar syrup. Beat
the custard with a wooden spoon to soften
slightly. Spread a third of the custard over the
cake, scatter with a third of the raspberries, then
top with more cake. Build up the layers,
finishing with a layer of cake. Cover and chill the
cake for at least 1 hour.
4 Preheat the oven to 250°C (500°F/ Gas 10).
Beat the egg whites in a small, dry, clean bowl
until stiff peaks form. Gradually add the sugar,
beating well after each addition until the sugar
has dissolved. Spread a thin layer of meringue
over the top and side of the cake. Press the
almonds all over the side of the cake. Using two
dessertspoons, make small ovals from the
remaining meringue by dipping the spoons
quickly into water, then scooping up some
meringue. Use the second spoon to scoop the
meringue from the first spoon, making an oval.
Scoop gently off the spoon around the edge of
the cake.
5 Bake for 2–3 minutes, or until the meringue
is just brown on the edges. You may need to
turn the cake halfway through cooking to ensure
even browning. Transfer to a serving plate. Heat
the apricot jam in a small saucepan, push
through a strainer and gently brush over the
meringue ovals. Fill the centre of the cake with
fresh raspberries and dust with icing sugar.

STORAGE: The cake can be stored for up to 2
days without the meringue topping. Top with the
meringue on the day of serving.

These meringue ovals, which are also called
quenelles, are shaped using two dessert spoons.

Scoop the meringue off the spoon and arrange
around the edge of the cake.

Use a pastry brush to coat the meringue ovals with
the strained jam glaze.

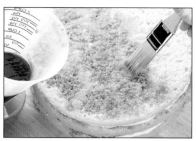

Brush generously with coffee syrup before adding another layer of mascarpone cream.

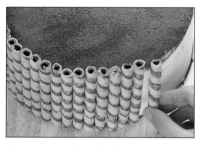

Arrange the chocolate wafer biscuits around the edge of the cake.

GATEAU TIRAMISU

Preparation time: 2 hours
Total cooking time: 10 minutes + cake
  cooking time

two 22 cm (9 inch) génoise sponges. We
  used the recipe on page 246.

190 g (6½ oz) caster sugar
1 tablespoon instant coffee powder
80 ml (2¾ fl oz) Kahlúa
4 egg yolks
500 g (1 lb) mascarpone cheese
300 ml (10 fl oz) thick cream
cocoa powder, to dust
220 g (7 oz) chocolate cream wafers (long
  thin cigar shapes)

1 Put 110 g (3½ oz) of the sugar and the coffee in a small saucepan with 250 ml (8 fl oz) water. Stir over low heat until the sugar has dissolved. Remove from the heat and leave to cool slightly, then stir in the Kahlúa.

2 Using electric beaters, beat the egg yolks and the remaining sugar in a heatproof bowl. Place the bowl over a saucepan of just simmering water, making sure the base does not touch the water. Beat for another 3 minutes, or until the mixture is thick and fluffy and leaves a trail on the surface. Remove from the heat and transfer to a cool clean mixing bowl. Beat for another 3 minutes, or until cool.

3 Gently stir the mascarpone in a large bowl to soften it. Add the egg yolk mixture, then the cream, beating slightly until thick.

4 Carefully slice both cakes in half horizontally. Place a layer of cake on a serving plate or board and brush generously with the coffee syrup. Spread one cake with about a fifth of the mascarpone cream. Top with another round of cake and continue layering with the syrup, mascarpone cream and cake, making sure to

finish with a layer of mascarpone cream. Refrigerate the cake and remaining portion of filling for 1 hour. Dust the top of the cake liberally with cocoa powder and spread the remaining mascarpone cream around the side. Trim the chocolate wafers to stand a little higher than the cake and press gently side-by-side around the cake. Tie a decorative ribbon around the cake and fasten with a large bow.

AHEAD OF TIME: This cake can be stored for a day, covered, in the fridge. Don't decorate with the wafers until ready to serve as they will soften if left to stand.

Remove the cake from the oven after 3 hours and decorate with fruit before baking again.

Dissolve the gelatine in boiling water and brush over the glacé fruit.

GLACE-TOPPED FRUIT CAKE

Preparation time: 50 minutes
Total cooking time: 3 hours 35 minutes

one uncooked fruit cake mixture. We used
the recipe on page 249.

725 g (1½ lb) mixed glacé fruit, roughly
chopped (try a mixture of apricots,
pineapple, ginger and cherries)
3 teaspoons gelatine

1 Preheat the oven to 150°C (300°F/ Gas 2).
Line the base and side of an 18 x 25 cm (7 x 10
inch) deep oval cake tin with two layers of brown
paper and then two layers of baking paper. Wrap
three layers of newspaper around the outside of
the cake tin, tightly securing with string.
2 Spoon the cake mix into the tin and smooth
the surface, using your hand dipped in water. Tap
the tin on the bench several times to remove any
air pockets from the mixture. Place in the oven
on top of several layers of newspaper and bake
for 3 hours, then arrange the glacé fruit over the
top. Bake for another 30 minutes, then cover
loosely with greased foil or baking paper to
prevent the fruit burning, and bake for another
hour, or until a skewer comes out clean when
inserted into the centre of the cake.
3 Put 2 tablespoons boiling water in a bowl and
sprinkle with the gelatine. Leave for 1 minute
until spongy, then stir briskly with a fork to
dissolve. Brush the gelatine over the hot cake,
cover the top with baking paper and wrap in a tea
towel. Cool completely in the tin, then turn out
and tie with a decorative ribbon.

STORAGE: This cake is perfect for making in
advance as it can be stored in an airtight
container for up to a year.

PASSIONFRUIT AND LEMON CURD SPONGE

Preparation time: 1 hour 30 minutes
Total cooking time: 40 minutes + cake cooking time

two 22 cm (9 inch) classic sponge cakes. We used the recipe on page 248.

50 g (1½ oz) white chocolate melts

PASSIONFRUIT TOPPING
185 g (6 oz) passionfruit pulp (see NOTE)
3 tablespoons orange juice
2 tablespoons caster sugar
1 tablespoon cornflour

LEMON CREAM
3 egg yolks
75 g (2½ oz) caster sugar
2 teaspoons finely grated lemon rind
90 ml (3 fl oz) lemon juice
180 g (6 oz) unsalted butter, chopped
300 ml (10 fl oz) thick cream

1 For the passionfruit topping, strain the passionfruit to separate the juice and seeds——you will need 125 ml (4 fl oz) passionfruit juice and 1½ tablespoons of seeds. Put the passionfruit juice, seeds, orange juice and sugar in a small saucepan. In a separate bowl, mix the cornflour with 3 tablespoons water until smooth and then add to the saucepan. Stir constantly over medium heat until the mixture boils and thickens, then pour into a small bowl, lay a sheet of plastic wrap directly on the surface, and refrigerate until cold.

2 Bring a saucepan containing a little water to a simmer, then remove from the heat. Place the chocolate melts in a heatproof bowl, then place the bowl over the saucepan. Make sure the base of the bowl does not sit in the water. Stir the chocolate over the heat until it has completely melted. Spoon the chocolate into a paper piping bag and pipe lattice patterns onto a sheet of baking paper. Leave to set, then peel away the paper.

3 To make the lemon cream, put the yolks and sugar in a jug and beat well. Strain into a heatproof bowl and add the lemon rind, juice and butter. Place the bowl over a saucepan of simmering water, making sure the base does not touch the water. Stir constantly for 20 minutes, or until the mixture thickens enough to coat the back of a wooden spoon. Cool the lemon curd completely before folding into the thick cream. Beat until the mixture has the texture of thick sour cream.

4 Slice each cake in half horizontally and place one cake layer onto a serving plate. Spread with a quarter of the lemon cream, then top with another cake layer. Repeat with the remaining lemon cream and cake, finishing with a layer of lemon cream. Use a fork to roughly spread the cream.

5 Stir the passionfruit topping slightly to make it pourable and, if necessary, add a little orange juice to thin it. Pour the topping evenly over the cake, allowing it to run down the side. Stand the chocolate lattices on top.

AHEAD OF TIME: The lemon curd and passionfruit topping can be stored for up to 3 days. Assemble the cake an hour before serving, and don't pour over the topping until ready to serve.
NOTE: You will need 6–8 fresh passionfruit for the topping.

Spoon the melted white chocolate into a piping bag and pipe lattice patterns.

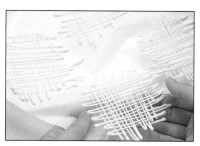

Once the chocolate lattice have set, gently peel away the backing paper.

Sprinkle the caster sugar over the petals, then shake off any excess.

Press a layer of petals around the base of the cake then overlap the layers upwards.

ROSE PETAL CAKE

Preparation time: 2 hours 30 minutes +
1–2 hours drying time
Total cooking time: 10–15 minutes + cake
cooking time

one cake made in a 2-litre charlotte tin. We used the butter cake recipe on page 244, but you could use the chocolate cake on page 247.

1 bunch pale pink roses
3 white roses
1 egg white
caster sugar, to coat

MERINGUE FROSTING
3 egg whites
165 g (5½ oz) caster sugar
250 g (8 oz) unsalted butter

1 Line two or three large trays with paper towel. Carefully separate the rose petals, discarding any that are very small or blemished. Lightly whisk the egg white until just foamy. Spread the caster sugar on a large plate. Use a small brush to paint the egg white lightly over each petal—make sure the entire petal is coated, but not too heavily. Sprinkle the petals with caster sugar, gently shake off the excess and put the petals on the tray to dry. Leave them for at least 1 or 2 hours. The drying time may vary according to the weather and the humidity.

2 To make the meringue frosting, put the egg whites and sugar in a heatproof bowl. Place the bowl over a saucepan of simmering water, making sure the base does not touch the water. Stir constantly to dissolve the sugar, but be careful not to cook the egg whites.

3 When the sugar has dissolved, remove the bowl from over the saucepan and beat the mixture with electric beaters for 3–5 minutes, or until stiff peaks form. Cut the butter into about 10 pieces and add, piece by piece, beating after each addition. The mixture should thicken when

you have about 2 pieces of butter left, but continue until you have added all of it.

4 Place the cake on a serving plate. Spread the frosting evenly over the cake, as smoothly as possible. Starting from the base, press a layer of pink rose petals around the cake. Start the next layer slightly overlapping the first and continue working up towards the top of the cake. In the final few layers, alternate white petals with the pink. The cake should look like an open flower from the top.

AHEAD OF TIME: This cake can be decorated up to a day in advance as long as the rose petals are dry. Store in a cool dark place in an airtight container.

Remove the rind from the sugar syrup when it is bright and transparent.

Turn the cake upside down on a wire rack and smooth the icing over the top.

CANDIED CITRUS CAKE

Preparation time: 1 hour
Total cooking time: 15 minutes + cake
  cooking time

one butter cake. We used the recipe on page 244 and made the cake in a 2-litre charlotte tin.

CANDIED RIND
2 oranges
2 tangelos
2 lemons
2 limes
310 g (10 oz) caster sugar

LEMON ICING
125 g (4 oz) icing sugar
20 g (³/₄ oz) butter, melted
1-2 tablespoons lemon juice

1 To make the candied rind, use a vegetable peeler to peel the rind from the fruit. Use a sharp knife to remove any pith (the bitter white layer of flesh just inside the rind). Cut the rind into long thin strips.
2 Put the sugar in a saucepan with 125 ml (4 fl oz) water and stir over low heat until completely dissolved. Bring to the boil, reduce the heat slightly, then add the rind in batches. Simmer each batch for 3–5 minutes, or until the rind is bright and transparent. Remove the rind with tongs and drain on a wire rack until cold.
3 To make the icing, put the icing sugar and butter in a small bowl. Mix in the lemon juice gradually, until the icing is just pourable but not too runny.
4 Use a serrated knife to cut the dome from the top of the cake to level the surface. Turn the cake upside down on a wire rack and smooth the icing over the top of the cake, allowing it to run down the side, but not completely cover the side. Leave the icing to set. Transfer the cake to a serving plate or stand and pile the candied rind on top of the cake.

AHEAD OF TIME: The cake can be kept, refrigerated, for 2 days after decorating. The candied rind can be stored for up to 3 days in an airtight container. Place in a single layer between sheets of baking paper. Refrigerate in hot weather.

SPOTTED COLLAR CAKE

Preparation time: 1 hour 15 minutes
Total cooking time: 10–15 minutes + cake
cooking time

one 18 x 25 cm (7 x 10 inch) oval cake. We
used the mud cake recipe on page 245,
but you could use the butter cake on page
244 or the chocolate cake on page 247.

cocoa powder, to dust

COFFEE BUTTERCREAM
2 tablespoons cream
75 g (2¹/₂ oz) white chocolate melts
100 g (3¹/₂ oz) unsalted butter, chopped
40 g (1¹/₄ oz) icing sugar
1 teaspoon instant coffee powder

COLLAR
30 g (1 oz) white chocolate melts
30 g (1 oz) milk chocolate melts
60 g (2 oz) dark chocolate melts
60 g (2 oz) dark chocolate

1 Cut the dome off the top of the cake to level
the surface. Turn the cake upside down on a
board so that the flat base becomes the top.
Measure the height of the cake. Cut a strip of
contact this wide, and long enough to wrap
around the cake.

2 To make the coffee buttercream, put the
cream and chocolate melts in a small heatproof
bowl. Place the bowl over a saucepan of
simmering water, making sure the base does
not touch the water. Remove the saucepan from
the heat and stir the chocolate until melted.
Beat the butter until light and creamy, then
gradually beat in the icing sugar until thick and
white. Beat in the cooled melted chocolate until
the mixture is thick and fluffy. In a cup, dissolve
the coffee powder in a teaspoon of hot water
and beat into the buttercream.

3 Spread the buttercream evenly over the top
and side of the cake. In warm weather you could
refrigerate the cake for 10–15 minutes to firm
the buttercream a little.

4 To make the collar, put the white and milk
chocolate melts in separate heatproof bowls and
melt as above. Alternatively, melt in the
microwave for 1 minute on high, stirring after 30
seconds. Spoon the melted chocolate into
separate paper piping bags. Pipe large and small
dots of chocolate over the shiny side of the
contact. Gently tap the contact on the bench to
flatten the dots and then leave them to set.

5 Melt the dark chocolate melts and dark
chocolate together, then cool slightly. Working
quickly, spread evenly over the entire strip of
contact, over the top of the dots. Be careful not
to press too hard or the dots may lift off the
surface. Leave to set a little, but you need to be
able to bend the strip without it cracking.
Quickly wrap the strip around the cake, making
sure the chocolate is on the inside. Seal the
ends of the contact and set aside in a cool place
or the fridge until set. Carefully peel the contact
from the collar and dust the cake with the cocoa
powder.

AHEAD OF TIME: You can decorate the cake and
keep it in the fridge for several hours before
serving. Don't attempt the chocolate collar on a
very hot day—you may find it too soft to work
with.

Melt the dark chocolate and spread all over the
contact, over the dots.

Wrap the collar around the cake with the chocolate
on the inside.

Once the chocolate has set, gently peel away the
strip of contact.

BOXES OF GIFTS

Preparation time: 4 hours–4 hours 30 minutes
Total cooking time: 5 minutes + cake cooking time

one 12 cm (5 inch) square and one 25 cm (10 inch) square fruit cake from the recipe on page 249 plus one 16 cm (6½ inch) square and one 30 cm (12 inch) square mud cake from the recipe on page 245.

80 g (2¾ oz) apricot jam
9 x 500 g (1 lb) packets ready-made soft icing
pure icing sugar, to dust
assorted food colorings
1 egg white

1 Cut three cardboard squares the same size as the three smaller cakes. Trim the tops off the cakes so they are similar heights. Invert the cakes onto the cardboard and place the largest on a covered cake board. Warm the jam, strain and brush over the cakes.
2 Knead 3½ packets of the icing on a work surface dusted with icing sugar. Tint the icing pale pink. Roll out the icing to about 5 mm (¼ inch) thick and large enough to cover the largest cake, dusting the bench and rolling pin with icing sugar to prevent sticking. Use a little icing to fill in any holes in the cake, to ensure an even surface. Roll the icing over the rolling pin and re-roll over the top of the cake. Gently press over the cake, using the palms of your hands dusted with icing sugar. Smooth and trim any excess. Add more pink coloring to the leftover icing to tint it darker pink and wrap in plastic.

3 Insert four skewers into the cake to support the layers (see NOTE). Knead 2½ packets of the icing and tint pale blue. Roll out to cover the 25 cm (10 inch) cake. Tint the leftover icing darker blue. Repeat the process with the skewers.
4 Knead 1½ packets of icing and tint it pale yellow to cover the 16 cm (6½ inch) cake. Keep a little pale icing and tint the rest darker. Repeat the process with the skewers.
5 Knead 1 packet of the icing and tint pale orange to cover the smallest cake. Tint the leftover icing darker orange.
6 Place the cakes on top of each other. Roll the darker icing out on an icing sugar dusted surface to about 3 mm (⅛ inch) thick. Cut small hearts from the pink icing and stick onto the pink cake with a little egg white. Cut strips from the blue icing and stick onto the blue cake. Using a cutter or knife, cut daisy shapes from the dark yellow icing and stick onto the yellow cake–cut small rounds from the pale yellow icing for the centres. Stick small dots of dark orange icing to the orange cake. Re-roll the remaining dark orange icing and cut into strips 3 cm (1¼ inch) wide. Stick to the cake to form a flat ribbon. Re-roll the remaining icing and cut two strips. Trim the ends as shown (see step photograph), fold in half and support with cotton wool. Wrap a small strip of icing over the centre of the join for the centre of the bow. Place in the centre of the 'ribbon'. Remove the cotton wool when set.

Cut strips of dark orange icing, then trim the corners and fold in half.

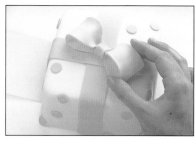

Wrap a small strip of icing over the centre of the join to make a bow.

FLOODWORK FLOWERS

Preparation time: 1 hour 30 minutes –2 hours
Total cooking time: 5 minutes + cake cooking time

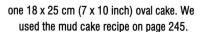

one 18 x 25 cm (7 x 10 inch) oval cake. We used the mud cake recipe on page 245.

FLOODWORK FLOWERS
1 egg white
250 g (8 oz) pure icing sugar
3 teaspoons lemon juice
assorted food colorings

WHITE CHOCOLATE BUTTERCREAM
80 ml (2¾ fl oz) cream
150 g (5 oz) white chocolate melts
200 g (6½ oz) unsalted butter
80 g (2¾ oz) icing sugar

1 To make the flowers, lightly beat the egg white with a wooden spoon. Gradually add the sifted icing sugar and beat to a smooth paste. Gradually add 2 teaspoons lemon juice until the mixture has a slightly stiff piping consistency. Cover the surface with plastic wrap to stop it drying out.

2 Draw 16 simple flowers on a sheet of paper and tape this to a flat work surface. Tape a sheet of baking paper over the top of the drawing sheet. Using a 1 mm piping nozzle, pipe carefully over the outlines. Remove the baking paper sheet and set aside to dry. Repeat with a second sheet of baking paper.

3 Gradually add more lemon juice to the icing until it is slightly thinner and will spread smoothly. Divide the icing into four bowls and add a different color to each (keep the bowls covered or the icing will dry out quickly). Using paper piping bags, pipe the icing inside the flower outlines. Place the sheets on baking trays and dry overnight.

4 To make the buttercream, bring a little water in a saucepan to a simmer and remove from the heat. Put the cream and chocolate in a heatproof bowl and place over the saucepan, making sure the bowl does not touch the water. Stir until smooth, then allow to cool slightly. Beat the butter until light and creamy, then slowly beat in the icing sugar until thick and white. Beat in the cool chocolate mixture.

5 Cut the dome off the cake and put the cake upside down on a serving plate. Spread two thirds of the buttercream over the cake, smoothing the surface. Carefully lift the flowers off the baking paper with a palette knife (be very careful as they break easily). Press the flowers around the top edge of the cake, so they stand up slightly higher than the cake. Arrange the remainder in a bunch in the centre.

6 Tint some of the remaining buttercream pink and the rest green. Using a paper piping bag, pipe green stems down from the flowers on the side of the cake and from the bunch in the centre. To make pointed leaves, cut the tip of the bag into a 'v', press firmly, then pull away. Pipe a pink bow in the middle of the bunch of flowers.

AHEAD OF TIME: The cake will keep for 3 days after icing. The flowers can be made up to a week in advance. Once dry, store them in a single layer in an airtight container.

With the thicker, colored icing fill in the petals and centres of the flowers.

Cut a 'v' in the tip of the piping bag to make pointed leaves on the stems.

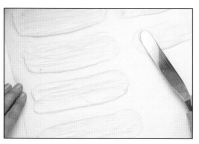

Spread the melted white chocolate in strips over a sheet of baking paper.

Break the end of each strip of chocolate, to give a flat base to stand it up on.

SWEET FIG AND CHOCOLATE CAKE

Preparation time: 1 hour
Total cooking time: 5 minutes + cake
**   cooking time**

one 20 cm (8 inch) round cake. We used the
    butter cake recipe on page 244, but you
    could use the mud cake on page 245 or
    the chocolate cake on page 247.

BUTTERCREAM
250 g (8 oz) unsalted butter
125 g (4 oz) icing sugar, sifted
1 teaspoon vanilla essence
2 teaspoons milk

Kirsch or other fruit-based liqueur
4 tablespoons raspberry jam
300 g (10 oz) white chocolate melts

5 fresh figs, quartered

1 To make the buttercream, beat the butter with
electric beaters until light and creamy. Gradually
add the icing sugar alternately with the vanilla
essence and milk, beating until smooth and
fluffy.
2 Use a serrated knife to slice the cake
horizontally into three even layers. Place the
bottom layer on a board or plate. Brush with a
little liqueur and spread with half the jam.
Spread with a thin layer of buttercream. Place
another cake layer on top and repeat the layers.
Top with the remaining cake layer, and spread
the rest of the buttercream evenly over the cake.
3 Put the white chocolate melts in a heatproof
bowl. Place the bowl over a saucepan of
simmering water, making sure the base does not
sit in the water. Remove the saucepan from the
heat and stir until the chocolate has melted.
4 Spread the melted chocolate in 5 x 11 cm
(2 x 5 inch) strips over a sheet of baking paper.
Leave to set completely before removing from
the paper—you will need about 20 of these

shapes but make a few extra in case of
breakages. Break one end of each strip or trim
with a knife to give a flat base, then stand them
upright around the edge of the cake, slightly
overlapping. Arrange the fresh fig quarters
around the edge.

AHEAD OF TIME: This cake can be decorated up
to 2 days in advance, but add the figs
immediately before serving. Keep in a cool dark
place in an airtight container or in the fridge
during warm weather.

For the icing to pour over the cake, whisk the egg white, then add lemon and icing sugar.

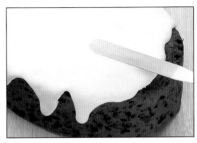

Smooth the icing over the cake, allowing it to run slowly down the side.

CHRISTMAS FROSTED FRUITS

Preparation time: 1 hour 20 minutes + drying time

one 18 x 25 cm (7 x 10 inch) oval fruit cake (page 249)

selection of seasonal fruits such as white and dark cherries, red or white currants, blackcurrants, apricots or
tiny plums or pears
1 egg white
caster sugar

ICING
1 egg white
1-3 teaspoons lemon juice
125 g (4 oz) pure icing sugar, sifted

1 Wash the fruit and make sure it is completely dry before starting. Line a tray with paper towel. Place the egg white in a shallow bowl and whisk until just foamy. Put some caster sugar on a large plate. Work with one piece of fruit at a time, except for the berries which can be sugared in small bunches. Brush the whisked egg white lightly over the fruit, making sure the entire piece of fruit is covered but not too heavily.

2 Sprinkle the sugar over the fruit and shake off any excess, then leave on the tray to dry. The drying time will depend on the humidity. Always frost more fruit than you need, so you have a good selection to choose from when arranging over the cake.

3 To make the icing, whisk the egg white in a shallow bowl until just foamy. Beat in 1 teaspoon of the lemon juice until well combined. Add the sifted icing sugar gradually, beating well after each addition. The icing should be thick and white–add a little more of the lemon juice if necessary, but be careful not to make it too runny.

4 Place the cake on a serving plate or stand. Working quickly, pour the icing over the top. Using a palette knife, carefully smooth the icing to the edge of the cake, allowing it to run slowly down the side. Leave the cake to stand for 10 minutes to let the icing set a little. Carefully arrange the frosted fruits on top of the cake.

AHEAD OF TIME: The fruits can be frosted several hours in advance.
NOTE: It is best to wash the fruit beforehand and leave to dry for several hours before frosting.

STRIPED CAKE WITH MANGO

Preparation time: 1 hour 30 minutes
Total cooking time: 5–8 minutes plus cake
cooking time

two 22 cm (9 inch) round classic sponge
cakes. We used the recipe on page 248.

SPONGE COLLAR
3 eggs, separated
135 g (4¹/₂ oz) caster sugar
¹/₂ cup (60 g/2 oz) self-raising flour
¹/₄ cup (30 g/1oz) cornflour
30 g (1 oz) butter, melted
1¹/₂ tablespoons cocoa powder

CHANTILLY CREAM
2¹/₂ cups (600 ml/20 fl oz) cream
2 teaspoons vanilla essence
¹/₄ cup (30 g/1 oz) icing sugar

icing sugar, to dust
2 mangoes

1 Preheat the oven to 180°C (350°F/ Gas 4). To
make the sponge collar you will need to make
three lengths of striped sponge to wrap around
the cake (you would need a very long baking
tray to make the collar in one section). Draw
three sets of two parallel lines 28 cm (11
inches) long and 7 cm (3 inches) apart on a
piece of baking paper and place upside down
on a baking tray. You might need to use two or
three separate baking trays, depending on their
size. Beat the egg whites in a clean, dry mixing
bowl until stiff peaks form. Gradually add the
sugar, beating well after each addition until the
sugar has dissolved and the mixture is glossy.
Beat in the egg yolks. Using a metal spoon, fold
in the combined sifted flours and butter until the
mixture is smooth. Divide the mixture between
two mixing bowls and fold the sifted cocoa into
one.

2 Place the plain half of the sponge mixture into
a piping bag fitted with a 1 cm (¹/₂ inch) nozzle.
On the baking paper, pipe lines at 1 cm (¹/₂ inch)
intervals between the three sets of parallel
pencil lines on the baking paper. Spoon the
cocoa sponge mixture into a second bag and
pipe between the white sponge lines. Bake for
5–8 minutes, or until the sponge is lightly
browned. Leave the striped sponge on the trays
to cool. You should have three striped sponge
strips.

3 To make the chantilly cream, place the cream,
vanilla essence and icing sugar in a large mixing
bowl. Beat the mixture until well combined and
soft peaks form.

4 Use a large serrated knife to slice each
sponge in half horizontally. Sandwich together
three layers of the sponge cake with the chantilly
cream, reserving some for the top and side.
(There will be one layer of the cake left over, but
it can be frozen or used for cake crumbs later.)
Place the assembled cake layers on a serving
plate. Trim one edge of each striped sponge
collar to make them the same height as the
cake. Cover the side of the cake with a thin layer
of the chantilly cream and spread the remainder
on top. Carefully place the sponge collars
around the side of the cake, placing the flat side
against the cake and the cut edge at the base.

5 Peel the mangoes and cut into slices. Dust
icing sugar over the top of the cake, then
decorate as desired with the mango slices.
Serve immediately.

STORAGE: This cake is best served on the day it
is made.

Pipe the chocolate sponge mixture between the
plain sponge rows.

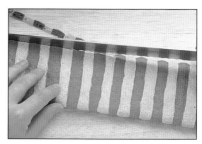

Trim the edge of the striped collar to make it the
same height as the cake.

SUGARED ROSES

Preparation time: 1 hour 30 minutes + drying time
Total cooking time: 5 minutes plus cake cooking time

one 22 cm (9 inch) round butter cake. We used the recipe on page 244.

WHITE CHOCOLATE GANACHE
150 g (5 oz) white chocolate melts
130 g (4¹/₂ oz) white chocolate, chopped
¹/₂ cup (125 ml/4 fl oz) cream
250 g (8 oz) unsalted butter, chopped

2 bunches roses
1 egg white
caster sugar, to coat

1 To make the ganache, put all the ingredients in a pan and stir over low heat until melted and smooth. Transfer the mixture to a small mixing bowl, cover the surface with plastic wrap and leave to cool completely. Do not refrigerate. Beat cooled mixture with electric beaters for about 3–5 minutes, or until thick, pale and creamy.

2 Line two large trays with paper towel. To sugar the roses, firstly make sure there is no water trapped between the petals as this will prevent the sugar hardening and may make the roses limp. If you are preparing the roses the day before, leave the stems on and put them back in water after sugaring so they will stay fresh. You will need to pull the petals from one of the roses. Choose some leaves also and set them aside.

3 Place the egg white in a bowl and whisk lightly until just foamy. Put the caster sugar on a large plate. With a small brush, lightly paint a rose petal with the beaten egg white. Make sure the entire petal is coated, but not too heavily. Sprinkle the sugar over the petal until completely coated, then shake lightly to remove excess sugar and put the petal on the tray. Repeat until all the petals and leaves are coated.

4 Carefully brush the whole roses with the beaten egg white, making sure to brush between some of the petals. Sprinkle with the sugar and shake off any excess. Stand the rose in a jar of water, making sure the sugared area doesn't get wet.

5 Leave the sugared roses, petals and leaves to dry for at least an hour. Drying time will vary depending on the humidity.

6 Place the cake on a serving plate and spread with ganache, making swirls with a flat-bladed knife. Trim the rose stems and arrange the roses and leaves on top. Scatter the sugared petals over.

NOTE: If you are using carrot cake, you might prefer to use a cream cheese frosting rather than the ganache. Simply beat 375 g (12¹/₂ oz) cream cheese and 75 g (2¹/₂ oz) softened butter with electric beaters until smooth and creamy. Gradually beat in 90 g (3 oz) sifted icing sugar and 1 teaspoon vanilla essence until thick and creamy.
The cake can be decorated up to 5 hours in advance. In hot weather, decorate just prior to serving. The roses can be sugared the day before.

Sprinkle the sugar over the petal, then shake to remove the excess.

Brush over and between the petals with egg white, then sprinkle with sugar.

As the sugar melts, sprinkle more sugar on top of it, stirring to melt the lumps.

Drizzle the toffee in circles over the lined baking tray and leave to set.

TOFFEE CIRCLES

Preparation time: 1 hour
Total cooking time: 5–10 minutes plus cake
cooking time

four 9 cm (3½ inch) round butter cakes. We used the recipe on page 244.

CREAM CHEESE FROSTING
375 g (13 oz) cream cheese
75 g (2½ oz) unsalted butter
¾ cup (90 g/3 oz) icing sugar, sifted
1 teaspoon vanilla essence

100 g (3½ oz) caster sugar
ground nutmeg, to dust

1 To make the frosting, beat the cream cheese and butter with electric beaters until smooth and creamy. Gradually beat in the icing sugar and vanilla essence, beating until thick and creamy. Spread the frosting over the top and sides of each cake.

2 To make the toffee, place a heavy-based saucepan over medium heat, gradually sprinkle with some of the caster sugar and, as it melts, sprinkle with the remaining sugar. Stir to melt any lumps and prevent the sugar burning. When the toffee is golden brown, remove the pan from the heat. Line a baking tray with foil. Using a metal spoon, drizzle 4 toffee circles on the tray, then leave until the toffee has set completely.

3 Sprinkle the top of each cake with nutmeg. Arrange a toffee circle on each cake just before serving.

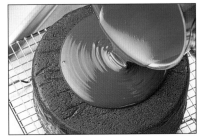

Pour the chocolate glaze over the cake, letting it run down to cover the side.

Remove pieces of gold leaf from the sheet with tweezers and decorate the cake.

GOLD LEAF CAKE

Preparation time: 30 minutes
**Total cooking time: 5 minutes + cake
    cooking time**

one 20 cm (8 inch) round cake. We used the
    mud cake recipe on page 245, but you
    could use chocolate cake on page 247.

DARK CHOCOLATE GLAZE
250 g (8 oz) dark chocolate, roughly
    chopped
125 g (4 oz) unsalted butter, chopped
2 teaspoons glycerine
2 teaspoons light corn syrup

24 carat edible gold leaf (see NOTES)

1 Use a serrated knife to cut the dome off the top of the cake and level the surface. Turn the cake upside down on a wire rack so that the flat base of the cake becomes the top. Stand the wire rack on a tray to catch any glaze that may drip.
2 To make the dark chocolate glaze, put the chocolate, butter, glycerine and corn syrup in a small saucepan. Stir over low heat until melted and smooth.
3 Pour the chocolate glaze over the cake, allowing it to completely cover the side. Leave on the wire rack in a cool place until the glaze has set completely, then carefully lift onto a serving plate or cake board. Use tweezers or a small brush to remove the gold leaf from the sheets and stick randomly over the cake. If the gold leaf won't at first stick, dab a little egg white onto the glaze first, then carefully stick the gold leaf to it.

STORAGE: The cake can be decorated up to 3 days in advance and stored in an airtight container in the fridge. Make sure you allow enough time for the cake to return to room temperature before serving.
NOTES: Edible gold leaf is available from art supply shops and some cake decorating shops. You will need 1–2 sheets for this recipe. You might need to buy several sheets in a pack, but it will keep indefinitely. The chocolate glaze may also be made in a microwave oven. Place all the ingredients in a heatproof bowl and melt on high for 1–2 minutes. Stir the glaze at 30-second intervals until smooth.

LEMON CURD MERINGUE CAKE

Preparation time: 1 hour 30 minutes + 2 hours refrigeration
Total cooking time: 2 hours 30 minutes

two 22 cm (9 inch) round gènoise sponges. We used the recipe on page 246.

4 egg whites
220 g (7 oz) caster sugar
pink food coloring
40 g (1¼ oz) flaked almonds
1 cup (250 ml/8 fl oz) thick cream
icing sugar, to dust

LEMON SYRUP
110 g (3½ oz) caster sugar
3 tablespoons lemon juice

LEMON CURD
5 egg yolks
150 g (5 oz) caster sugar
1 tablespoon grated lemon rind
⅔ cup (170 ml/5½ fl oz) lemon juice
180 g (6 oz) unsalted butter, chopped

1 Preheat the oven to 120°C (250°F/ Gas ½). Cover four oven trays with non-stick baking paper. Mark a 21 cm (8½ inch) circle on three pieces of the baking paper and turn over. Place the egg whites in a mixing bowl and beat until soft peaks form. Gradually add the sugar, beating well after each addition, until the mixture is smooth and glossy. Add a few drops of food coloring until the meringue mixture is pale pink. Spoon a quarter of the meringue mixture into a piping bag fitted with a 1 cm (½ inch) plain nozzle. Pipe strips at 1.5 cm (⅝ inch) intervals along the length of the unmarked tray and sprinkle with the almonds. Spread the remaining meringue over the circles marked on the trays (they will spread slightly during cooking). Bake in two batches for 1 hour each and then turn the oven off and leave the meringues to cool with the door ajar. Break each strip into three pieces and store in an airtight container for up to 2 days, until required.

2 For the lemon syrup, put the sugar and lemon juice in a small pan with 3 tablespoons water and stir over a medium heat until the sugar has dissolved. Leave to cool.

3 To make the lemon curd, beat the egg yolks and sugar in a jug and strain into a heatproof bowl. Add the lemon rind, juice and butter and place the bowl over a pan of barely simmering water, making sure the bowl does not sit in the water. Stir over the heat for 20 minutes, or until the mixture thickens enough to coat the back of a spoon. Cool slightly then cover the surface with plastic wrap and leave until completely cold.

4 Cut the cakes in half horizontally. Place one layer on a plate, brush with the syrup and spread with a thin layer of lemon curd. Top with a round of meringue, trimming the edge to fit. Spread with lemon curd and top with another layer of cake. Repeat the layers, finishing with the last round of cake and syrup. Chill for several hours to soften the meringue.

5 Beat the cream into stiff peaks and spread over the cake. Pile the meringue fingers on the top and dust liberally with icing sugar.

STORAGE: Ideally, make this cake a day in advance so that the meringue layers will have time to soften. However, the decorated cake will not keep for longer than 2 days.

Stir the lemon curd over the heat for 20 minutes, or until it coats the back of a spoon.

Spread the cake with a layer of lemon curd, then top with a meringue circle.

DAISY CAKE

Preparation time: 2 hours + drying time
Total cooking time: 5–10 minutes + cake
** cooking time**

two 20 cm (8 inch) round butter cakes. We
  used the recipe on page 244.

1 bunch of yellow daisies
1 egg white
caster sugar
3 tablespoons jam of your choice
yellow and green food coloring

MERINGUE FROSTING
3 egg whites
$^2/_3$ cup (160 g/5$^1/_2$ oz) caster sugar
250 g (8 oz) unsalted butter

1 To frost the daisies, place the egg white in a
shallow bowl and whisk until just foamy. Put
some caster sugar on a large plate. Line a tray
with paper towel. Trim the stalks from the
daisies, making sure they are dry and
unblemished. Working with one flower at a time,
brush the egg white lightly over and between
the petals, making sure the flower is completely
coated but not too heavily. Sprinkle over the
caster sugar, shake off any excess and dry on
the lined tray. It could take up to an hour to dry
depending on the humidity. It is very difficult to
sugar flowers successfully if the weather is
humid.

2 To make the meringue frosting, put the egg
whites and sugar in a heatproof bowl. Bring a
small pan of water to a simmer, remove from the
heat and place the bowl over the pan, making
sure the bowl doesn't sit in the water. Stir
continuously to dissolve the sugar, but be
careful not to cook the egg whites.
3 When the sugar has dissolved, remove from
the heat and beat with electric beaters for 3–5
minutes, or until stiff peaks form. Cut the butter
into about 10 pieces and add, piece by piece,
beating well after each addition. The mixture
should thicken when you have about two pieces
of butter left, but continue until you have added
it all.
4 Using a serrated knife, trim the domed tops
from the cakes to give a flat surface. Place one
cake, upside down, on a serving plate or cake
board and spread jam over the top. Place the
second cake on top. Set aside 3 tablespoons of
the frosting. Add a few drops of yellow food
coloring to the remaining frosting until it is a
very pale egg yellow. Spread the frosting evenly
over the cake, using a palette or flat-bladed knife
to make faint furrows up the side of the cake.
5 Add the green food coloring to the reserved
frosting until it is light green then spoon into a
small icing bag fitted with a small plain nozzle.
Pipe flower stems over the cake and attach a
sugared daisy to the end of each stem. Snip a 'v'
into the end of the piping bag to pipe little
leaves onto the stems. Remove the daisies
before eating!

NOTE: This cake can be decorated several hours
in advance if kept in a cool, dry place. Sugared
flowers do not keep well, so should be prepared
on the day and, if necessary, kept in an airtight
container in a cool dry place.

Using a flat-bladed knife, spread the frosting over
the cake and make furrows up the side.

Use the pale green frosting to pipe flower stems
over the cake then add sugared daisies.

TRIPLE TRUFFLE CAKE

Preparation time: 1 hour 30 minutes + 45 minutes refrigeration
Total cooking time: 20 minutes + cake cooking time

one 22 cm (9 inch) round cake. We used the chocolate cake recipe on page 247 but you could use the mud cake on page 245.

CHOCOLATE GLAZE
1²/₃ cups (250 g/8 oz) dark chocolate, chopped
¹/₂ cup (125 ml/4 fl oz) cream
165 g (5¹/₂ oz) sugar

TRUFFLES
300 g (10 oz) Madeira cake crumbs
2 tablespoons jam
¹/₄ cup (60 ml/2 fl oz) cream
60 g (2 oz) unsalted butter, melted
2 cups (300 g/10 oz) milk or dark chocolate, melted
2 tablespoons rum
1 cup (150 g/5 oz) each of white, milk and dark compound chocolate
1 egg white
24 carat edible gold leaf (see NOTE)

1 Cut the dome off the cake to give a flat surface. Turn the cake upside down on a rack and place over a tray to catch the glaze that runs over.
2 To make the glaze, put the chocolate, cream and sugar in a pan and stir over low heat until smooth. Bring to the boil, then reduce the heat and simmer for 4–5 minutes, stirring occasionally. Remove from the heat and stir gently, to cool a little.
3 Pour the glaze over the cake, letting it run evenly down the side. Tap the tray on the bench to level the surface. Leave to set completely.

4 Line a baking tray with baking paper or foil. To make the truffles, mix together the cake crumbs, jam, cream, butter, melted chocolate and rum, stirring until moistened. Refrigerate for 20–30 minutes, or until firm. Roll teaspoons of the mixture into balls and place on the tray. Refrigerate for 10–15 minutes, or until firm.
5 Line three trays with baking paper or foil. Place the white chocolate in a heatproof bowl. Bring a small pan of water to a simmer, remove from the heat and place the bowl over the pan, making sure it doesn't sit in the water. Stir the chocolate until melted. Repeat with the milk and dark chocolate.
6 Using a fork, dip the truffles in the different chocolates, tapping gently on the edge of the bowl to drain away the excess. Dip a third of the truffles in the white chocolate, a third in the milk and the rest in the dark. Leave on the baking trays to set. Make sure the chocolate is not too hot, or the truffles may melt and the chocolate discolor. If you find the chocolate too thick, melt and add 15 g (¹/₂ oz) copha (white vegetable shortening).
7 Dab a spot of egg white onto the dark chocolate truffles, then remove the gold leaf from the sheet with tweezers and press onto the egg white. Put the cake on a serving plate and pile the truffles on top.

STORAGE: The cake can be glazed up to a day in advance. Pile with the truffles just prior to serving (use a little melted chocolate to stick them to the cake). The truffles can be kept for 2–3 days in an airtight container in a cool, dry place.
NOTE: Edible gold leaf is available from art supply shops and some cake decorating shops. You will need 1–2 sheets for this recipe. You might need to buy several sheets in a pack, but it will keep indefinitely.

Place the glaze ingredients in a pan and stir until smooth before bringing to the boil.

Pour the glaze over the cake, letting it run down to completely cover the side.

CONTINENTAL WEDDING CAKE

Preparation time: 2 hours 30 minutes + refrigeration
Total cooking time: 20 minutes + cake cooking time

one 18 cm (7 inch) and one 25 cm (10 inch) gènoise sponge. We used the recipe on page 246.

WHITE CHOCOLATE GANACHE
1 cup (150 g/5 oz) white chocolate melts
135 g (4¹/₂ oz) white chocolate
¹/₂ cup (125 ml/4 fl oz) cream
250 g (8 oz) unsalted butter

CUSTARD FILLING
75 g (2¹/₂ oz) cornflour
¹/₂ cup (60 g/2 oz) custard powder
²/₃ cup (160 g/5¹/₂ oz) caster sugar
2 teaspoons vanilla essence
1¹/₂ cups (375 ml/12 fl oz) cream
2 cups (500 ml/16 fl oz) milk
2 egg yolks

³/₄ cup (185 ml/6 fl oz) Cointreau
2 cups (300 g/10 oz) white chocolate melts, melted
²/₃ cup (160 g/5¹/₂ oz) sugar

1 To make the ganache, put all the ingredients in a saucepan and stir over low heat until smooth. Transfer to a bowl, cover with plastic wrap and leave until cooled–don't refrigerate. Beat for 3–5 minutes, or until the mixture is light and fluffy.

2 To make the custard filling, put the cornflour, custard, sugar and vanilla essence in a pan. Gradually add the cream and milk, whisking until smooth. Stir over low heat until coming to the boil. Reduce the heat and simmer for 3 minutes. Remove from the heat and quickly stir in the egg yolks. Transfer to a bowl, cover with plastic wrap and refrigerate for 30 minutes, stirring occasionally.

3 With a serrated knife, slice each cake horizontally into three layers. Put the bottom layer of the large cake on a plate. Brush with Cointreau and spread with a third of the custard filling. Top with another layer of cake, Cointreau and custard. Brush the underside of the top layer of the cake with Cointreau and place on top. Cover with two-thirds of the ganache.

4 Place the bottom layer of the small cake on top of the larger cake. Brush with Cointreau and spread with half the remaining custard. Top with the next layer of cake, brush with Cointreau and spread with the rest of the custard. Brush the underside of the top layer of cake with Cointreau and place on top. Cover with the remaining ganache. Chill.

5 Lay out two sheets of plastic wrap. Wrinkle the surface and spread with two rows of chocolate about 10 cm (4 inches) wide. Leave to set. Break into pieces. Place around the cakes, overlapping the pieces slightly.

6 Cover three baking trays with foil. Put a heavy-based pan over medium heat and sprinkle with a little sugar. As the sugar melts, add the rest gradually. Stir to melt any lumps and prevent burning. When golden brown remove from the heat. Drizzle toffee on the trays, cool, then peel away the foil. Tie a cream ribbon around the cake and top with toffee.

AHEAD OF TIME: The cake can be kept for 2 days once assembled but don't add the toffee until you are ready to serve or it will soften.

Using a serrated knife, slice each of the cakes horizontally into three layers.

Brush the cake liberally with Cointreau, then spread with custard filling.

BUTTER CAKE

Preparation time: 20 minutes
Total cooking time: 1 hour 15 minutes

280 g (9 oz) butter
225 g (7 oz) caster sugar
1½ teaspoons vanilla essence
4 eggs
225 g (7 oz) self-raising flour
150 g (5 oz) plain flour
¾ cup (185 ml/6 fl oz) milk

1 Preheat the oven to 180°C (350°F/ Gas 4). Lightly grease a deep 20 cm (8 inch) round cake tin and line with baking paper.

2 Place the butter and sugar in a mixing bowl and beat with electric beaters until light and creamy. Add the vanilla essence then the eggs, one at a time, beating well after each addition.

3 Sift the self-raising and plain flours together into a mixing bowl. Using a large metal spoon, add the combined sifted flours alternately with the milk into the butter mixture, folding until smooth. Spoon into the prepared tin and smooth the surface. Bake for 1¼ hours, or until a skewer comes out clean when inserted into the centre of the cake.

4 Leave the cake in the tin for at least 5 minutes before turning out onto a wire rack to cool completely.

STORAGE: This butter cake can be kept in an airtight container in the fridge for up to a week, or for 3–4 days in an airtight container in a cool dry place. It can be frozen for up to 2 months.

VARIATIONS: To make a 22 cm (9 inch) round cake, bake for 1 hour 5 minutes.

CHOCOLATE MUD CAKE

Preparation time: 30 minutes
Total cooking time: 1 hour 45 minutes

250 g (8 oz) butter
1²/₃ cups (250 g/8 oz) dark chocolate
2 tablespoons instant espresso coffee
  powder or granules
150 g (5 oz) self-raising flour
150 g (5 oz) plain flour
¹/₂ cup (60 g/2 oz) cocoa powder
¹/₂ teaspoon bicarbonate of soda
550 g (1lb 2 oz) caster sugar
4 eggs
2 tablespoons oil
¹/₂ cup (125 ml/4 fl oz) buttermilk

1 Preheat the oven to 160°C (315°F/ Gas 2–3). Lightly grease a deep 22 cm (9 inch) round cake tin and line the base and side with baking paper, making sure the paper around the side extends at least 5 cm (2 inches) above the top edge.

2 Put the butter, chocolate and coffee in a pan with 185 ml (6 fl oz) hot water. Stir over low heat until smooth. Remove from the heat.

3 Sift the flours, cocoa powder and bicarbonate of soda into a large mixing bowl. Stir in the sugar and make a well in the centre. Add the combined eggs, oil and buttermilk and, using a large metal spoon, slowly stir to incorporate the dry ingredients. Gradually stir in the melted chocolate mixture.

4 Pour the mixture into the tin and bake for 1 hour 45 minutes. Test the centre with a skewer—the skewer may appear just slightly wet. Remove the cake from the oven unless the centre looks raw. If the cake needs a little longer, give it an extra 5–10 minutes. Leave the cake in the tin until completely cold, then turn out and wrap in plastic wrap.

STORAGE: Keep in the fridge in an airtight container for up to 3 weeks or in a cool dry place for up to a week. Can be frozen for up to 2 months.

GENOISE SPONGE

Preparation time: 20 minutes
Total cooking time: 25 minutes

2¹/₃ cups (290 g/10 oz) plain flour
8 eggs
220 g (7 oz) caster sugar
100 g (3¹/₂ oz) unsalted butter, melted

1 Preheat the oven to 180°C (350°F/ Gas 4). Brush two shallow 22 cm (9 inch) round cake tins with melted butter. Line the bases with baking paper, then grease the paper. Dust the tins lightly with a little extra flour, shaking off the excess.

2 Sift the flour three times onto baking paper. Mix the eggs and sugar in a large heatproof bowl. Place the bowl over a saucepan of simmering water, making sure the base doesn't touch the water, and beat with electric beaters for 8 minutes, or until the mixture is thick and fluffy and a ribbon of mixture drawn in a figure of eight doesn't sink immediately. Remove from the heat and beat for 3 minutes, or until slightly cooled.

3 Add the cooled butter and sifted flour. Using a large metal spoon, fold in quickly and lightly until the mixture is just combined.

4 Spread the mixture evenly into the prepared tins. Bake for 25 minutes, or until the sponge is lightly golden and shrinks slightly away from the side of the tin. Leave the cakes in their tins for 5 minutes before turning out onto a wire rack to cool. The cake can be lightly dusted with sifted icing sugar just before serving, if desired.

STORAGE: The sponge can be kept in an airtight container in the fridge or a cool dry place for up to a day.
NOTE: The Gènoise sponge is traditionally made in a tin with sloping sides and served dusted with icing sugar. However, it is often baked to be used for a decorated gateau or celebration cake, in which case it is generally baked in two sandwich tins. In this case, you can ensure you have exactly half the mixture in each tin by weighing each tin first, then dividing the mixture between the tins before weighing the tins again to make sure they are equal.

CHOCOLATE CAKE

Preparation time: 25 minutes
Total cooking time: 1 hour 15 minutes

185 g (6 oz) butter
330 g (11 oz) caster sugar
2½ teaspoons vanilla essence
3 eggs
75 g (2½ oz) self-raising flour, sifted
225 g (7 oz) plain flour, sifted
1½ teaspoons bicarbonate of soda
¾ cup (90 g/3 oz) cocoa powder
280 ml (9 fl oz) buttermilk

1 Preheat the oven to 180°C (350°F/ Gas 4). Lightly grease a deep, 20 cm (8 inch) round cake tin and line the base with baking paper.
2 Beat the butter and sugar with electric beaters until light and creamy. Beat in the vanilla essence. Add the eggs, one at a time, beating well after each addition.
3 Using a metal spoon, fold in the combined sifted flours, bicarbonate of soda and cocoa powder alternately with the buttermilk. Stir until mixture is just smooth.
4 Spoon the mixture into the tin and smooth the surface. Bake for 1 hour 15 minutes, or until a skewer comes out clean when inserted into the centre of the cake. Leave the cake to cool in the tin for at least 5 minutes before turning out onto a wire rack to cool completely.

STORAGE: Store in an airtight container in the fridge for up to a week, or for 3 days in a cool dry place. The cake will freeze for up to 2 months.

CLASSIC SPONGE

Preparation time: 20 minutes
Total cooking time: 25 minutes

75 g (2¹/₂ oz) plain flour
150 g (5 oz) self-raising flour
6 eggs
220 g (7 oz) caster sugar
2 tablespoons boiling water

1 Preheat the oven to 180°C (350°F/ Gas 4). Lightly grease two deep 22 cm (9 inch) round cake tins and line the bases with baking paper. Dust the tins lightly with a little extra flour, shaking off the excess.

2 Sift the flours three times onto baking paper. Beat the eggs in a large mixing bowl with electric beaters for 7 minutes, or until thick and pale.

3 Gradually add the sugar to the eggs, beating well after each addition. Using a metal spoon, fold in the sifted flour and hot water. Spread evenly into the prepared tins and bake for 25 minutes, or until the sponge is lightly golden and shrinks slightly from the side of the tin. Leave the sponges in their tins for 5 minutes before turning out onto a wire rack to cool completely.

STORAGE: This sponge is best eaten on the day it is made. It won't keep well as it only contains a very small amount of fat.
Unfilled sponges can be frozen for up to one month and make sure you freeze the cakes in separate freezer bags. Thaw at room temperature for about 20 minutes.

NOTES: The secret to making the perfect sponge lies in the folding technique. A beating action, or using a wooden spoon, will cause loss of volume in the egg mixture and result in a flat, heavy cake.
Another very important factor is the amount of air incorporated in the flour. To make a light textured sponge, you must sift the flour several times. Sifting not only removes any lumps in the flour but incorporates air.
A lot of eggs are used in making sponges and they should be at room temperature before adding them to the mixture. Remember to take the eggs out of the fridge for at least an hour before required.

FRUIT CAKE

Preparation time: 30 minutes + overnight soaking of fruit

Total cooking time: 3 hours 15 minutes

500 g (1 lb) sultanas
375 g (12 oz) raisins, chopped
250 g (8 oz) currants
250 g (8 oz) glacé cherries, quartered
1 cup (250 ml/8 fl oz) brandy or rum, plus 1 tablespoon to glaze
250 g (8 oz) butter
230 g (7½ oz) soft dark brown sugar
2 tablespoons apricot jam
2 tablespoons treacle or golden syrup
1 tablespoon grated lemon or orange rind
4 eggs
350 g (11 oz) plain flour
1 teaspoon ground ginger
1 teaspoon mixed spice
1 teaspoon ground cinnamon

1 Put the fruit in a bowl with the brandy and soak overnight.

2 Preheat the oven to 150°C (300°F/ Gas 2). Lightly grease a deep 22 cm (9 inch) round cake tin. Cut two strips of baking paper long enough to fit around the outside of the tin and wide enough to come 5 cm (2 inches) above the top of tin. Fold down a cuff about 2 cm (1 inch) deep along the length of each strip. Make diagonal cuts up to the fold line approximately 1 cm (½ inch) apart. Fit the strips around the inside of the tin, pressing the cuts so that they sit flat around the bottom edge of the tin. Cut two circles of baking paper, using the tin as a guide, and line the base. Wrap a folded piece of newspaper around the outside of the tin and tie securely with string.

3 Beat the butter and sugar in a large bowl with electric beaters until just combined. Beat in the jam, treacle and rind. Add the eggs one at a time, beating after each addition.

4 Stir the fruit and the combined sifted flour and spices alternately into the mixture.

5 Spoon into the prepared tin and smooth the surface. Tap the tin on the bench to remove any air bubbles. Dip your hand in water and level the surface. Sit the cake tin on several layers of newspaper in the oven and bake for 3–3 hours 15 minutes, or until a skewer comes out clean when inserted into the centre. Brush with the extra tablespoon of brandy. Cover the top of the cake with paper and wrap in a tea towel. Leave to cool completely in the tin.

STORAGE: Can be kept, tightly wrapped in plastic wrap, in a cool dry place for up to 8 months or frozen for at least 12 months.

Cake Tins & Linings

Cakes can be an easy way to impress, but don't let your masterpiece be spoiled at the last minute as you turn it out of the tin. Follow these simple instructions for perfect results every time.

Cake tins are greased and lined to prevent the mixture from sticking to the tin. Always prepare the tin according to the instructions before preparing the cake.

Check the size of your cake tin by measuring the diameter or width and length of the base. It is important to use the tin size specified in the recipe or at least one of the same cup capacity—check by measuring with water. Aluminium tins give consistently good results. Avoid using dark-colored tins as they may brown the cake before it cooks through.

Remember—when you start to make your cake, it is very important to read through the recipe first to be sure you have all the necessary ingredients and equipment. Preheat the oven and put the cake on the middle shelf once it has reached the correct temperature.

GREASING AND LINING THE CAKE TIN

Grease the tin using melted unsalted butter or a mild-flavored oil. Apply just enough to evenly coat the base and sides of the tin using a pastry brush, making sure there is no excess dripping back to the base of the tin —oil sprays are a quick and easy alternative (spray away from the heat source in a well-ventilated area).

Greaseproof paper is the preferred baking paper for lining cake tins.

Lining the tin

Average-sized cakes generally only need the tin base to be lined, after a light greasing with either melted butter or oil (don't use a strong-flavored oil), or a light coat of vegetable oil spray. This is because they don't have a particularly long cooking time. Simply place

the tin on top of a piece of baking paper, draw around it and cut out the traced shape to fit the base of the tin. Other cakes, such as fruit cake, which are cooked for a much longer time or those with a high sugar content, require extra protection, both around the side and under the base. Generally, with these cakes the oven temperature will be quite low so the best way to do it will be to tie a few layers of newspaper in a cuff around the outside of the tin, and to sit the tin on a wad of newspaper in the oven in addition to greasing and lining it as described before. Because the oven temperature stays low, this is quite safe. When lining the inside of the tins, use a good-quality baking paper, making sure that it is free of any wrinkles that could spoil your cake's smooth finish.

Making a collar

Some of the cakes in this book are cooked with a collar. This extends the height of the cake, giving a more dramatic result. Collars can also give extra protection during cooking.

As a general rule a single layer of baking paper is enough for a collar on an average-sized cake. Larger cakes and fruit cakes will need a double layer of baking paper to make the collar and line the base.

To make a collar, lightly grease the cake tin. Cut a strip of paper long enough to fit around the outside of the tin and tall enough to extend 5 cm (2 inches) above the top of the tin. Fold down one cuff, about 2 cm (1 inch) deep, along the length of the strip. Make diagonal cuts up to the fold line about 1 cm ($^1\!/_2$ inch) apart. Fit the collar around the inside edge of the tin, with the cuts in the base of the tin, pressing them out at right angles so they sit flat around the bottom edge of the tin. Cut a circle of baking paper using the bottom of the tin as a guide. Place the circle of paper in the base of the tin, over the cuts in the collar. Make sure that the paper is smooth and crease-free before pouring in your cake batter or the base and side of your cake will come out with the creases baked into them.

Lining a round cake tin

Step 1: To line the side of a round tin, cut a strip of baking paper long enough to cover the outside of the tin and up to 6 cm (2$^1\!/_2$ inches) wider than the height. Fold down a 2 cm ($^3\!/_4$ inch) cuff, then cut the cuff on the diagonal at 2 cm ($^3\!/_4$ inch) intervals.

Step 2: Grease inside of the tin and place the strip of baking paper against the inside with the cut cuff sitting neatly on the base—the cut cuff will act like pleats, ensuring that the paper sits snug against the side of the pan.

Step 3: Place the cake tin on a sheet of baking paper and trace around the outside, then cut out with a pair of scissors. Place, pencil-side down, onto the base of the tin over the pleats and smooth out any bubbles. If just lining the base, complete step 3 only.

Fold down a cuff on one edge of the baking paper and cut the cuff up to the fold line.

Lining a square cake tin

Step 1: Place the cake tin on a sheet of baking paper and trace around the outside with a pencil.

Step 2: Cut out the paper and place, pencil-side down, onto the base of the tin, smoothing out any air bubbles.

Step 3: If lining the sides of the tin as well, cut a strip of baking paper the same length as the outside of the tin and 1 cm ($^1\!/_2$ inch) wider than the height. Place against the inside around the sides, smoothing out any bubbles.

Use the base of the cake tin to accurately trace the shape onto the baking paper.

Grease the tin, then fit the paper into the base, eliminating air bubbles as you go.

Fold down a cuff in one edge of the collar, then make diagonal cuts at intervals up to the fold.

Place the baking paper along the greased side of the tin, with the cut cuff sitting on the base.

Place the collar around the edge of the tin, pressing the cuts onto the base of the tin.

Cut a circle of baking paper to fit into the base of the tin and put in place.

Cut pieces of baking paper to fit the sides of the tin and smooth them into place.

USEFUL INFORMATION

The recipes in this book were developed using a tablespoon measure of 20 ml. In some other countries the tablespoon is 15 ml. For most recipes this difference will not be noticeable but, for recipes using baking powder, gelatine, bicarbonate of soda, small amounts of flour and cornflour, we suggest that, if you are using the smaller tablespoon, you add an extra teaspoon for each tablespoon.

The recipes in this book are written using convenient cup measurements. You can buy special measuring cups in the supermarket or use an ordinary household cup: first you need to check it holds 250 ml (8 fl oz) by filling it with water and measuring the water (pour it into a measuring jug or even an empty yoghurt carton). This cup can then be used for both liquid and dry cup measurements.

Liquid cup measures

$^1/_4$ cup	60 ml	2 fluid oz
$^1/_3$ cup	80 ml	2$^1/_2$ fluid oz
$^1/_2$ cup	125 ml	4 fluid oz
$^3/_4$ cup	180 ml	6 fluid oz
1 cup	250 ml	8 fluid oz

Spoon measures

$^1/_4$ teaspoon	1.25 ml
$^1/_2$ teaspoon	2.5 ml
1 teaspoon	5 ml
1 tablespoon	20 ml

Nutritional information

The nutritional information given for each recipe does not include any garnishes or accompaniments, such as rice or pasta, unless they are included in specific quantities in the ingredients list. The nutritional values are approximations and can be affected by biological and seasonal variations in foods, the unknown composition of some manufactured foods and uncertainty in the dietary database. Nutrient data given are derived primarily from the NUTTAB95 database produced by the Australian New Zealand Food Authority.

Oven Temperatures
You may find cooking times vary depending on the oven you are using. For fan-forced ovens, as a general rule, set oven temperature to 20°C lower than indicated in the recipe.

Note: Those who might be at risk from the effects of salmonella food poisoning (the elderly, pregnant women, young children and those suffering from immune deficiency diseases) should consult their GP with any concerns about eating raw eggs.

Alternative names

bicarbonate of soda	—	baking soda
capsicum	—	red or green (bell) pepper
chickpeas	—	garbanzo beans
cornflour	—	cornstarch
fresh coriander	—	cilantro
cream	—	single cream
eggplant	—	aubergine
flat-leaf parsley	—	Italian parsley
hazelnut	—	filbert
plain flour	—	all-purpose flour
prawns	—	shrimp
sambal oelek	—	chilli paste
snow pea	—	mange tout
spring onion	—	scallion
thick cream	—	double/heavy cream
tomato paste (US/Aus.)	—	tomato purée (UK)
kettle barbecue	—	Kettle grill/Covered barbecue
zucchini	—	courgette

Weight

10 g	$^1/_4$ oz	220 g	7 oz	425 g	14 oz
30 g	1 oz	250 g	8 oz	475 g	15 oz
60 g	2 oz	275 g	9 oz	500 g	1 lb
90 g	3 oz	300 g	10 oz	600 g	1$^1/_4$ lb
125 g	4 oz	330 g	11 oz	650 g	1 lb 5 oz
150 g	5 oz	375 g	12 oz	750 g	1$^1/_2$ lb
185 g	6 oz	400 g	13 oz	1 kg	2 lb

Published by Murdoch Books Pty Limited.

Murdoch Books Australia
Pier 8/9, 23 Hickson Rd, Millers Point NSW 2000
Phone: +61 2 8220 2000 Fax: +61 2 8220 2558

Murdoch Books UK Limited
Erico House, 6th Floor North, 93-99 Upper Richmond Road
Putney, London SW15 2TG
Phone: +44 (0)20 8785 5995 Fax: +44 (0)20 8785 5985

ISBN-13: 978 1 921208 31 7
ISBN-10: 1 921208 31 7

Printed in China by Midas Printing (Asia) Ltd. in 2006.

Reprinted 2006.

© Text, design and photography Murdoch Books Pty Limited 2006.